ALSO BY GEORGE M. TABER

*Judgment of Paris: California vs. France and the Historic 1976
Paris Tasting That Revolutionized Wine*

TO CORK OR NOT TO CORK

Tradition, Romance, Science,
and the Battle for the Wine Bottle

GEORGE M. TABER

SCRIBNER
New York   London   Toronto   Sydney

SCRIBNER
1230 Avenue of the Americas
New York, NY 10020

First Scribner hardcover edition October 2007

SCRIBNER and design are trademarks of Macmillan Library Reference USA, Inc.,
used under license by Simon & Schuster, the publisher of this work.

For information about special discounts for bulk purchases,
please contact Simon & Schuster Special Sales at
1-800-456-6798 or business@simonandschuster.com.

DESIGNED BY ERICH HOBBING

Manufactured in the United States of America

1   3   5   7   9   10   8   6   4   2

Library of Congress Cataloging-in-Publication Data is available.

ISBN-13:   978-0-7432-9934-3
ISBN-10:   0-7432-9934-5

PHOTO CREDITS

p. 17: Photo courtesy of António Amorim; p. 71: Photo courtesy of Pascal Chatonnet; p. 81: Photo by
Edward Gajdel; p. 109: Photo courtesy of António Amorim; p. 127: Photo courtesy of Grosset Wines;
p. 145: Photo courtesy of John Stichbury; p. 157: Photo courtesy of Bonny Doon Vineyard; p. 165:
Photo courtesy of Lara Taber; p. 181: Photo courtesy of Jean Arnold; p. 195: Photo by Kevin Judd;
p. 209: Photo courtesy of Domaine Laroche; p. 221: Photo courtesy of Ridge Vineyards;
p. 243: Photo courtesy of Penfolds

CONTENTS

FOREWORD BY KAREN MACNEIL

I have to admit that when George Taber asked me to write this foreword, I thought: *a whole book dedicated to cork?* But then, I knew cork to be genuinely amazing: what could compare with a substance that contains roughly 200 million fourteen-sided air-filled cells in just a one-inch cube of the stuff? What other common material is lighter than water, virtually impervious to air, difficult to burn, resistant to rot, and so elastic it can snap back into shape after withstanding 14,000 pounds of pressure per cubic inch? Indeed, cork is rather miraculous.

What I didn't know was the centuries-long story behind cork. And who better to tell it than George Taber whose skillful, incisive reporting thirty years ago exposed the behind-the-scenes story of the so-called Paris Tasting? That legendary tasting, which made global headlines and changed forever the course of the California wine industry in the process, became the basis of George's seminal book *Judgment of Paris*. *To Cork or Not To Cork* is his next big achievement.

Part good storytelling, part investigative journalism, this new book is George at his best. Maybe it's one wine woman's passion for the subject, but I was glued by the intrigue, complexity, and drama of an untold story that has literally been "under our noses" for two centuries. Along the way George gives us fascinating "I didn't know that!" moments that keep the book lively.

In the end, I am a researcher who loves the fine details of wine. And so it is that George's new book was something I could not put down. On last count, I've pulled (sometimes struggled to pull!) 90,000 corks. After reading this book, every one of those *thwocks* took on new meaning.

TO CORK OR
NOT TO CORK

PROLOGUE

The David Bruce Winery has long made one of America's most prestigious Chardonnays. Founder David Bruce, a California wine pioneer, was originally trained as a medical doctor with a specialty in dermatology. His real passion, though, was making wine, and for years after starting his own winery in 1961 he practiced medicine by day so that by night and on weekends he could make wine. He only retired from medicine and became a full-time winemaker in 1985. Bruce's vineyards are in the Santa Cruz Mountains south of San Francisco. Early on, he became convinced that his cool, western side of the mountain range facing the Pacific Ocean was ideally suited to making wines in the style of Burgundy—fruity Chardonnays and elegant Pinot Noirs that reach their peak after five or six years. Paul Masson, one of the first winemakers in the area, called it the Chaîne d'Or because of the similarity he saw to Burgundy's Côte d'Or, where Chardonnays and Pinot Noirs excel. Bruce in the 1980s easily sold out his annual production of some twenty thousand cases of Chardonnay and an additional ten thousand of Pinot Noir and regularly won awards for both wines.

In the fall of 1987, Bruce was about to begin the harvest when he started getting reports from his distributor, the San Francisco Wine Exchange, that stores were returning an unusually high number of Chardonnay bottles with complaints that the wine had cork taint. As a winemaker for more than two decades, Bruce was familiar with the problem of random bottles acquiring a musty odor resembling wet newspapers or moldy cardboard. At the time, winemakers and wine drinkers considered getting a "corked" bottle just a minor annoyance in a field they loved. Bruce, along with other winemakers around the world, didn't know what caused taint or whether anything could be done to stop it. Since they felt helpless, they just lived with the problem and made few attempts to control the quality of their cork.

Anywhere from 3 to 5 percent of bottles supposedly had the off taste. Cork taint poses no health threat to the consumer, but it can still ruin a wine experience. Today the purpose of the ritual of tasting a little wine from a bottle in a restaurant before accepting it is to see whether the wine is corked. To cork's critics, the failure rate is both outrageous and unacceptable. They repeatedly argue that if 3 to 5 percent of Toyota cars or IBM computers failed, those companies would be out of business.

Another problem caused by corks is random oxidation. Just as an apple or a pear left out on a kitchen countertop turns brown and develops a woody taste, wines can also go bad if excessive air gets into the bottle. Corks that seal imperfectly cause oxidation. No one knows how often it happens, but since cork is a natural product and no two corks—just as no two snowflakes—are exactly alike, it occurs from time to time. Some wine experts consider random oxidation to be an even worse problem than corkiness. Oxidation takes place when wine is exposed to excessive air, sometimes through a malfunctioning cork, and is most obvious in white wines, which can turn amber or brown and take on a woody taste. It's the same phenomenon that happens when a cut apple turns brown after being exposed to air. Random oxidation, though, did not seem to be the problem with the David Bruce Chardonnay.

Shortly after the distributor sent those early warnings came the avalanche. From all over the country more and more bottles of the Chardonnay were returned. The explanation was always the same: the wine had cork taint. The staff of the David Bruce tasting room were also noting a lot of bad bottles. A shocking seven of the twelve bottles in a case were often affected. "We got returns after returns after returns," Bruce says with a pain he still feels today.

Bruce knew that he had a disaster on his hands. His first reaction was to pull back as much of the Chardonnay as he could, but he was only able to retrieve about seven thousand cases—at a cost to him of $400,000. That left some thirteen thousand cases out in the marketplace destroying his winery's reputation one bottle at a time, as an unknown number of consumers, who might not be able to determine exactly what was wrong with the wine except that they didn't like it, turned away from David Bruce Chardonnay.

The David Bruce Winery got its corks from Portugal, the world's leading producer. When he checked around the California wine fraternity, Bruce heard that such large wineries as Robert Mondavi, Inglenook, Gallo, and Beaulieu Vineyard were rejecting a significant share of their corks because of taint problems. Bruce concluded that cork suppliers were probably not shipping those back to Portugal but passing them along to another winery in a game akin to old maid. He figured he had been stuck with tainted corks that other wineries had rejected. Once the corks were his property, they were his problem. He had no recourse.

The 1987 cork disaster ultimately cost Bruce $2 million in lost business and an inestimable amount of lost customer loyalty. "We didn't have any money in those days," he recalls ruefully. In a final attempt to rescue at least a little from the catastrophe, the winery owner sold the returned wine to the discount retailer Trader Joe's for $1 a bottle. "That was a terrible mistake, since our label was still on the bottles. I may have gotten a few dollars for them, but it put the nail in the coffin, at least temporarily, by telling consumers that they couldn't trust David Bruce with Chardonnay." Bruce says it took him years to win back the customers. "The market has a very long memory," he still laments. As a result of the cork-taint problem, the winery was almost forced out of the Chardonnay business and had to turn its attention more to Pinot Noir.

David Bruce was the victim of 2,4,6-trichloroanisole, a chemical compound that has been around for centuries but had only been identified six years before in Switzerland. TCA, as it is commonly known, is one of the most intensely aromatic substances in the world. Just one teaspoon of it is enough to taint the entire annual American wine production. An expert wine taster can note cork taint when only one part per trillion is present in a wine, and an average consumer will usually detect it at about 5 parts per trillion. One part per trillion is the equivalent of one second in 320 centuries! But it's enough to ruin a bottle of wine.

For nearly four hundred years, corks like the ones that failed David Bruce have been almost the exclusive way to close a wine bottle. But because Bruce's problem has been repeated so many times at so many wineries, today cork is challenged as never before. The world of wine is now embroiled in an often highly emotional multibillion-dollar battle for the bottle. Says Brian Croser, one of Australia's leading winemakers, "It's scary how passionate people can be on this topic. Prejudice and extreme positions have taken over, and science has often gone out the window."

CHAPTER ONE

Nature's Nearly Perfect Product

When Robert Hooke first saw
cork under a microscope,
the structure reminded him
of a monk's cell.

In the early 1660s, Robert Hooke, the Curator of Experiments for the newly founded Royal Society, a group leading the scientific revolution in England, labored for hours over his new, exciting instrument. It was called a microscope, and just as Galileo had opened new worlds by looking far into space in the early 1600s with a telescope, Hooke was now discovering new worlds in the opposite direction, minute ones that had previously been too small for the human eye to see.

Hooke, a physically unattractive and often unpleasant person who collected enemies as easily as friends, would later be called England's Leonardo da Vinci because of the breadth of his scholarship. After graduating from Oxford in 1663, he worked with scientist Robert Boyle developing the theory of gases that bears his collaborator's name. He also worked with court architect Sir Christopher Wren in the reconstruction of London after the Great Fire of 1666 and on such historic projects as rebuilding St. Paul's Cathedral and the Royal Observatory at Greenwich, where world time starts. In addition, Hooke discovered the spring control of the balance wheel for watches, which finally made accurate time-telling possible, the reflecting telescope, and the pedometer.

Through his microscope, which had a fifty-times magnification, far more than others at the time, Hooke studied some of the most basic natural objects around him: fleas, sponges, bird feathers, and more. Observation Eighteen, as he carefully noted it, particularly fascinated him. It was a piece of cork, a product that had been around for centuries but was only recently being used widespread as a stopper in bottles. He first selected what he described as a "good clear piece" and then with a penknife "sharpened as keen as a razor" cut off a slice to leave "the surface exceedingly smooth." Then he sliced an "exceedingly thin piece" and placed it on a black plate so that the pale cork would stand out in contrast. As he peered at the material through his lens, the cork seemed to take on magical characteristics. He later wrote, "I could exceeding plainly perceive it to be all perforated and porous, much like a honey-comb."

The structure of the piece reminded Hooke of cells where monks in a monastery slept and prayed, and so he called the boxes cells, coining the term since given to the building blocks of all living things. He went on to calculate with awe that there must be "twelve hundred million" cells in a cubic inch of cork. Swept away with the excitement of the moment, Hooke later wrote, "These pores, or cells, were not very deep. . . . I no sooner discerned these (which were indeed the first microscopical pores I ever saw, and perhaps that were ever seen, for I had not met with any writer or person that had made any mention of them before this) but me thought I had with the discovery of them presently hinted to me the true and intelligible reason of all the phenomena of cork."

In 1665, when Hooke was twenty-nine, the Royal Society published his *Micrographia,* a book recounting his experiments, which became a best seller and laid the foundation for using microscopes in biology and medicine. Hooke was also an artist and drew detailed illustrations for the book of what he had seen through his microscope, including the cross section of a cork that indeed resembled a honeycomb. One of his book's early readers was English diarist Samuel Pepys. After working at his job as Secretary to the Admiralty Commission until past midnight on January 21, 1665, Pepys stayed up at home until two in the morning reading what he called "the most ingenious book that ever I read in my life."

People since then have been just as fascinated by cork as Robert Hooke was the day he saw it for the first time under a microscope, for there is no other product in nature quite like it. Later scientists with better microscopes have learned a lot more about cork. The cells that Hooke first saw are fourteen-sided, or tetrakaidecahedrons, so tightly joined together that there is no empty space between them. The cell walls are made up of five layers of material: two outer ones are cellulose; the central one has a woody quality and provides the structure; two inner ones are impermeable. Suberin, a complex fatty acid, is the basic material in cork. Hooke was off only a little on the number of cells; a wine cork contains some 800 million.

Cork cells are filled with microscopic amounts of air. Nearly 90 percent of cork's volume is made up of those tiny, trapped air pockets, and that gives the product its unique buoyancy and compressibility. Air gets into a bottle closed with a cork, but three and a half centuries after Hooke, scientists still don't know how that happens. Some believe it comes through or around the cork, but others think compressed cork cells release it.

Because of the air pockets, cork is among the lightest of all solid substances, which is why it has been used for millennia as floats. If a cork is pushed in one direction, it does not bulge out in another, unlike rubber or plastic. Cork simply contracts. But then it also quickly returns to its original shape because of its unique elastic memory. Even if cork is strongly compacted, it will return to 85 percent of its original volume almost immediately and to 98 percent after a day. In addition, cork can withstand extreme high and low temperatures, but does not conduct either heat or cold. It also absorbs vibration and is extremely long lasting. Cork floors or cork bottle stoppers are good for decades. In 1956, twenty bottles of vintage 1789 wine were found with corks in them in a French cave. The corks were still in fine condition. The wine was slightly brown and obviously overaged, but still well preserved.

Cork comes from the cork oak tree, known to scientists as *Quercus suber.* The tree has two layers of bark. The inner one is alive, while the outer one has died. As successive layers die, the outer bark becomes thicker. This outer layer can be harvested about every decade without doing damage to the inner tree.

Although attempts have been made to cultivate cork elsewhere in the world, it still grows mainly around the western-Mediterranean region. It is thought that cork was originally harvested around the whole basin, but in more recent times it has been grown primarily in the western part on both the northern and southern shores—from Italy to Portugal in the north and from Tunisia to Morocco in the south. The two major cork-producing countries are Portugal and Spain, accounting for more than 80 percent of total world production.

No one knows exactly when the first person put the first cork in a wine container. Archaeologist Patrick McGovern of the University of Pennsylvania and author of *Ancient Wine* is a leading expert on the history of winemaking. According to his research, the Chinese made a product that consisted of wine, beer, honey, and other products about nine thousand years ago. Western wine was first produced about a millennium later somewhere in the mountainous area stretching from eastern Turkey across the Taurus, Caucasus, and Zagros mountains to northern Iran. The first wine was probably made by accident when bunches of grapes were left too long in a container and mysteriously turned into a light, fruity wine. McGovern labels that Stone Age Beaujolais Nouveau, speculating that it was made by carbonic maceration much like the short-lived, but popular, drink now made each fall in France.

The Greek historian Thucydides wrote, "The peoples of the Mediterranean began to emerge from barbarism when they learned to cultivate the olive and the vine." The discovery of pottery in roughly 6000 BC made it possible for people to store wine for the first time, and so the history of pottery coincides with that of wine. Pottery also made wine trade possible. The vast majority of trade in ancient times was in just three products: wine, grain, and olives or olive oil.

Winemakers soon learned that air is the enemy of wine. While some air is crucial to get fermentation started and turn the sugar in grape juice into alcohol, the resulting wine will become vinegar if it stays in contact with air. Ethanol, the intoxicating ingredient in wine, in the presence of the bacterium *Acetobacter aceti* turns into acetic acid, which gives vinegar its astringent smell and taste. The English word *vinegar* comes from the French *vinaigre*, which literally means "sour wine."

Thus winemaking for millennia was an endless struggle to halt the natural process of wine turning into vinegar. Vintners soon developed containers that not only held wine but also kept out most air. The most popular were amphoras made of reddish brown clay, which carried a variety of both dry and liquid products. They remained in use for nearly six thousand years and came in all sizes, with the most popular being about two to three feet high and containing between eight and sixteen gallons of liquid. The larger ones weighed about 130 pounds when full of wine.

Amphoras had two handles and a pointed end, which served as a third handle that helped in carrying and pouring them. They also had long, narrow necks that made it hard for air to enter the container, but during winemaking the amphora's neck had to be left at least partially open so that carbon dioxide, a by-product of fermentation, could escape. Fermentation was a haphazard development that early winemakers could neither understand nor control. They learned from bad experiences that if they sealed amphoras too tight, pressure built up, and the vessels exploded. Early winemakers learned that once fermentation ended, though, they had to seal amphoras to keep out air. This was often done by putting a glob of wet clay onto the top of the neck. Many early winemakers also stored amphoras partly in the ground to keep the contents cooler and thereby slow the change to vinegar.

By 3000 BC, Egypt, the superpower of its day, was the center of wine. At first the Egyptians imported wine, probably from southern Palestine, but eventually they planted their own vines and took the rudimentary craft they inherited to a much higher level. Egyptian methods of making wine were clearly described on fresco paintings that still exist today. In addition, many amphoras dating back to 3000 BC have survived.

By the golden age of Egypt, about 1500 BC, winemaking had become fairly sophisticated. Vintners now had a much better mastery of the process, especially the crucial task of keeping out air. A fresco in a tomb in Thebes from 1400 BC gives a colorful picture of contemporary viticulture. Along the back wall of the winery are rows of amphoras at various stages of winemaking. Some of the vessels are open and are probably still undergoing early fermentation. Above them are jugs with the neck containing straw or grass to let off carbon dioxide while keeping air out, a process similar to the one used today in wineries around the world. Off to the side are rows and rows of wine in amphoras with flat or cylindrical tops on them, where fermentation has been completed.

Colin Hope of Monash University in Australia has done extensive studies of Egyptian stoppers. These show that after fermentation finished, chopped-up organic material such as leaves and reeds was stuffed into the neck of the amphora, a piece of pottery was placed on top of that, and finally moist clay went over the opening to create a totally sealed container.

The Egyptians also discovered that by closing amphoras tightly after fermentation was completely finished the wine usually became much better over time. Thus the Egyptians first developed a taste for aged wines. An Egyptian prisoner named Onkhsheshonqi in the fourth century BC scribbled winemaking notes on pieces of clay to his son, writing on one, "Wine matures as long as one does not open it."

Egyptians are believed to have used cork as early as the fourth century BC for fishing buoys, but there is no evidence that they used it as a stopper for amphoras or in other wine containers.

The rise of Greek city-states as the major political powers of the Mediterranean beginning about 800 BC resulted in the shift of viticultural innovation to that area. Tree resins had been used to seal wine containers before the Greeks, but they developed the practice into an art form. One of the most popular resins came from terebinth trees, which are part of the cashew family and grow widely in the Mediterranean basin. The resin became a standard way for the Greeks not only to seal the inside of amphoras to make sure no air seeped through porous jar walls, but also to fix in place the clay stoppers at the top of jars. In addition, the Greeks added resin to the wine to impede the growth of bacteria and for flavoring. The result was retsina, which is still drunk today in Greece.

Grape cultivation spread to Italy with the rise of Rome, and the Romans loved their wine. As one epitaph of the day said, "Baths, wine, and sex ruin our bodies. But what makes life worth living except baths, wine, and sex." The Romans left the world the most detailed evidence of ancient viticulture. Pliny the Elder, who wrote in the first century of the modern era, dealt extensively with wine in his thirty-seven-book treatise *Natural History,* going into detail about various ways of dealing with what he called "wine disease." He offers plenty of practical advice: "It is a proof that wine is beginning to go bad if a sheet of lead when dipped in it turns a different color."

Pliny credited the Celtic tribes in the Alpine valleys of what is now Switzerland with introducing the wooden barrel as a replacement for amphoras. Barrels were easier to both make and transport than the earlier jugs, although unfortunately for archaeologists they disintegrate and are lost over time. Pliny called them "wooden casks" and noted the use of cork stoppers to keep air out of them. He also gave a detailed account of harvesting a cork tree and wrote that its bark was "used chiefly for ships' anchor drag-ropes and fishermen's drag-nets and for the bungs of casks, and also to make soles for women's winter shoes."

The Bible has numerous references to viticulture and winemaking. The gospel of Luke 5:37 notes, "No one puts new wine into old wineskins, or else the new wine will burst the wineskin and be spilled, and the wineskins will be ruined." Wineskins, which were stoppered with a plug to keep out air, were a popular method in the ancient world for short-term wine storage and for transferring it into larger containers. Pictures of them remain in frescoes and on ancient jars, but the skins disintegrate over time and no remnants remain.

Corks have been found in Roman shipwrecks dating from the fifth century BC to the fourth century AD. Professor Vernon Singleton of the University of California, Davis, believes the Romans first used cork as a way to protect wine from air. Amphoras dating from 500 BC show cork being used to seal the containers, but Singleton says, "This does not appear to have been the usual ancient method of closure." He adds that old corks were very different from the ones we know today. In ancient times the cork was a large piece of raw bark, which might be an inch or two thick, and was fit into the mouth of an amphora and fixed in place with resin. These, however, still let some air into the vessel through lenticels, thin, horizontal slits in the bark. Today's smooth corks are made by punching plugs parallel to the bark, which cuts across the lenticels and provides a much tighter seal.

Resin discovered in the necks of amphoras indicates that ancients realized the cork alone was not sufficient to seal the jar properly. Archaeologists found fifteen jars dating back to the third century BC on a sunken ship off the east coast of Sicily that had cork stoppers sitting flush with the top of the container. They had been sealed tight to the jar with pitch. The Roman poet Horace, who lived in the last century of ancient times, writes in Ode VIII of having a joyous banquet for Bacchus, the god of wine, where they "remove the cork fastened with pitch." Rome's ruling class was fond of aged wines, and Falernian, a wine from near Naples and the First Growth of its day, was aged for ten to twenty years in amphoras with cork stoppers covered with clay or cement.

Corks, however, fell into disuse after the fall of the Roman Empire in the fifth century when the Dark Ages descended upon Europe. There was much less trade in the millennium between 500 and 1500, and cork farmers from the Iberian Peninsula had difficulty selling their product in other parts of the continent. An additional blow to the use of cork with wine was the rise of the Moors, who were forbidden by their holy book—the Koran—from drinking alcoholic beverages. They began conquering Europe from the south starting in the eighth century, an invasion that reached its apogee at the Battle of Tours on October 10, 732, when the Franks led by Charles Martel defeated the Moors only 130 miles southwest of Paris. It would take another seven centuries before the invaders were expelled from Iberia and a wine culture—and cork—returned to that area.

Although barrels were the main vessel for making and transporting wine during the Dark Ages, the containers no longer had a stopper made of cork as in Roman times. In its place were a variety of inferior substitutes such as wooden plugs, which were pounded into a barrel and generally provided a leaky closure at best. Rags made of hemp or other textiles were also soaked in olive oil and stuffed into the bunghole of a barrel to keep out air. Sometimes pieces of leather were similarly used. Often the stoppers were held in place by pieces of string that were tied down onto the container, and sometimes sealing wax was poured over the plug to reinforce the seal.

German winemakers used large wine casks to reduce the amount of air in the barrel in relation to the level of wine and thus lessen the danger of its going bad. In some cases they put rocks into barrels to keep the level of liquid high and reduce the amount of air.

A popular peasant solution for keeping air away from wine was to pour a little olive oil in the container. The oil floated on top of the wine and blocked any contact with air. When the wine was served, a small amount of liquid was poured off the top to remove the oil. The custom of tasting wine before serving it actually started as a way of making sure all the oil was gone and goes back to before the birth of the modern cork.

During its millennium without cork, wine had to be consumed quickly, and there was a constant race to drink it before it went bad. The value of wine decreased inexorably after it was made, and it was considered worthless once the next year's vintage was available. Without exception, from 500 to 1500 old wine meant bad wine.

Cork was first exported to England in 1307. Its most popular use in medieval Europe was as soles for footwear because it provided insulation against bitterly cold castle floors in winter. Not until the late 1500s was cork used as a stopper for bottles holding liquids, in particular wine. One of the first known uses of the word *cork* as a stopper in English was in Shakespeare's play *As You Like It,* which is believed to have been written in late 1599 or early 1600. The character Rosalind at one point says to Celia, "I pray thee, take the cork out of thy mouth, that I may drink thy tidings."

The serendipitous union of corks and inexpensive glass bottles took place first in England and then spread to the Continent starting in the seventeenth century. Ancient Egyptians and Romans made glass containers, and the Venetians had been producing them since the early thirteenth century. But that glass was both expensive and fragile. The most commonly used bottles at the time were made of heavy pottery or stoneware. Wine in those days was shipped in wooden barrels and served to customers in decanters that didn't need a stopper since the wine was quickly consumed.

In 1632, Kenelm Digby, the eccentric owner of a glassworks and a sometime privateer, introduced a bottle-making technology that produced both a strong and much less expensive glass container. The bottles were manufactured in a furnace heated with coal, rather than wood, resulting in a much hotter fire. In addition, the glass contained a higher ratio of sand to potash and lime than previously. There was later a patent fight over Digby's role in developing the new bottles, but a court ruled in his favor. The vessels became known as English Bottles, and the technology was quickly copied elsewhere. The dark green or brown containers had a so-called string rim on the neck so that a piece of twine could be tied over the cork to hold it in place. Corks were left sticking out of the bottle so they could easily be removed.

Early bottles were individually blown, and the size was determined by the glassblower's lung capacity. This led to a great disparity in the capacity of containers and the widespread practice of claiming that more liquid was in the bottle than was actually the case. Sir Boyle Roche tried to rectify that problem with the straightforward proposal to the Irish House of Commons that "every quart bottle should hold a quart." Nonetheless, for many years it was illegal to sell wine in bottles because of misrepresentations about their contents.

The English upper class bought wine in barrels and then moved it to bottles, which carried the family name or seal on the front and had a cork in the neck. In the most privileged manors, the top servant was charged with going to the wine cellar and bringing back one of the glass bottles filled with wine. He was called the bottler, but over time his title evolved into *butler.*

The quality of cork, though, was often questionable. John Worlidge, an early English agronomist, wrote in his 1676 book *Vinetum Brittannicum or A Treatise of Cider,* "Much liquor being absolutely spoiled through the only defect in the cork."

In about 1700, inexpensive bottles appeared in France. The first encyclopedia of Denis Diderot in 1751 included a drawing of a man carving a cork into the shape to fit a bottle as well as a detailed description of cork making. It said corks were used for shoes and slippers "but above all to close jugs and bottles."

One bit of cork folklore is that the French Benedictine monk Dom Pérignon rediscovered corks for the Western world as a perfect closure for the Champagne that he had just invented. According to the story, two Spanish monks on their way to Sweden stopped at the Abbey of Hautvillers in northern France, where Dom Pérignon was the cellar master from 1668 to 1715. The French monks asked the visitors about the cork stoppers they had in the necks of their water gourds. The Spaniards explained they came from the bark of a tree that grew in Catalonia and were a wonderful way to seal a container hermetically. Dom Pérignon supposedly immediately saw this as a superior way to close Champagne bottles and ordered a supply of corks. At the time he was sealing his bottles with wooden pegs wrapped in hemp soaked in olive oil.

Like many other stories about Dom Pérignon, this one is false. André Simon, the British wine merchant, connoisseur, and historian, writes that the wine from Champagne was "first bottled, sold, and drunk as a sparkling wine in London during the sixties and seventies of the seventeenth century." The Duke of Bedford's household accounts for March 25, 1665, showed expenditures for "Champaign [sic] wine, also 2 dozen glass bottles and cork." That was three years before Dom Pérignon entered the monastery. The story about how Dom Pérignon invented Champagne is likewise false, but that's a tale for another book.

Corks and the new bottles got a major boost in 1703 with the signing of the Methuen Treaty between Portugal and England. This was both a military and a commercial accord that gave privileged trade access to both countries in the other's market. Portuguese wines, especially Port, which improved with years of aging in corked bottles, were taxed less than French imports and were soon popular in English manors. The Portuguese often put wax or pitch on top of the cork to make the seal even more airtight.

The original English bottles were almost pear-shaped with long necks and a wide base. That made them stable when sitting on a table, but inconvenient for storage in bins. So in the early eighteenth century, bottle design changed, with the neck becoming shorter and the sides narrower and flat, much like today's bottles. This made it much easier to stack them on their sides. An added advantage was that it kept the cork moist, thus protecting its seal. If a bottle is stored standing up, the cork quickly dries out and air can leak into the container.

The English bottles were used for much more than just wine and were soon the container of choice for medicine, perfume, liquor, cider, and other liquids. The closure was usually a cork.

The only thing left to do once a better bottle had been developed and cork had been rediscovered was to find a better way of getting the cork out of a bottle. For many decades there were only two ways to remove the cork, and both of them were bad. The first was to leave it sticking out of the neck, but that made it harder to store and decreased the effectiveness of the seal. The second solution, if the cork had been pushed entirely into the bottle, was to slice the glass off below the end of the cork with a special set of prongs. An anonymous poem printed in London in 1732 relates the heroic attempts by one wine enthusiast to get the cork out of a bottle: "Sir Roger set his teeth to work / This way and that he ply'd / And wrench'd in vain from side to side." Sir Roger then burned the cork from the top and pushed the remainder into the bottle—only to get his thumb stuck in the neck. Some modern wine consumers might commiserate with Sir Roger.

Fortunately the English soon came up with better ways to remove a cork, which also allowed it to be put in flush with the bottleneck. Initially they used a tool called a steel worm or gun worm, which was designed to pull unspent bullets out of a gun barrel. Later devices for pulling a cork carried a variety of names, including cork drawer, bottle screw, and bottle worm. The first English patent for a corkscrew (#2061) was given to Samuel Henshall, a clergyman, on August 24, 1795. Ever since, inventors around the world have spent endless hours developing new contraptions for getting a cork out of a bottle.

By the end of the eighteenth century, the bottle, the cork, and the corkscrew had opened a new age in wine history. For the first time since the Romans with their tightly sealed amphoras, it was possible to enjoy aged wine. Consumers no longer had to drink wine in a hurry before it spoiled. Wrote Britain's Hugh Johnson in 1966, "The invention of the cork is the most important event in the history of fine wine. . . . However well our ancestors may have been able to make their wine . . . it could never have reached anything like the point of soft, sweet perfection which a claret or burgundy can, if it is given the chance, today."

In the entire world, only a few sounds bring joy to all but the most jaded. One is the purring of a kitten. Another is the thwack of a well-pitched baseball hitting a perfectly swung bat. And a third is the pop of a cork being pulled from a bottle of wine.

CHAPTER TWO

The Making of a Cork

Recently harvested cork bark
is now stored on stainless steel pallets
to avoid contamination.

In the childhood classic *The Story of Ferdinand* by Munro Leaf, the friendly young bull is happy to sit in the pasture under a cork tree all day and smell the flowers rather than get into the bullring and fight a matador. Illustrations in the book show a happy Ferdinand sitting in the shade of a tree, smelling flowers. Above him are bunches of cork stoppers looking very much like clusters of grapes. Cork does grow on trees, but not the way that illustrator Robert Lawson and generations of young children thought.

Cork comes from the bark of the cork oak tree, which grows most abundantly in the Iberian Peninsula countries of Spain and Portugal. At first, Spain was the world's leading cork producer, and even today many experts believe the best cork comes from Catalonia in eastern Spain. The cork grown there is considered superior because of its high density. The first company to make industrial cork was started around 1750 in Anguine,

Spain. The country, though, eventually lost its predominant position to Portugal, where cork oak trees grow more abundantly. The Spanish Civil War of the 1930s and its aftermath also cut the country off from most of its markets and helped the Portuguese take over as the industry leader, a position it has held ever since.

The structure and operation of the cork industry changed little for some three hundred years until the beginning of the twenty-first century. This large and diffuse business, with many small players and few internal controls, operated mainly on handshakes. Before Portugal joined the European Union in 1986, the country was almost a third-world nation, and much of its industrial production, even for cork, its most important export, took place in hundreds of small factories, many of which were located in a family's backyard. Producers followed practices that had developed over the centuries and saw no need to change since they had a virtual monopoly on the world's market for closing wine bottles.

The first Portuguese cork-growing areas were in the southernmost part of the country in the Algarve and just north of Lisbon. Later, the rural Alentejo area northeast of Lisbon became the epicenter of cork forests, while a region about fifteen miles south of Oporto in the north became the main location for cork production. The Alentejo, which means "beyond the Tejo" River in Portuguese, is a rolling plain with an abundance of pine, eucalyptus, olive, and cork oak trees. Most residents live in villages or small towns in whitewashed houses with adobe-tile roofs. The summer temperature regularly tops 105°F, but it is usually a dry heat. It rains little during the cork harvest, between early June and the end of August.

Cork oak trees grow haphazardly throughout the area with pine trees often interspersed among them. Even along the sides of roads in the Alentejo stand harvested cork trees. Farmers cut the light underbrush in the forests periodically to reduce the danger of fire, their greatest threat. The most distinctive sight in the Alentejo is the white, hand-painted number on the side of a tree, indicating the last numeral of the year in which it was last harvested. Sometimes there are also initials on a tree, indicating its owner.

Alentejo forests are a favorite place for wildlife. During the fall, the trees are stopping-off spots for birds on their north-to-south migration and then in the spring on the south-to-north route. A number of endangered animals such as the Iberian lynx live in the cork forests, which has made the habitat a favorite cause of conservationists. Another resident, though not an endangered one, is the black pig, which provides a delicious ham, air-cured for several years, called *pata negra* in both Spanish and Portuguese. Large herds of pigs roam between Portugal and Spain with no regard for national borders, and the animals also rummage around for acorns under the cork oak trees.

Unlike American oaks, cork oaks are evergreens with gray-green leaves that look something like a holly, although they are much softer to the touch. While some forests have trees planted in rows, they usually grow in a haphazard way simply where nature dropped the acorns.

Portugal's wealthiest clans own most of the plantations, called *montados,* which have usually been in families for generations. The trees are generally on spreads that run for thousands of acres. Many families once also ran cork-manufacturing facilities, but in recent years have concentrated on growing trees.

Under Portuguese law, a cork tree cannot be harvested until it grows to 70 centimeters (27.6 inches) in diameter and 1.2 meters (3.9 feet) in height, which usually takes about twenty-five years. The quality of cork from the first harvesting, however, is poor, and that material ends up in lesser-quality goods such as tiles or shoes, and not in stoppers. After that, the tree grows taller and thicker at the base, but by law can only be harvested every nine or ten years. With the third harvest—after the tree has been alive for about fifty years—the bark is sufficiently dense to be used to make cork stoppers. Wealthy families with little need for quick cash are particularly well suited for cork farming because of the long harvesting cycles. Ask a Portuguese cork farmer his production, and he will give you the total for the past ten years. While it varies somewhat from farmer to farmer, most harvest about one-tenth of their forests each year on a rotating basis.

The harvesting of cork and the production of bottle stoppers has changed little over the years. By the time a tree is ready to be harvested, the outer of the two layers, which provides the cork material, is usually about two inches thick. Farmers and their laborers used to pull wagons through the forest to pick up the bark, but now tractors or trucks do that work. Otherwise much remained the same until recently.

Harvesting takes place during the summer, when the weather is dry and the two parts of the bark are easy to separate. The field workers are hired from the surrounding area, and some people take vacations from their regular jobs to work in the cork harvest, where pay is better. A project manager finds the men to work the fields and is often paid on the basis of the quality of the cork harvested. Workers generally earn about €90 ($119) a day. About twenty workers make up a team and cut the bark from trees in a designated area of a forest. Half the members carry a sharp, fan-shaped ax with a four-foot handle. Those are the cutters, and they are always men. The other half of the team are the stackers, who collect the wood left by the cutters. An occasional woman or two is among the stackers.

The cutters work in groups of two. One man goes up the tree and begins whacking his ax into it at the highest point where cutting is permitted under national regulations. With one hand he holds the tree, while he cuts with the other. If it's an old tree, he may also climb out onto the limbs and cut those as well. The cutter chops deep into the wood until he sees he has reached the inner layer of the bark. As he pulls his ax out of the tree, the cutter twists the head and begins prying the bark away. Then he continues cutting in a straight line around the tree, prying more and more bark from what is called the mother tree. The goal is to pry a final piece of bark as big as possible, since larger ones are more valuable. While the first cutter is up the tree, his partner stays on the ground doing the same kind of stripping at a lower level, cutting from the ground up toward the point where the worker in the tree has started. Eventually a piece of bark in a long, round sheet separates from the tree and falls to the ground. A stacker then picks the piece up and carries it to a truck or flatbed trailer. The pieces may be several yards long and several feet wide, but are very light.

The teams carry out this whole operation with the focus, skill, and speed of an urban gang stripping a stolen car by the side of a highway. There's little talking while the work goes on. The only thing you hear in the forest is an occasional bird chirping and the thunk, thunk, thunk as the axes slash into the trees. From time to time, one of the workers may stop for a minute to take a drink of water from a bottle stored in a cork box, which keeps the water cool even in the hot Alentejo sun. Workers start early in the morning, when it's still cool, and on the hottest days they stay on the job only until lunch. At the beginning and end of summer, they also work in the afternoon, but as Alentejo weather gets hotter and hotter in midsummer, workers generally quit at about three thirty.

After the harvesting of the cork, the mother tree standing in the forest looks naked. The upper area, where cutting is not permitted, is still full of leaves and thick bark, but below that is only bare wood. A visitor almost feels embarrassed for the tree, as if he's looking at a victim exposed for all to see. In reality, though, the tree will soon be growing more bark and restarting an ancient cycle.

According to a traditional saying of cork cutters, the best trees have inner cores that are as smooth as the stomach of a beautiful young woman. Cork from those trees gets the highest grade and brings the best prices. The more common trees, though, have a bumpy inner bark, and some are even scarred from past cuttings when the ax slipped and sliced the interior bark.

The average life span of a cork oak is about 150–200 years, which means a tree could be harvested fifteen times before it is cut down and burned to make charcoal. The oldest known cork oak is Whistler Tree, which has been harvested every nine years since 1820. It yielded more than one hundred thousand corks in its latest harvest in 2000, and there are no signs that it won't be harvested again in 2009 or 2010.

The process of turning raw cork into stoppers and then shipping them off to winemakers around the world changed little for centuries. Traditionally, once the bark was cut and stacked, it was left on the ground in the forest for months so any residual sap and moisture would be lost. Rain also removed bitter tannins from the wood. During this drying, defects in the cork could also be noted. While it was lying there, cork-stopper producers from Oporto sent buyers to the forests, looking at the wood and considering whether to bid at an auction on this or that lot, which could be several tons of cork. Middlemen known as *preparadores* also bought cork from farmers and handled the first stages of production before passing it off to companies further down the process. In the past decade, though, many middlemen have lost their role, and the power of cork manufacturers and exporters has increased.

After months of sitting out to dry, the raw cork was shipped to many locations around the country to begin manufacturing. Most of those were just south of Oporto in the north. The primary purpose of cork production was to make stoppers for wine and other bottles since that is the highest value-added product. Stoppers account for only 20 percent of cork production in terms of volume, but some 70 percent in terms of value. So every piece of cork bark was looked at first to see whether it could be used to make stoppers. If it could not, then it went onto another production path.

The cork that doesn't go into stoppers is used in a myriad of different products primarily because of the material's lightness and insulation. One of the biggest uses is cork flooring. Architect Frank Lloyd Wright designed it into many projects, and the White House's Oval Office had a cork floor for years until President Ronald Reagan had it pulled up and a rug put down. The two Mars Exploration Rovers, which landed on the red planet in January 2004, had heat shields made of cork and other materials. Chicago Cubs slugger Sammy Sosa on June 3, 2003, was ejected from a baseball game for using a corked bat that gave him greater bat speed. Birkenstocks, the shoes of Generation X, have cork soles. According to the company, cork provides "the orthopedic contours feet need for maximum comfort." And, of course, countless classrooms and kitchens around the world have cork bulletin boards carrying urgent messages or a child's first artwork.

The first step in manufacturing was to classify the cork into one of six categories based primarily on the thickness of the wood, because that determined its future use. Thick wood brings the highest price, but visible defects such as too many holes can reduce the value.

Then the bark went into large vats of water and was boiled for about an hour. This removes most of the cork's volatiles and phenolics and flattens out the pieces of bark, which would otherwise still have had the curved shape of a tree. It also added moisture back to the wood that evaporated during the months of drying. That made the bark easier to work with and reduced the amount of breakage during stopper manufacturing.

After the boiling, the bark was put aside for about a month to bring the moisture content down from about 40 percent to between 15 and 20 percent, the right level for punching corks out of the bark. The cork was then shipped to punching companies, which produced the raw corks. There were formerly hundreds of big and small punching companies around Portugal with higher or lower levels of machinery and expertise. Many of them, just as in the boiling businesses, were mom-and-pop operations run sometimes at home at night and on weekends by people who had day jobs working for bigger punching companies. Today, however, punching is concentrated in far fewer firms.

Workers wielding long, sharp knives first trimmed the edges off the pieces of bark and cut the pieces into rectangular slabs about two feet by four feet. The pieces of bark were then fed into a lathe that can be operated either by hand or by machine that stamped out the corks. No matter how the process was done, the goal was to get the maximum number of cork stoppers out of a piece of bark by having a minimum space between them. The cork stoppers were then put in a bag while the remnant material, looking something like pieces of Swiss cheese, was sent to a grinder that ground it into small pieces to be used for other cork products. In the early days of Chicago slaughterhouses, it was said that meatpackers used every bit of the hog except for the squeal. Cork manufacturers likewise used every part of the cork bark.

After the punching, the rough cork stopper went through a finishing to smooth the surface and make sure it conformed to standard sizes. Starting in the 1950s, punched corks were generally treated with chlorine to whiten them. Chlorine was legally eliminated as a whitening agent in 1982 because it could cause cork taint, but it took several years before the practice was stopped. The corks were then dried again, although winemakers want corks to be fairly moist so they will slip easily into bottles.

Finally the corks were graded for quality, again based entirely on appearance, dependent on the number of holes. White corks were usually more highly valued, although some wineries preferred darker and more natural-colored ones. Women manually—and with blinding speed—used to classify the corks into one of seven grades, going from one for the best looking to seven for the least attractive. In recent years, three more classifications were added at the top, and most of that manual process was taken over by machines. A human eye then made the final quality call, and each cork went into a container for that grade.

Cork stoppers are now divided into six categories. The top of the line is natural corks, which contain nothing but pure cork material and come in ten quality grades. A second type is agglomerated corks, which are made of ground up cork particles that come from the remnants of natural cork manufacturing. The pieces are bound together with glue. A new generation of agglomerates, which have come out in the past five years, are much better than the first ones introduced in the 1990s. Technical corks are made of both cork particles and disks of natural cork at the top and bottom. The large corks used for Champagne and sparkling wines are technical corks, but are considered a separate category. Colmated corks are imperfect natural ones with either holes or cuts filled with cork dust and glue. Colmated corks are inexpensive and a favorite of wineries producing wines such as Beaujolais that do not undergo extended bottle aging. The last group is the so-called T-tops, which have tops ranging from plastic to silver attached to a piece of cork. These are used for Sherry, Port, and expensive tequilas and Cognacs.

After the corks were produced by hundreds of manufacturers, a few large exporting companies bought them and shipped them to destinations around the world. The most expensive corks found their way to the wealthiest wine producers in countries such as France, while the lower grades were bought by wineries in the poorer countries of Eastern Europe.

•

The traditional decentralized system for growing cork and then turning the raw material into stoppers that operated in Portugal for centuries
made quality control impossible. Hundreds of growers and manufacturers operated on their own without any industry standards or verification,
and they turned their corks over to exporters who passed them along to the
world with no questions asked. Exporters bought most of their corks from
small suppliers where they had no control over production. But why
should anything change? The Portuguese had a monopoly on the stoppers
that went into the world's wine bottles. The system had worked for
nearly four hundred years, and there was no reason to think that it
wouldn't go on like that for another four hundred.

MESSAGE IN A BOTTLE: LONDON

Britain's Hugh Johnson is the most popular wine writer in history. Starting with the groundbreaking book in 1966 titled simply Wine, *which demystified the beverage and gave it a global view, Johnson has been a Sherpa to oenophiles around the world, guiding them to ever higher pleasures and saving them from falling into the pits of plonk.*

Some of Johnson's most pleasant wine experiences have been with members of The Bordeaux Club, a group founded by British wine merchant Harry Waugh and Sir John Plumb, a historian and master of Christ's College, Cambridge. Three times a year, six club members hold dinner meetings at one of their homes to enjoy outrageously good food and equally impressive wines.

As recounted in Johnson's autobiography, A Life Uncorked, *the meeting of The Bordeaux Club a decade ago was typical of their gatherings—except for one thing.*

The dinner was held at the residence of Sir John, who was attired in a velvet smoking jacket, and started with a 1976 Jacquesson Champagne that Johnson thought was "a bit sweet and oddly raw." The group then moved to the candlelit dining room for a first course of grilled fillet of Dover sole that was accompanied by a 1985 Château Haut-Brion blanc, which the group found "not very lively." Next came pheasants, roast, celeriac puree, Brussels sprouts, brown game chips, and gray bread sauce. The first red Bordeaux to accompany these courses was a 1982 Château Canon from St.-Émilion that Johnson noted had a "minty fresh finish." That was followed by a 1978 Château Pichon Longueville Comtesse de Lalande that Johnson labeled "rather simple," and then a 1975 Château Latour that some at the table liked, while others found disappointing. After that came a 1961 Château Malescot St.-Exupéry that Johnson described as "dark, sweet and spicy . . . and finishing on a note of sweet decadence."

All of this, though, was only a prelude to what was expected to be the pièce de résistance: a 1953 Château Haut-Brion to accompany the Welsh rabbit. As soon as the wine was poured from an elegant decanter, everyone at the table knew it was corked. Making matters worse, there was only one bottle, so there was no backup. "There is no hiding the disappointment when this happens," Johnson wrote. "Of course Jack should have tasted it when he decanted it, as we told him."

The Bordeaux Club members then discussed the problem with tainted corks and how to handle it when a bad bottle appears in the middle of a gastronomic extravaganza. Johnson is highly critical of the cork industry's inadequate performance in removing the problem from wine drinking. In his autobiography he laments, "If all wine-drinkers recognized it, and rejected every tainted bottle, the wine-trade would go bust. It is worrying to think that its profits depend on its customers' ignorance."

At the same time, though, Johnson told me he finds screwcaps "so esthetically unsatisfactory."

CHAPTER THREE

Science in the Service of Wine

For most of its nine-thousand-year history, winemaking was only a small step above witchcraft. Vintners didn't really understand what was happening as grape juice turned into wine and then became vinegar. Rome's Pliny the Elder in *Natural History* advised coating wine barrels with pitch "immediately after the rising of the Dog Star" and not opening wine jars "when a south wind is blowing or at a full moon." Such sorcery and folklore were passed on from generation to generation, and other tidbits of tradition were added as time passed. Straining a wine at the table was de rigueur for centuries because remnants of fermented yeast, seeds, and other wandering matter were usually floating amid the nectar. While ancient wines might seem romantic in history and literature, today's consumers would certainly reject them with disdain.

Only in the middle of the nineteenth century were new tools of science first used to help winemakers improve their product. The father of wine science was the Frenchman Louis Pasteur, who still ranks as the greatest wine researcher of all time. Pasteur was born in 1822 to a tanner in the mountainous Jura region of eastern France and didn't show great promise as a youngster. He received a "mediocre" grade in chemistry in the local lycée or high school. While dean of the University of Lille in northern France, Pasteur began studies that would eventually lead him to resolve the riddle of fermentation. He did his initial work not on grapes but on sugar beets, a major crop around Lille. Like Hooke two centuries earlier, Pasteur was fascinated by the microscope and what it could tell about how nature worked. He first realized that crushed grapes only started to ferment when they came in contact with air. He then discovered that the secret to fermentation was tiny microorganisms, living yeast cells. They floated in the air and fell on the skin of ripening grapes, then later started turning the fruit's sugar into alcohol. Before Pasteur, conventional wisdom was that fermentation occurred because of some kind of spontaneous generation. Starting in 1857, Pasteur published a series of papers on fermentation.

In July 1863, Emperor Napoléon III commissioned Pasteur to study what was troubling French wines. Shortly before that, France had signed a trade treaty with England, and Paris had expected its wine sales there to increase rapidly. Instead, English wine merchants complained about the poor quality of the French wines they were receiving and were refusing to take delivery of orders because of spoilage.

Pasteur immediately set up an experimental winery in Arbois in his native Jura, where he bought a small vineyard and studied winemaking for the next three vintages. He watched the winemaking practices closely, tasting wines but also examining them under his microscope. The scientist was shocked by what he found. Storage barrels were often covered with mold, and wine frequently contained parasites that vintners never saw but were visible under a microscope. Pasteur was particularly interested in the role air played in enology. He wrote, "It will be obvious to everyone that air has always been considered the enemy of wine and that all the practices of vinification invite us to adopt this point of view." Yet at the same time, he was intrigued by how air helped mature wines. He concluded that wooden barrels were the best storage vessels because they permitted slow and steady aeration. "In short, in order to keep a wine young, one must keep it away from oxygen; in order to make it age, one must oxygenate it," wrote Pasteur's biographer Patrice Debré.

In the fall of 1865, Pasteur presented his conclusions to the emperor and his wife, Eugénie, at the château of Compiègne in northern France. The following year, Pasteur published his research under the title *Studies on Wine*. He lumped all the problems of French viticulture together, calling them "wine sicknesses" and was tough in his critique: "There may not be a single winery in France, whether rich or poor, where some portions of the wine have not suffered alteration."

The breakthrough in Pasteur's work was his conclusion that the way to fight wine sicknesses was to heat wine to a high temperature for a short time to kill the microbes causing the contamination. He took out a patent for the process, calling it simply pasteurization.

The French wine industry was aghast. How could wine be heated without destroying its bouquet and wonderful tastes? As a result, Pasteur's recommendation was never widely adopted by vintners, but pasteurization was used in many other fields, particularly the dairy industry. Pasteur, though, always steadfastly believed in the "improvement of wine through heating."

The scientist's guiding philosophy during his studies was that winemaking was an art, but now had to become a scientific art form. He wrote, "It is desirable to attain that goal, for wine can rightly be considered with good reason as the most healthful, the most hygienic of all beverages."

Pasteur's work on wine lasted only about four years before he moved on to research rabies and other major maladies. France's wine scientists, though, were soon struggling with an even more difficult problem that threatened the very survival of European wine: a tiny yellow bug that had been imported from America.

In 1862, a merchant and winemaker named Borty lived in the Rhône Valley village of Roquemaure near Avignon, a town famous for a song about its bridge that every French child learns. In the spring, he unexpectedly received a shipment of 154 rooted vines from someone in upstate New York named Carle, who had visited him the year before. French winemakers at the time were fighting a fungus called oidium that was killing vines. American plants, though, were reportedly resistant to the disease, and so Borty decided to plant the New York vines, which had names such as Clinton and Post-Oak. The imported plants, though, were carrying a small bug that ate the roots of grapevines. American vines were resistant to the bugs in a classic case of Darwinian survival of the fittest, but the French vines had no such immunity. The leaves on infected vines first turned yellow and then red before the plant died. The plague moved up both sides of the Rhône River, then farther north into Beaujolais and Burgundy and west to Bordeaux. Diseases don't recognize national borders, and soon it was also in Portugal, Spain, Germany, Italy, and was moving east toward Russia.

As recounted by Christy Campbell in his book *The Botanist and the Vintner,* the government and people of France tried everything to kill the aphid that was destroying their national treasure. The center of research about the disease, which was named *Phylloxera vastatrix* or dry-leaf devastator, was the agricultural department of the University of Montpellier in the Rhône Valley. Professor Jules-Émile Planchon headed a national committee studying the problem and possible solutions. The Ministry of Agriculture in 1870 offered an award of twenty thousand gold francs to anyone who came up with a way to stop the blight and only four years later raised the prize to three hundred thousand gold francs.

Nothing was too outrageous to try. Bottles of holy water from the new shrine of Lourdes, where the ill were miraculously cured, were placed among the rows of sick vines. Everything from arsenic to tar was also poured on plants. In Beaujolais twice a day male students left class and went into the vineyards to urinate on the vines in hopes that might stop the plague. It didn't.

The government, though, placed its faith in science to come up with a solution, and the national agricultural department in an 1881 report said, "Science will emerge victorious from this great struggle."

Soon two camps developed on how to fight the disease: the *américanistes* and the *sulfuristes*. The first group, championed by Henri Bouschet, was centered at the University of Montpellier and argued for planting disease-resistant American rootstock, the base of the vine, and then grafting French vines on top of that. Since the bugs attacked the roots, the plant would survive and grow French-style grapes.

The *sulfuristes,* which included mainly Paris bureaucrats and the wealthy owners of France's most prestigious wineries, argued for injecting sulfur and insecticides into the ground near the plants with an instrument that looked like a small jackhammer. That process, though, was expensive, even if the national government was generously subsidizing it, and only seemed to deter, and not defeat, the disease.

The argument went on for years at a host of meetings until October 1881, when a showdown took place over six days at the International Phylloxera Conference in Bordeaux. By then the costly strategy of the *sulfuristes* was weakened because it didn't seem to work for a prolonged time. The *américanistes* argued persuasively for the grafting solution. In a last line of defense, the *sulfuristes* offered the ultimate objection: wines from the grafted vines tasted terrible. "Foxy" was the pejorative term used to describe wines made from grapes grown on American rootstock.

On the last day of the conference, the results of a comparative tasting of grafted and ungrafted wines were announced. The final decision between the two sides was going to come down to a question of taste. The head judge concluded, "As for the French wines produced by vines grafted onto American roots, they seemed to present their original character." The *américanistes* had carried the day: the vines resisted the disease—and the wines still tasted good.

Momentum soon shifted to a strategy of replanting all of France's vineyards on American rootstock. It was a long and costly process, but it worked. Nevertheless, some of Bordeaux's wealthiest wineries were still pumping insecticides into the ground in 1914 at the outbreak of World War I.

The best evidence that the Montpellier solution had worked came in

1894 when a Meursault Goutte d'Or, a white Chardonnay from one of Burgundy's prized premier cru vineyards, won a gold medal at a Paris wine competition. The vine had been grafted three years before on American rootstock.

As a result of the battle against the dry-leaf devastator, several research centers were opened around the world almost simultaneously to bring better science to winemaking. In 1872, the Research Institute Geisenheim was started in the Rheingau region of Germany. Then in 1880, the Institute d'Oenologie opened in Bordeaux, the same year as a similar one was inaugurated at the University of California, first on the Berkeley campus and later in the town of Davis near the state capital, Sacramento. In 1890, the Swiss set up the Federal Research Station for Fruit-Growing, Viticulture, and Horticulture in the small town of Wädenswil near Zurich.

Research at the institutes helped winemakers improve their work and their wines. Geisenheim soon became well-known for breeding new pest-resistant grape varieties. Ulysse Gayon, who had worked with Pasteur, was the first director of the Bordeaux wine center and was followed by the highly esteemed academic duo of Jean Ribéreau-Gayon and Émile Peynaud. They all did groundbreaking research into the basics of wine production, working both with students and winemakers in the field. French winemakers used Peynaud's book *Knowing and Making Wine* for years.

Davis came into its own after the end of Prohibition, thanks to a remarkably small, but influential, group of hands-on researchers. The most important work was a modest monograph entitled *Composition and Quality of Musts and Wines of California Grapes*. By comparing the temperatures of various regions of California with those in France, Professors Maynard Amerine and Albert J. Winkler essentially gave a new generation of winemakers a map of where in California to grow the world's leading grape varietals. Later in the post–World War II era, Cornelius Ough, Vernon Singleton, and Harold Olmo made the University of California the leading center of wine research.

In the late 1960s, Hans Tanner, who had previously headed the research operation for a large Swiss food company, began looking into the problem of cork taint at the Wädenswil institute. Swiss winegrowers regularly came there with their problems, and one of the worst was the offensive smell and taste that they often found in bottles of both their red and white wines. Because of the country's challenging growing conditions far from the warm climates of southern Europe, the Swiss make generally light, fruity wines. The most popular white is Chasselas, a dry wine that does particularly well in the Valais area and is also known as Fendant. The favorite red is Dôle, which is made primarily from Pinot Noir and Gamay grapes. Both had trouble with what winemakers called cork taint.

The problem was nothing new; corks had been known to cause problems since the late seventeenth century. Researchers, however, had not been able to suggest what to do about it. In the late 1970s, Tanner thought the trouble was getting worse, and the German company Gültig Corks joined Swiss winemakers in asking Wädenswil to find out more about cork taint.

Tanner was typical of the serious, hardworking German Swiss. Without much fanfare or recognition, he labored in his lab twelve hours each day from early in the morning to early evening. Near the end of his career he was forced to take on the job as head of research, but for most of his life he did what he liked best: working in the lab on concrete problems. His wife, Magdalena, was used to his coming home late to a cold dinner. After dinner, he often wrote technical studies, eventually publishing more than two hundred.

Tanner had been working on the cork problem without much success for nearly fifteen years when Hans-Rudolf Buser, one of his colleagues at the institute, became interested in gas chromatography–mass spectrometry (GC-MS), a technology for the separation and identification of chemical compounds that had first been used in the 1950s. The equipment consisted of two instruments coupled together that first separate the individual components in a mixture (gas chromatography) and then identify individual components by their fragmentation pattern (mass spectrometry). Buser thought the new equipment might be just the thing Tanner had been looking for to isolate the chemical causing cork taint. Also working on the project was Carla Zanier, a research assistant whose salary was paid by Gültig Corks.

Tanner and Zanier started off by collecting sixteen bottles of various wines, including some that were badly tainted. The levels of contamination were so high that even the most inexperienced person would have recognized that something was wrong. They also found bottles of the same wines that did not have the bad smell. Among the paired samples were a 1978 Chianti Classico from Italy, a 1973 Rioja from Spain, and a 1979 Dorin, another Swiss wine made from Chasselas grapes. The wines were all bought in the open market.

Tanner and his group then made a first study of the two Chianti Clas-sicos because one bottle had a particularly obvious bad smell. The GC-MS equipment identified thirteen major compounds in the wine. The chro-matograms of the two wines were indistinguishable except for one varia-tion. The researchers found an extremely high level of a chlorinated compound in the tainted Chianti, but not in the good bottle of the same wine. The mass spectrum of the chlorinated compound indicated the presence of three chlorinated atoms at a temperature of 86°C (186.8°F) to 89°C (192.2°F). Later Tanner labeled the trouble-making compound trichloroanisole (TCA) because of the three chlorine atoms. The complete formal name was 2,4,6-TCA because the chlorine atoms are found at positions two, four, and six on the compound's benzene ring. The researchers then tested the other wines and found the same compound in all the offending wines, but not in the good bottles.

In the computer-reconstructed graphs of the bad Chianti, the offend-ing ions literally soared off the chart. Tanner later determined the wine had a trichloroanisole concentration of 100 nanograms per liter (ng/L) or 100 parts per trillion (ppt). Tanner's original work in 1981 gave the TCA inci-dence in both ways. Scientists generally prefer to use nanograms per liter, while non-scientists normally use parts per trillion. The numerical values, though, are exactly the same: 100 nanograms per liter equals 100 parts per trillion. In the test of a bad bottle of Refosco, an Italian red wine, the level was 370 parts per trillion. A bottle of Ruländer, a German white wine, had 73 parts per trillion.

The researchers then did some tests with average outsiders in an attempt to see at what level people would recognize the trichloroanisole. They determined that anyone would recognize it at 100 parts per trillion. At 10 ppt only half of the testers detected musty, off flavors, and nine out of ten noted them at 30 ppt.

The extremely low levels of TCA needed to spoil wine greatly surprised Tanner and his associates, and they began trying to come up with analo-gies about what they had found. One of their favorites was that it was like putting two sugar cubes into nearby Lake Constance and having the water taste sweet.

In early 1981, the Tanner research appeared in the *Swiss Review of Fruit and Wine,* the institute's official publication. The study was in German, with abstracts also in English, French, and Italian. As authors, the paper carried the names Buser, Zanier, and Tanner, who had written the report at night at home after he had finished his work at the lab. The conclusions were straightforward and clear:

- 2,4,6-TCA was found as a major component responsible for the musty cork taint occasionally found in cork-bottled wines.
- Cork taint in wine was caused by concentrations of 2,4,6-TCA in the ppt (parts per trillion) range.
- The presence of 2,4,6-TCA at those small levels in wine poses no toxicological risk; nevertheless, it could destroy the quality of the wine.

Tanner also thought he had a pretty good idea of what caused the offending compound to develop in some corks, although he admitted in the paper the origins were "not yet fully known." In 1975, he had been in Portugal visiting the cork industry as part of his ongoing work on the taint problem. While there, he noticed workers in the manufacturing plants boiling batches of cork in large containers of chlorinated water to make the corks whiter. He recalled that after putting the cork into a vat of boiling water, they would toss in a handful of chlorine powder. Since a chlorine compound was now recognized as causing the trouble, it seemed only logical to Tanner that this was the cause of 2,4,6-TCA. He even offered the cork industry a solution, writing in his paper, "If this proves to be true, replacement of chlorine treatment in the processing of cork should remedy the cork-taint problem."

In papers published in 1981 and in 1983, Tanner looked into another taint problem similar to 2,4,6-TCA. Several Swiss wineries were having troubles that were traced to a wood preservative painted on wine barrels and vats. The second compound was less potent than the original, but was at least as serious because the taint affected the company's entire wine production since it seeped into the barrels and onto walls. He called the second one 2,3,4,6-tetrachloroanisole (TeCA). A cellar cleanup was the only way to rid a winery of the offending material.

Tanner's original paper was published in English in 1982 in the American *Journal of Agricultural Food Chemistry*. He was also invited to make speeches about his work in Austria, Italy, and Germany. But not in Portugal. Tanner never received any awards or other honors for discovering TCA. That oversight was probably because the research was done in a small country and published first in a language that is no longer in the mainstream of academic research.

After his study was made public, Tanner received a letter from the head of Gültig Corks saying that he shouldn't have made his work public because it would give cork a bad image. A quarter century after his work was originally published, I asked Tanner why the Portuguese cork industry had ignored his work. He replied, "They felt that if they ignored the problem, it would go away. They were also afraid that if they examined their corks, too many of them would be rejected."

That reaction from cork-industry leaders was to plague the wine business and delay for two decades action to alleviate a problem first identified and named in 1981.

CHAPTER FOUR

The Long Search for an Alternative

*The drawing accompanying
John Mason's November 30, 1858,
patent application for his
"screw-neck bottle"*

From their first use in the seventeenth century until the mid-nineteenth century, corks were the closure of choice for bottles no matter what their content. Whether the liquid inside was medicine, distilled liquor, carbonated beverages, or wine, a cork stopper usually held it in place. As some of cork's shortcomings became evident over time, however, the search for a better closure developed.

English clergyman/scientist Joseph Priestley in 1767 invented soda water by injecting carbon dioxide into plain water or, as he called it, "impregnating water with fixed air." That became the innovative drink of its day, but a cork was not sufficiently tight to hold the effervescence because carbon dioxide escaped through the cork. As a result, the bubbling water quickly went flat. The beverage particularly intrigued Benjamin Franklin, who tried to seal a bottle with a wooden stopper sealed with wax, but that didn't work either.

The second half of the nineteenth century, however, was a golden age of new closure technology. On November 30, 1858, John L. Mason, a New York City tinsmith, received U.S. patent 22,186 for an "improvement in screw-neck bottles." He claimed it could be used for a "jar or bottle" and would provide an "air and water tight" seal. His innovation was a glass thread on the outside of the neck that worked with a reusable piece that Mason in his application called a "screw-cap." The mason jar and screw-cap is the primogenitor of today's screwcap.

August Voege of Brooklyn, New York, on June 4, 1878, received patent 204,463 for "an improvement in screw-caps for bottles, jars, etc." The drawing accompanying his application looks amazingly like today's short screwcap. It had a "water-tight packing," which would now be called a liner. Voege's application said it would be useful for "ale, beer, mineral water, and other effervescing liquids as the screw-cap is air-tight, can be unscrewed in an instant, and is at all times ready for use."

William Painter, an Irish-born American inventor living in Baltimore, who earned eighty-five patents in a lifetime of tinkering, on February 2, 1892, received U.S. patent 468,258 for a device he called a crown cap because it looked like the thing monarchs wore on their heads. He wrote in the application that it was "for use with liquids bottled under maximum pressure." The cap was a simple round piece of steel crimped in twenty-four places that was placed around the top of a bottle and then tightened by machine under an external lip at the top of the bottle's neck. At first glassmakers were reluctant to manufacture special bottles with the lip, but they soon changed their attitude because the crown cap made a wonderfully tight seal on popular carbonated drinks such as Schweppes Tonic in Britain or Coca-Cola in the United States.

Advocates of crown caps, though, did not totally turn their back on cork. In fact, in the early days, Painter called his product a "crown cork," and for many decades the new closures had a thin liner of cork inside the cap, where it provided safe and reliable insulation between the bottle's contents and the metal cap. The cork liner was later replaced with a plastic one.

Until early in the twentieth century, liquor bottles all came with traditional corks. In 1913 William Manera Bergius, a member of the family that made Britain's Teacher's Highland Cream Scotch whisky, got a patent for the T-top: a cork with a wooden or plastic top that makes it look like the letter *T.* Teacher's called it a "self-opening bottle," with the marketing slogan "Bury the Corkscrew."

Britain's White Horse Scotch whisky in 1926 sold the first hard liquor under screwcap, and it was a runaway market success. Quickly, a large segment of the spirits industry worldwide moved to screwcaps, although many prestige brands stayed with T-tops.

After Prohibition in the United States ended in 1933, leading California winemakers such as Gallo became big users of screwcaps. At a meeting with his sales staff in October 1959, cofounder Ernest Gallo proudly told employees that since April of that year the company had been "using Alcoa pilfer-proof closures on the entire Gallo line." In fact, Gallo used them exclusively until the 1980s, when it began trying to improve its image and go upmarket by using corks. Screwcaps were inexpensive and fitted the two styles of wines mass-production wineries were turning out. The first were cheap, low-quality table wines carrying the nickname Dago Red and consumed mainly by recent immigrants. The other was high-alcohol, fortified wine popular with alcoholics known as winos, who consumed them frequently on the street in small bottles out of paper bags. Convenience was a key factor for that market since winos didn't normally carry corkscrews.

As early as 1950, a modest test was done at the University of California, Davis, to see how well screwcaps preserved wines. Dr. Cornelius Ough used that seal on a few bottles of a wine, made with Tinta Madeira grapes grown in California, that had been fortified with distilled alcohol to make it like a Port. Ough can't remember much about the test and says he never published anything about it. The wine was still sitting in the Davis wine cellar in 1992, when Mike Dunne, a wine writer for *The Sacramento Bee*, called on Ough to interview him about the new plastic corks. After the interview, Ough suggested they go down to the cellar and try some of the screwcap wine that was now forty-two years old. Dunne carefully reported the professor's reaction: "Ough raised to the light one glass of each of the two wine samples. The one poured from the bottle with the screwcap was tawny red, still bright but thinner in hue, with more of a brownish tinge. The other was ruby red, also bright but deeper in intensity. He swirled, he sniffed, he tasted. Gradually, he began to prefer the wine from the cork-finished bottle. 'It doesn't seem quite as old,' he concluded. He was quick to note that both had withstood the past four decades quite well." As for himself, Dunne thought the screwcap wine was fresher, but as a good journalist, he didn't put his own views in the story.

One of many companies making screwcap closures for spirits, aperitif, and Cognac bottles was France's Le Bouchage Mécanique, a subsidiary of the large French glass company Saint-Gobain. The product's brand name was Stelcap, a combination of the words *stellar* and *cap*. In 1959, the management of Le Bouchage Mécanique decided to make a simple product-line expansion by taking the technology used in its Stelcaps and applying it to wine bottles. At almost the same time, Cebal, a subsidiary of the French aluminum firm Pechiney, began work on a similar project, and for the next few years the two companies worked independently on it. Eventually the two efforts were combined after Saint-Gobain and Pechiney merged in 1964 and the product continued under the Pechiney brand. The driving motivation for the new closure was not cork taint but the search for a modern and less expensive way to seal a wine bottle.

The brand extension, though, did not turn out to be as easy as it looked at first glance because of one crucial difference between low-alcohol wines and high-alcohol drinks such as Cognac. If a screwtop seal malfunctions and a little air gets into the Cognac or Scotch, it's not a problem because the high alcohol content protects the liquid. The same amount of air would ruin a bottle of wine. The biggest challenge for Pechiney was developing the liner that goes inside the capsules, the point of contact between the wine and the closure. Research showed that acids in the wine could corrode the caps, and flavors in some liner materials got into the wine.

An early liner trial used cork. A thin layer of agglomerated cork was pressed out of cork particles and placed inside the cap. Several other liners used different kinds of food-grade plastics. The use of plastic was not surprising because at the time the *vin ordinaire* that the average Frenchman drank with his lunch and dinner was sold in liter bottles sealed with a small half-inch plastic cup that was topped with a thin, light-metal cap. The consumer simply pulled off the metal and removed the cup. Far more wine was drunk out of those kinds of bottles than out of ones with a cork in them.

Starting in the 1960s, a sampling of wines from all regions of France were bottled with the new closure, which was at first called Stelcap-vin but was later shortened simply to Stelvin. The bottles were stored in locations around the country to see how the wines would age and how the cap performed.

In early April 1968, a case of vintage 1967 red Mouton Cadet, an inexpensive Bordeaux produced by the owners of the famed Château Mouton

Rothschild, was placed in the cellar of La Tour d'Argent restaurant. Six bottles had Stelvin closures and six had cork. A year later on April 21, 1969, the first verdict on the new Stelvin closures was passed at a blind tasting at the restaurant. The judges were some of France's leading wine experts, including Claude Terrail, the owner of La Tour d'Argent, and Raymond Oliver, the owner and chef of Le Grand Véfour restaurant. Using a common sensory system called a triangle taste test, the judges were presented with three wineglasses. Two of them were the same type, Stelvin or cork, and the third was the other. The twenty-two judges were then asked to identify which of the two were the same and which was different. Twelve said there was no difference between the three wines, five had a slight preference for the Stelvin, and five gave a similar nod to the cork. Not a clear victory, but certainly a respectable showing for the new closure.

Other test bottles found their way into all sorts of places. Christian Vannequé, then the chief sommelier at La Tour d'Argent, still remembers the day when two cases of 1970 Château Gruaud-Larose, one with corks and one with Stelvins, were placed in a small vault in a wall of the cellar and then cemented off. Some bottles of 1969 vintage Château Haut-Brion, a First Growth of Bordeaux, were also sealed in 1971 with Stelvin and stored at the winery. The Haut-Brion trial went well for several years, but as it headed toward a decade the screwcaps deteriorated because of the failure of the liner. The study was stopped shortly thereafter. Other bottles with Stelvin were shipped to wine research centers in Alsace, Bordeaux, and Burgundy, and experiments were done with such wines as 1964 Nuits-St.-Georges and 1966 Mercurey, two top Burgundies.

Many other tastings were conducted during the late 1960s in France with varying results, as Pechiney technicians continued trying to come up with a better liner. At best, the results of all the testing were inconclusive, but they were good enough for Pechiney to keep the research project going.

While Pechiney was still working on its development project, an American and Italian joint venture was already introducing its screwcap to the market with great success. Banfi is a New York–based company founded in 1919 by John Mariani Sr. to import Italian wines into the United States. The company struggled through Prohibition, but became one of the largest importers after the dry years. In 1950, nine wine producers in the Emilia-Romagna region formed the Cantine Cooperative Riunite. The group made light, slightly fizzy wines through the Charmat process, which has a second fermentation in a tank, rather than in a bottle, as is done with Champagne.

In December 1967, Banfi imported its first Riunite wines, a Lambrusco—just one hundred cases. The bottles, naturally, had a cork in them.
The wine was an immediate hit, and by the end of 1968, annual sales were
more than twenty thousand cases.

John F. Mariani Jr., who was by then running the company his father
had started, was soon looking for a cork replacement for Riunite for several reasons. The first was that cork did not provide a good seal for the
wine because pressure from the effervescence sometimes pushed corks out
of bottles. Champagne also has the problem, but its corks are held in
place by a wire cage. Mariani, who had been watching the evolving
market for beer and soda closures, thought the screwcaps they were
using might also be good for Riunite, which was designed to be an
informal, fun product. The convenience of screwcaps was particularly
attractive for larger bottles.

After coming up with the marketing concept, Mariani turned the
implementation of it over to the Riunite cooperative, which developed the
product with the help of Italian manufacturers on the model of beer and
soda screwcaps.

Banfi and Riunite, though, ran into problems with Italian wine regulators. As a way to protect Italy's cork industry, the government had in
1963 passed a regulation that appellation wines under the DOC (Denominazione di Origine Controllata) system had to be sold in bottles with
corks. Riunite Lambrusco was a DOC wine. Mariani tried to convince the
Italian Trade Commission to let it be sold in the United States with a
screwcap but failed. So Banfi decided to declassify the wine and called it
a simple table wine or *vino del tavola*. Riunite began shipping screwcap bottles to the United States in late 1969.

Helped by the popular jingle "Riunite on ice . . . that's nice," sales
exploded. Riunite wines were a hit with neophyte American drinkers
transitioning from soft drinks to wine. Nothing stuffy or complicated. An
easy wine for easy living, and just twist off the top. If you didn't finish the
bottle, put the top back on and put it in the refrigerator. Banfi did no test
marketing to see if the public wanted screwcaps. Mariani thought the new
closures didn't need any explanation. He was right. Sales rose steadily, and
by 1975 Riunite was the top-selling imported wine in the United States,
a position it held until 2000, when another Banfi import, Concha y
Toro from Chile, replaced it. In the mid-1980s, Riunite was selling 11.5
million cases annually around the world.

Despite Riunite's tremendous market success, however, winemakers in other countries did not pay much attention to Banfi's alternative closure. Whatever interest there was in a replacement for cork was focused on France's Stelvin.

The first company to use that product on a commercial wine was Switzerland's Hammel, which did its initial bottling in 1972. Hammel, along with all other Swiss wineries, had the taint problem with its Fendant and Dôle wines. When Hammel's manager complained to his cork supplier, he was told that cork was a natural product in increasingly short supply, and that ended the story. It was an answer winemakers heard regularly from cork salesmen. The Swiss owner, though, was furious and went on a search for an alternative to cork, which led him to Pechiney. Hammel was happy to be a pioneer, and soon many other Swiss wineries adopted screwcaps as a solution to their cork-taint problems, especially for daily drinking wines sold in liter bottles. Quickly, about half of Swiss wines were being bottled in screwcaps, but the Swiss wine market was too small for its pioneering innovation to have much of an impact on the global closure market.

At the same time Stelvin was becoming a hit in Switzerland, it was also popular with airlines. Starting in the early 1970s, the world's airlines began serving 185-milliliter (6.3 ounces) bottles of wine sealed with screwcaps on flights in economy class. First-class passengers in the front of the plane still enjoyed top-quality wines served in a glass and poured from a bottle with a cork in it. But back in economy class, less affluent travelers got their wines in the smaller bottles with the new twist-off tops. Airline stewardesses loved the new bottles because they no longer had to struggle with a corkscrew at thirty-five thousand feet, at least in economy class. Passengers liked the convenience.

Australian winemakers at this same time were also seriously looking for an alternative to cork. Many were convinced that they were the dumping ground for the world's cork suppliers, who kept their better products for customers close to home in Europe. There's no evidence and plenty of denials of that charge, but there is no doubt that Australian wineries had major cork failures. Some cork suppliers said the Australians were having problems because they bought mainly low-quality cork. The trouble could have come from the long sea voyages across the equator, when cargo was subjected to high temperatures that brought out the worst in cork. Whatever the cause, winemakers down under were fed up.

Australian society and its wines were then going through dramatic changes. The first grapes were planted in the country in the 1790s, but until the 1960s Australia produced mainly fortified Sherry- and Port-style wines that were rarely seen outside the British empire. Most of that cheap, low-quality wine was sold in screwcap bottles just as in California. The comic group Monty Python, in a television skit, gave the early Australian wines a well-deserved put-down when a character says with great umbrage, "This is not a wine for drinking—this is a wine for laying down and avoiding."

Post–World War II immigrants from countries such as Italy became a driving force in the movement toward both better food and better wines. Australia's traditional British-influenced food-and-drink culture was on the way out as people went from drinking tea, beer, and fortified wines to enjoying table wines, bottled water, and coffee along with an increasingly sophisticated cuisine.

Australian winemakers were also developing new wine techniques suited for their conditions, such as night harvesting and adding oak chips to tanks as an inexpensive way to obtain the flavors Europeans got from costly oak barrels. If there was something new to try, an Australian wine-maker was ready to give it a go. They were also introducing strict quality control standards in a way never practiced in Europe, where wine was still considered more an art than a science.

The showcase for Australia's new wineries was the annual circuit of wine shows. Every state capital from Perth to Hobart had an event where wineries presented their wares and were judged against their peers. Winning wineries soon bragged in their marketing about their gold medals. The wine shows, though, were also a place where faulty wines were on display warts and all, and in-your-face Aussies were not shy about expressing their distaste for corked bottles.

When Australian winemakers visited with their European colleagues at international wine conferences and complained about the problem, the Europeans didn't seem to know what they were talking about. The French dismissed it as just a mysterious smell that gave wine its magic je ne sais quoi.

At the time, The Yalumba Wine Company in the Barossa Valley was a leader in Australian wine research. Its production manager, Peter Wall, had originally studied accounting but switched to winemaking and graduated from Roseworthy Agricultural College, the country's top wine education center, which is now part of the University of Adelaide. Wall went to work at Yalumba in 1963, while still studying at Roseworthy, and became head of winemaking in 1972. His goal was to produce good, clean, fresh wines that would win medals at the shows. He used all the latest international equipment such as new filters to remove unwanted residues. Riesling was one of his favorites since the nearby Clare and Eden valleys were ideally suited for that subtle wine.

As he tried to make truly great wines, Wall became increasingly unhappy with the cork that he put in the bottle. Too many wines were either tainted or oxidized, and the culprit, he thought, was the cork. During his studies at Roseworthy, Wall had learned about the impact excessive oxygen has on wines, especially Rieslings, by robbing them of aromas and flavors. "That was a very powerful realization, and it always stuck with me," Wall says. "If I was really going to avoid those oxidative characters that spoiled wines, what was I going to do?"

Wall looked at all sorts of things in his search for a better closure. He tried gluing various metals onto corks in an attempt to make them more impermeable to air. He also worked with a variety of plastic closures to eliminate the cork taint and tried bonding those onto aluminum. He also tested crown caps. In 1964, he wrote to Le Bouchage Mécanique in Paris to ask about Stelvin, but was told that the wine version of the closure was still in the early stages of development. Wall was not easily put off, and in 1970 he visited Le Bouchage Mécanique's office in Chalon-sur-Saône, where he tasted several Bordeaux red wines under Stelvin.

Also in 1970, Australian Consolidated Industries, a huge conglomerate that manufactured bottles, obtained the right from the French company to manufacture Stelvin in Australia. Before launching it in the Australian market, however, company officials decided to undertake a major study with the help of the country's leading winemakers on how wines aged in bottles under Stelvin compared with those under cork. The Australian Wine Research Institute was brought on board to give the work credibility and independence. ACI and the AWRI devised a long-term tasting program to be carried out at the ACI laboratories in Melbourne. The tasting panel included three of the country's top winemakers: Don Ditter of Penfolds; Bruce Tyson of McWilliam's Wines; and Peter Weste of B. Seppelt & Sons. Bryce Rankine, head of Technical Services at the AWRI, joined them. Peter Wall worked with the ACI staff on the oxygen transfer aspects of the trials.

Penfolds, McWilliam's, and Seppelt donated the wine, and researchers described their methodology clearly in a study published later: "A total of 2,880 bottles were obtained, according to an experimental design requiring 60 bottles each of six wines (three white and three red), with four closures and stored at two temperatures [12°C or 53.6°F and 22°C or 71.6°F]." From Penfolds came 1974 Bin 365, a white wine made with

Semillon grapes; and 1972 Bin 333 Dry Red, a Shiraz. From McWilliam's there was 1973 Private Bin 46 Hock, made from Semillon; and 1972 Private Bin 35, made with Shiraz. Seppelt provided 1972 White Burgundy, made with Semillon and Tokay grapes; and 1971 Moyston Claret, which came from Shiraz, Malbec, and Cabernet Sauvignon grapes. The bottles were stored horizontally in equal lots.

Pechiney was still wrestling with the nagging problem of finding a perfect liner, and the Australians helped the French company by developing several new ones. Three types of liners were eventually used. Two were identified as LBM 358 and LBM 323, which were made primarily with polyethylene and PVDC, a plastic film sold commercially as Saran wrap. The third was Celloseal, a widely used commercial product made of polyethylene and film that was considered a good barrier to moisture.

The screwcap was the long version (60 mm or 2.4 in.), made of aluminum. The cork in the trials was a commonly used one in the Australian market, and a tin capsule covered it, as was standard with commercial bottles.

Tastings of the bottles were conducted every six months, and each participant was given four glasses of a wine that had been sealed with each of the closures. The red wines were served at room temperature, while the whites were poured at 13°C (55.4°F). The glasses were coded with numbers.

The tastings were blind, meaning the judges did not know which wines they were examining. It took seven hours to taste ninety-six wines, which came in twenty-four flights of four wines each. Scoring was on a five-point scale. The top wine of the four was given five points.

The April 1976 issue of *The Australian Grapegrower and Winemaker,* a leading trade magazine, published a report entitled "Stelvin—Evaluation of a New Closure for Table Wines." The authors were Bryce Rankine and two ACI executives, Bora Eric and David Leyland. It reported the results after eighteen months and three tastings. The article gave detailed results for ullage, the wine level in the bottle; the torque pressure needed to break the seals; the amount of both total and free SO_2 in parts per million after eighteen months; and finally the taste tests.

The summary conclusions were stated carefully but clearly: "The metal closure with 358 wad [liner] performed well on the wines tested in comparison to cork and the other two wadding materials, justifying its use as a commercial closure for table wines." A close examination of the tasting part of the trials showed the Stelvin caps with the 358 liner handily winning over cork, with the 323 one placing second. Stelvins with those two liners and cork all did better than the Stelvin with the Celloseal liner.

After the study was released, ACI began a major marketing campaign to promote the new closure on which it had by now placed a large bet. The goal was to change the image of screwcaps from cheap to quality, and ads ran in both newspapers and women's magazines.

Even before the results were published, Peter Wall had already tried out Stelvins. In the early summer of 1973, he did an experimental bottling of 1972 Pewsey Vale Riesling, the company's most prized version of that varietal, in a bottle with both a cork and a screwcap. In the fall of 2006, I saw some of those bottles still in storage in the company's museum collection. The company's idea at the time was that the use of both screwcaps and corks would be a good way to ease customers into accepting screwcaps on premium wines, and it continued the practice for four years.

When the ACI study was released, wineries all over Australia studied it carefully, and many decided to jump on the screwcap train that seemed to be leaving the station. By the end of the decade, more than thirty wineries were using Stelvin on all or part of their production.

The decision, though, was not taken lightly. In the fall of 1977, British-born David Armstrong, the winemaker at both Reynella and Hungerford Hill, two wineries owned by the Rothman cigarette company, had to make a presentation to his Australian board of directors on screwcaps. He was ready to propose that the wineries start by doing all their white wines in Stelvin, which seemed best adapted to the new technology. Years before, a mentor had counseled him that in making a pitch like that to a board, he should always be prepared to answer the three most likely objections. So Armstrong went into the meeting at the Reynella Winery armed with responses to the expected criticism.

After concluding his speech, Armstrong stepped back and prepared to take questions, fully confident that he was ready for whatever would come his way. Nonetheless, he grew nervous when Chairman Colin Hazelgrove raised his hand to signal he had a question. This looked bad. Hazelgrove had studied winemaking in the 1930s at Montpellier in France and was a master of wine technology. He asked Armstrong why he wanted to do only white wines with Stelvin. The chairman explained that when he was at Montpellier he had seen a lot of experiments with crown caps on wine that showed them to be clearly superior to cork as a wine closure. Hazelgrove said Stelvin caps would undoubtedly be the same. Armstrong had prepared for tough questions, but not for that one. After a short discussion, the board decided that the white wines at both wineries would go into screwcaps starting with the 1978 vintage. At the same time, Armstrong would begin doing tests of reds under screwcaps. Despite Hazelgrove's question, it was considered too risky to do the reds without more research.

Yalumba was also ready to expand its Stelvin program. Every afternoon the half dozen members of the executive committee met informally over a glass of wine to discuss business. The closure trials at ACI were a frequent subject of conversation, and support for the Stelvin closures was gathering strength, although some people there were still fearful of the change. Wall always backed the move to Stelvin. In 1976, Yalumba enlarged its use of Stelvin to other wines, including both reds and whites. In the winery museum is a bottle, with both a cork and a screwcap and a label reading, "This is the first bottle of commercially packaged wine in Australia with a Stelvin closure—May 1976."

Not unexpectedly, all wineries faced some new issues with Stelvin closures. After nearly four centuries of corks, every little old winemaker in his backyard could run a corking machine because cork was such a forgiving product and easily adjusted to suit an imperfect bottle or bungled incision. Stelvins were much more complicated. First, a slightly different bottle had to be manufactured with much more demanding specifications, especially for its neck. Bottling lines also had to be more carefully monitored. Screwcap operations were much more industrial, and the machinery had to be regularly and carefully maintained. The torque, or pressure, at which the screwcap was installed had to be finely calibrated. Wineries generally concluded that the bottling line had to be slowed down by about 15 percent to accommodate the new method of closing. Storage was also carefully watched so that bottles didn't bump into each other and nick the caps, thus breaking the seal. Previously bottles at most wineries had been stored in cages before labeling and frequently banged into each other. That was not a problem with bottles containing cork, but could be a serious issue for those with screwcaps.

When the first wave of wines under Stelvin reached the Australian market in the spring of 1979, everyone seemed entranced with the new closures. Winemakers liked screwcaps because they promised to rid them forever of the twin problems of cork taint and oxidation. Stores liked them because they didn't have to worry about keeping the corks moist by resting bottles on their sides or upside down. Bottles could be stored upright. Restaurant staff liked them because they were convenient to open and close—no more fumbling with corkscrews or fighting with broken corks. Winery owners liked screwcaps because they were significantly cheaper than corks.

Everybody seemed to favor the Stelvin caps with the exception of the Australian wine-drinking public. Within a few months the sales staffs at wineries were reporting problems in the market. Consumers still liked corks and associated screwcaps with cheap wines. After the first reports of consumer rejection came in, top management and the winemakers asked salespeople to give the new product a little more time. By six months after introduction, however, the results were clearly bad for screwcaps. But by that time, the next vintage was almost ready to be bottled and the Stelvin closures had already been ordered. So the 1979 vintage also went into screwcap bottles.

As early as the 1980 vintage some Australian wineries were switching back to cork. David Armstrong at his two wineries did the full 1978 and 1979 vintages in Stelvin and part of the 1980. But then he moved entirely back to cork. Peter Wall and Yalumba held out longer, only going back to cork in 1984. That year nature and the winemakers in Australia served up a terrific Riesling that was a huge market success—in bottles with a cork. The company's marketing people naturally pointed to the closure as part of the reason for the good sales.

Bryce Rankine in April 1980 in *The Australian Grapegrower and Winemaker* magazine published a second article entitled "Further Studies on Stelvin and Wine Bottle Closures." It reported on continued tastings of wines with both corks and Stelvin in November 1976, 1977, and 1979. The members of the tasting panel were the same, although the wines were different. This time they were 1976 Kaiser Stuhl Clare Riesling, 1977 Yalumba Moselle, 1975 Yalumba Galway Claret, and 1975 Stonyfell Cabernet Shiraz. The conclusions this time were even more categorical in favor of screwcaps: "The results obtained in this study confirm the superiority of the Stelvin 358 and 323 closures over cork. . . . These results point to the suitability of certain of these closures as replacements for the traditional bark cork, where the wine stored under these closures matured better than under cork."

The 1980 report, though, had little impact. The market had already spoken loudly. Consumers wanted cork in wine bottles, no matter what experts told them.

Two professors at Victoria University of Technology, Wayne J. Mortensen and Brian K. Marks, later wrote a study entitled "The Failure of a Wine Closure Innovation: A Strategic Marketing Analysis." The report was heavy on MBA jargon about the "technology adoption life cycle." In simple terms the authors said that the Stelvin "technology enthusiasts" and "visionaries" had not been "effective as opinion leaders" to convince the "mainstream market" of their superior product. The professors concluded, "Thus no collective strategy was evident and the key stakeholders (screwcap manufacturers, winemakers, and wine retailers) allowed the screwcap to become associated with cheap wine and economy airline travel."

In 1989, Sutter Home, a California maker of low-quality wines best known for introducing white Zinfandel, began using Stelvin caps for its 187-milliliter bottles. Then in 1993, the winery also adopted them for its liter-and-a-half ones. In 2001, though, Sutter Home went back to cork. Stan Hock, the spokesman for the winery, explained the move by saying, "A lot of distributors said we were losing out in the very competitive market because our closure looked downscale."

Bruno de Saizieu, the commercial director of Alcan Packaging Capsules, the current manufacturer of Stelvin, says that screwcap advocates in the 1970s made an early strategic error by targeting their product toward the inexpensive, quick-consumption part of the wine market and thus creating the market perception that screwcaps were only for cheap wines.

The Stelvin story, however, was far from over.

MESSAGE IN A BOTTLE:

BLOCK ISLAND, RHODE ISLAND

Arnold Weinstein, a professor of comparative literature at Brown University in Providence, Rhode Island, is a lover of wine, particularly French reds. He looks back fondly on his early teaching days in the late 1960s, when he could buy allegedly off-vintages of France's First Growths such as Château Latour or Château Lafite Rothschild for $3.99 or $4.99 a bottle in the Boston area. In 1990 to celebrate his fiftieth birthday, Weinstein drank a 1945 Latour that had been given to him as a present. Now that First Growths are selling for $200 or $300 a bottle and more, he's drinking them less frequently, but he still adds fine wines to the collection he stores in the cellar of his home near the Brown campus.

Weinstein's wife, Ann, in 1970 gave him a bottle of 1961 Château Lafite Rothschild as a present in honor of the birth of their son Alexander. It then cost a pricey $22. The 1961 Lafite is widely regarded as one of the great vintages of the twentieth century, and so Weinstein guarded the wine carefully as he moved from house to house and from cellar to cellar in Providence.

In early 2005, though, he began seeing signs in the bottle that worried him. The ullage, the headspace in the bottle between the bottom of the cork and the top of the wine, was growing ever larger and was now down from the neck of the bottle to the shoulder. He worried that he might have waited too long to drink it. The magic 1961 Lafite was probably over-the-hill, lost in the mist of time.

Nonetheless, he brought the bottle to his vacation home on Block Island, Rhode Island, in mid-November 2005 and invited my wife and me plus another couple to come over and see what mysteries the bottle held. "It is a real question mark," he told his guests. It could be a great wine; or it could be a great disappointment.

First Weinstein invited people to a table where the bottle was sitting. With his hands slightly shaking, he then began to open the forty-four-year-old wine. First he removed the tin capsule, the wrapping at the top of the bottle that covers the cork, and was discouraged by what he saw. Part of the cork was sticking out of the bottle, perhaps a sign that it had not been keeping a good seal. The cork's top was also black, another bad sign.

Undaunted, Weinstein used a classic, long corkscrew to pull out the closure, which slipped out of the bottle easily and unbroken. Almost the entire cork was moist with wine.

The host quickly smelled the wine. "It is pure nectar," he said with elation.

Weinstein then poured glasses for his five guests and himself. For nearly an hour the group sat with a fire burning nearby talking about little else than this wonderful old wine. The literature professor was not at a loss for words, describing the wine as "fragrant, fresh, rich, sweet, deep, strong, intact." It even seemed to improve in the glass as time passed. The 1961 Lafite had lived up to its exalted reputation; it was still truly a great wine.

CHAPTER FIVE

A Disastrous Decade
for Portuguese Cork

In the late 1980s, James Laube, a senior editor for the *Wine Spectator,* was working out of the publication's San Francisco office covering the booming Napa Valley scene. From that forum, he was becoming one of the most powerful voices in American wine. Laube had grown up in Southern California, graduating from San Diego State. In 1978, he was a general reporter for the *Vallejo Times-Herald* in charge of its Napa office. His biggest story was naturally the young California wine business, which was so small that you could still get all the players into one room and not feel crowded. In those days before superstar winemakers, reporters had virtually total access to everyone in the valley. Legendary figures such as Robert Mondavi and André Tchelistcheff even took time to teach Laube how to taste wine. It was a bit like a young Roman Catholic taking catechism lessons from the pope.

In those days before the *Wine Spectator* had offices in other parts of the globe, the San Francisco one was in charge of tasting wines from not only California but also from Italy, France, Germany, Australia, and elsewhere. Each week Laube might taste one hundred wines and give them the scores that readers used to help them decide what to buy.

As Laube remembers, in 1988 he and his colleagues were tasting the 1986 vintage of French wines and also their California counterparts when they started to detect a markedly higher level of cork taint. He was surprised by the sudden uptick because it was such a contrast from his experience of only a few years before when he was working on a two-volume compendium, *California's Great Cabernets* and *California's Great Chardonnays.* While researching the books, he set out with the goal of tasting every one of those two classic varietals ever produced in California, and he had tried famous wines, such as a 1939 Beaulieu Georges de Latour Private Reserve, to which he gave only 83 points out of 100, and a 1933 Inglenook Napa Valley Rutherford, which got 95. While tasting thousands of wines, Laube rarely found a tainted bottle, but now suddenly the problem was popping up every day in tasting the 1986 wines.

There had seemingly always been some cork taint in wines, but it was a minor problem that happened too rarely to be much more than a nuisance. In a 1957 French book *Le Liège et les Industries du Liège* (Cork and the Industries of Cork), author Charles Pouillaude wrote about what he called "cork tastes." He cited the findings of a study done by a major Champagne house between 1933 and 1956, which showed the maximum level of corked bottles was three in a thousand or 0.3 percent. Pouillaude concluded that the problem was most common in wines from Alsace, Burgundy, and Champagne, which meant white wines, light reds, and sparkling wines.

Christian Vannequé remembers taint being an insignificant problem at La Tour d'Argent in Paris during the 1970s. He and his staff of sommeliers used to open and test between eight hundred and a thousand bottles a week in those years, but rarely found more than five of those corked. If there were problems, he says, it was almost always wines from the 1960s, rather than from the 1930s, '40s, or '50s. "If you had a problem with a 1929 wine, for example, it was never cork taint," he notes. "It might have a crumbly old cork that was hard to get out of the bottle. But it wasn't corked."

No one has any statistics to back up a personal point of view, but all around the world starting in the 1980s, wine consumers, just like Laube, began running into more and more corked bottles. What had been a minor irritant was turning into a major problem. Brian Croser, Australia's leading winemaker, dates it to "mid to late 1980s." Denis Dubourdieu, a Bordeaux winemaker as well as a professor in the wine program at the University of Bordeaux, told me in 2006 it started "maybe thirty years ago." The *Oxford Companion to Wine,* edited by Jancis Robinson, states categorically, "The problem of corkiness was perceived by the wine industry to have increased in the 1980s."

A wide variety of causes came together at that time, and the reason for the greater incidence of cork taint in that period cannot be laid to just one or two factors. It's also important to remember that any problems dealing with corks will take years to show up in the market because of long industry lag times. It takes nine or ten years to grow the raw material for a cork, and then it's another couple of years before the cork is put into a bottle, and finally it may be one, ten, twenty years or even longer before the cork is pulled and the sommelier or consumer discovers that taint has at some time in the past ruined the bottle.

So why did things get so much worse during the 1980s?

The first cause was a lingering effect of the greatest political and social upheaval Portugal has ever gone through. On April 25, 1974, a group of mainly junior officers in the Portuguese armed forces staged a coup and overthrew the fascist regime whose reign had started in 1932, when António Salazar seized power. The trigger for the revolt was their opposition to the country's colonial wars in Africa. It was called the carnation revolution because adoring civilians showered the suddenly popular soldiers with fresh red carnations and even shoved the flowers down the barrels of their G3 assault rifles, the icons of the wars. During the next two years, Portugal went through a political happening. I remember the heady days well because I covered those exciting times as a reporter for *Time* magazine.

The Portuguese weren't just throwing off the fascist regime, they were really shucking centuries of repressive or corrupt kings and dictators who had preceded Salazar. The nation had little experience with democracy, and people took to the streets to stridently support the cause du jour. While the country was waiting for its first free election, politicians and military leaders jockeyed for power and called their followers into the street to demonstrate their political clout. The general who first headed the interim government was soon replaced by a troika of military officers with varying degrees of leftist leanings. Outsiders such as American secretary of state Henry Kissinger seriously worried that the country would fall under communist control. For months Portugal hardly functioned; people were too busy protesting in the streets. Cynical journalists covering endless demonstrations during the long, hot summer of 1975, when the country seemed to be on the brink of a leftist takeover, used to quip, "A demo a day will keep democracy away." On the main road from the political capital of Lisbon to Oporto, the country's second-largest city, armed irregular militias stopped cars and inspected them, looking for weapons and enemies of the interim government.

In that almost circus atmosphere, the cork industry, the country's most important economic sector, was a prime target for politically inspired insurgents. Strikers "liberated" the cork forests Soviet-style from their owners, and labor committees began running them, while many landlords fled abroad. An industry with a profound and necessarily long view was soon being run by amateurs who wanted to get the most out of the forests as fast as possible. The new managers tried to get production up as a way to support the left-wing government, by using fertilizers and insecticides containing little-understood ingredients that stimulated tree growth and killed underbrush. Untrained workers hacked at sections of the trees that had previously been off-limits. Harvests were taking place long before the normal nine or ten years.

The family of Francisco Almeida Garrett, a cork farmer in the village of Aldeia Velha in the Alentejo region, has owned a thousand-hectare (2,471-acre) cork forest for five generations, but in 1975 people from the village, as he says, "just took over." He didn't get back total control of his property until 1989. The new "owners" recommended cutting down cork trees and planting wheat and barley to "feed the people," even though the land was totally inappropriate for that use. Then they dropped that idea and planted new trees in areas where they had never grown before—and wouldn't grow this time either. Almeida Garrett says that inexperienced workers seriously damaged trees through improper harvesting, and some of them today still show the bad effects of the 1970s.

Worker groups occupied the cork forests owned by the Amorim family, the largest Portuguese cork company, and the interim legislature in 1975 passed a law to nationalize the family holdings as part of a plan to control all international trade in cork. In April 1975, the provisional government passed agricultural reform legislation that expropriated all land of more than five hundred hectares (1,235.5 acres) of unirrigated terrain and more than fifty hectares (123.6 acres) of irrigated property. The Amorim family owned three thousand hectares (7,413 acres) at the time. The legislation was sitting on the desk of Prime Minister Vasco dos Santos Gonçalves waiting for his signature when Américo Amorim, the company chairman, visited the Soviet ambassador in Lisbon, who seemed to have considerable influence on the left-leaning government. Amorim had been doing business with the Soviet Union for more than fifteen years and was the country's largest exporter to the Soviet Union. No one knows what transpired, but the expropriation legislation was never signed.

Then in June of the same year a Soviet delegation arrived in Portugal to place a large order with the new Fundo Fomento da Exportação (Export Trading Institute), which was going to administer all cork exports. Américo Amorim again went to work. On a Sunday, the day before the Soviets were to place the order, he and the head of the delegation held two long meetings in Espinho and Figueira da Foz in northern Portugal. After the second session, the Soviet official returned to the Dom Manuel Hotel in Lisbon and left for Paris and Moscow the next day.

Following the April 1976 election of the government led by Socialist Mário Soares, the country began a long and slow return to stability and the undoing of the revolutionary chaos.

Not that the cork industry before the revolution had been the epitome of industrial efficiency and quality. Because of the longtime fascist government, Portugal had been an outcast from the political and economic mainstream of Western Europe for decades. Portugal in many ways looked more to underdeveloped Africa, where it had colonies, and Brazil, which spoke its language, than to modern Western Europe. For centuries many of the country's best and brightest went abroad to seek a better life. Portugal at the time of the 1974 revolution was an almost feudal society where a few wealthy families held vast power. At its roots, Portuguese cork was still a backward, peasant industry.

In 1982, Terry Lee, who was about to take over as director of the Australian Wine Research Institute and would later head wine research for Gallo in California, went to Portugal for the first time and was appalled by what he found. "The conditions under which they were handling cork was abominable," he recalls. Chlorine was still being used to wash cork to make it look whiter so that it could get a higher price despite the warning of Switzerland's Hans Tanner that chlorine was the main cause of cork taint. Raw bark was left out in the open for weeks, and mold, a key ingredient for TCA, grew freely. "Molds were ubiquitous in the environment of the cork towns of northern Portugal," says Lee. "Everywhere you could see this luxurious mold growth." He still remembers looking at planks of cork with a snowlike covering of mold.

At the same time a backward industry was trying to recover from a runaway revolution, the demand for Portuguese cork was reaching new heights. In the old wine countries of Western Europe, where only top-quality wines had been in bottles with a cork while daily *vin ordinaire* or table wine was in containers with plastic stoppers, change was sweeping over wine consumption. "Drink less, drink better" was the mantra, and the French, Italians, and Germans were drinking more wine with corks and less sealed with plastic.

In addition, new wine countries such as Australia and the United States were becoming major consumers of Portuguese corks. Australia was not only drinking its own wines at home in bottles with corks but also sending more of its exports to Britain, its most important export market, in bottles with them. The U.S. wine boom was in its takeoff phase, and consumers were looking for wines with a cork because that meant quality.

Gallo for years sold its red Hearty Burgundy wine in five-gallon jugs with screwcaps. But it began selling it in standard 750-milliliter bottles after a marketing genius suggested that the company could put a ten-cent cork in the bottle and charge an additional dollar for the same amount of wine.

The new wine producers, though, were in markets far from the traditional ones Portugal had been serving for centuries. It was much more difficult to ship corks from the epicenter of the industry in Oporto thousands of miles across the equator and under humid conditions in cloth bags, where mold loves to grow, to new markets in Australia and New Zealand. There were numerous accounts of whole shiploads of Portuguese cork being contaminated. Wood preservatives containing chlorine that had been painted on slats in a ship's hold would interact with mold on the corks to cause TCA. There is no proof that the Portuguese dumped inferior products on distant markets, but that's widely believed. John Forrest of New Zealand's Forrest Estate still complains today, "The Portuguese stepped back and said, 'Let's just send those suckers whatever we can. They won't know the difference.' If you look at French corks, they're always better than what we got."

Portuguese cork-company executives deny it, but industry insiders confirm that marginal production areas of the forests and parts of the trees near the base that had previously been off-limits started being harvested during the revolution and after world demand increased. Consumers around the world wanted more and more cork, and the producers were not going to turn them down even if that meant lowering industry standards. Says cork farmer Almeida Garrett, "In order to fulfill orders in those years, product got through that shouldn't have. They were boiling cork sometimes in dirty water that they used four or five times before changing it. Work was being done at home or anywhere. There were no controls at all."

Brian Croser, who was running the Australian winery Petaluma during those years, sees the advent of a more industrial atmosphere in wineries as another of the causes for the decline of cork. High-speed bottling was introduced at around this time. Corks were given a coating of silicone to make it easier to get them into bottles on the production line. Previously there might have been a light coating of wax or nothing at all on the natural corks. Croser thinks the silicone can sometimes give unwanted tastes to wine. Paul Draper, the winemaker at Ridge Vineyards in California, shares that view. In addition, by making it easier to get the cork in the bottle, the coating also made it easier for air to enter the bottle as well. Oxidation, which had also been relatively rare, became a much more common problem during the 1980s.

Another possible cause for increased corkiness in the 1980s was the style of wine being made in the new wine-producing countries. The New World wines were cleaner and lighter, especially the whites. Those wines, such as Riesling and Sauvignon Blanc, are more delicate than big reds and have traditionally been more susceptible to TCA, and more of them were on the market.

Finally, by the late 1980s, there was a greater public awareness of TCA. It helps to have a name for a problem to bring it more into the public consciousness. As long as TCA was vaguely dismissed as an unknown romantic smell, it was easy not to pay it much heed. Hans Tanner, however, had given the problem a name, and wine critics, sommeliers, and eventually the general public were starting to identify troubled wines and talked about them more. When Australian winemakers in the late 1970s introduced screwcaps to answer TCA, they were proposing a solution for a problem that not many average wine consumers or even critics had ever experienced or could recognize. By the end of the 1980s, though, not only was more TCA out there, but the wine-consuming public was more aware of it.

Everyone was conscious of the problem, with the exception of the monopoly cork industry. It's easy for everyone in a business to ignore an issue if there is no competition. At the end of the 1980s, cork was still the only available closure for quality wines or wines that had aspirations of quality. Low-tier wines might not be in a bottle with a cork, but that was the commodity market where only price mattered.

Since the cork industry's pricing system was based solely on the product's appearance, rather than on its effectiveness as a closure or its freedom from TCA, cork makers were not encouraged to do anything to improve the quality of their product or eliminate taint. Making the situation even worse, the hundreds of small producers making corks didn't have the technology to do it. They didn't really understand why some corks spoiled wines and others didn't. But it didn't really matter because they could sell all the corks they made.

Given the industry's inability to control the quality of its product and its market monopoly for closures, it's not surprising that the cork industry as a whole chose to do nothing and to blame any problems on its customers or just ignore them. Winemakers complaining that they were getting an increasing number of corked wines were told that they weren't storing them properly or that they had dirty cellars, where good corks were contaminated. Cork salespeople regularly replied that TCA didn't come from their corks, but from equipment used in the wineries. Many winemakers and their cork suppliers became the closest of enemies, trading barbed complaints and blame. The final line of defense for the cork salesperson to the endless criticism was to point out that cork, after all, was a natural product in increasingly short supply. And that, by the way, was the reason that the price was going to be raised again, as it was regularly during the 1980s, sometimes by up to 20 percent a year. From 1982 to 1989, total Portuguese cork exports increased from 100,000 to 111,000 tons, or 11 percent, but the value of that cork increased by 340 percent.

Competition has been the magical engine of progress throughout the entire saga of mankind. People run faster, work smarter, and try harder because they know that someone out there is gaining on them. Nature gave the cork-producing countries of the Mediterranean the gift of an efficient and inexpensive way to seal a bottle, and for centuries that product had no competition. As a result, the cork industry never ran faster, worked smarter, or tried harder. Its members happily counted their profits confident that no one could come along to take away their business even if the quality of their product was declining and it often smelled bad.

By the end of the 1980s, some winemakers and wine consumers, especially in the new wine world countries, were starting to get mad . . . really mad. Just like the television news anchor in the 1976 movie *Network*, they were ready to throw open their windows and shout out to the world, "I'm mad as hell, and I'm not going to take it anymore!"

As Australian winemaker Brian Croser told me in the fall of 2006 while we drove to see the new Pinot Noir vineyard he was planting on the Fleurieu Peninsula south of Adelaide, "Many winemakers had a hatred of cork because of what it had done to their wines, and some of them were willing to throw cork away without thinking about what it contributed to wine's aging and without working to solve the systemic cork problems that had emerged during the 1980s."

CHAPTER SIX

The Rise of Australia

During the 1980s, Australia came of age as a power in the world of wine. With big brands such as Penfolds and Hardy as well as renowned boutique wineries such as Petaluma and Leeuwin Estate, its wines were gaining wide respect. Then a disaster in Europe on April 26, 1986, gave the land down under an unexpected market opportunity. The Soviet Union's Chernobyl nuclear accident spread radioactive contamination across the wine-growing regions of Western Europe. Quickly nonproducing or low-producing countries such as Sweden, which had previously been big buyers of bulk wines from France, looked around for countries that might not have been affected by the nuclear fallout. The obvious producer was Australia, a country half a world away in the southern hemisphere. Its vineyards had been untouched by Chernobyl, and Australia that year also had a large surplus of wine, which had been destined for distillation into industrial alcohol. Spurred on by the unexpectedly large exports to Switzerland and Sweden as well as to its always important market in Britain, Australian exports took off—and the Aussies have never looked back. Australia in 2000 passed France to become the largest exporter to the British market. By then some Aussie wines such as Penfolds Grange and Henschke Hill of Grace were achieving prices that matched those of France's best.

At the same time, the center of world wine research was moving from the University of California, Davis, to the Australian Wine Research Institute. In the immediate decades after World War II, Davis ruled supreme in viticultural and enology studies, surpassing France's University of Bordeaux, which had dominated the field for the better part of a century. During the 1960s and early 1970s, a well-funded golden age of research flourished at Davis with such academic stars as Maynard Amerine and Ralph E. Kunkee, who even had a wine microorganism named after him—*Lactobacillus kunkeei*. Much of the money for the academic work came from giants such as Gallo, which looked to Davis to supplement its large, in-house research operation. Amerine, in particular, had close relations with the Gallo family, and both sides served each other well. The Davis faculty, though, also worked well with smaller wineries such as Beaulieu Vineyard and even such Napa newcomers as Stag's Leap Wine Cellars.

Within a short time, however, the generation that had led Davis from the end of Prohibition in 1933 through the Napa Valley boom of the 1970s and into the 1980s retired and a new one took over. The newcomers were equally talented scientists and, in some cases, were even more esteemed academics than their predecessors. The new group, though, lacked personal connections to the winemaking community, especially to the big companies that had deep pockets to pay for research. Those corporations began complaining privately that Davis was becoming too academic in its studies and too far removed from business. Winery owners said they wanted real-world solutions to real-world problems and not arcane studies that might sit on the shelf unread.

The priorities of academia and business, of course, are different and often conflict. In the publish-or-perish world of universities, life is all about getting studies peer-reviewed and then published in serious journals. Everything has to be transparent or open to the public, even though the funding that makes the research possible often comes from a private company not particularly interested in having its winemaking problems outed even in scholarly publications.

The big companies were also increasingly concerned about international competition and wanted to keep their secrets secret. Unlike in an earlier era, California wineries were no longer fighting to get world attention as a major wine area. The camaraderie that had marked the period of the California wine industry when it was recovering from the ravages caused by Prohibition was now less evident in a world where companies were not only competing fiercely against each other but also with winemakers abroad. Professor Vernon Singleton still recalls a study he did on a contamination problem that Manischewitz, a prominent maker of kosher wines, had with one of its Loganberry hybrids. Company officials called him on the carpet after he published a paper on his research, complaining that they didn't want that information to get out to the public—or their competitors.

Davis was not as much in touch with a new type of winery owner then rising to prominence in California. This was the proprietor of a smaller boutique winery who had dreams of producing one of the cult wines such as Harlan or Diamond Creek that could sell for $100 and more a bottle. These people, who had often made their fortune in another field, were a world away from the Gallo brothers, Ernest and Julio, or the Mondavi brothers, Robert and Peter. More often than not, the aspiring cultists hired their winemakers rather than doing the job themselves, and they were quick to support them with outside consultants, whether it be American Helen Turley, Frenchman Michel Rolland, Australian Richard Smart, or one of many others. The advisers were called flying winemakers because they seemed to spend as much time in airliners as they did in vineyards or wineries. The new owners weren't interested in the science of winemaking and the topics Davis promoted; they were looking for the recipe for success that would get them high scores from critics such as Robert M. Parker Jr.

By the mid-1980s, funding from California's large wine companies to pay for Davis research, which had been so plentiful for a generation, began drying up. The major wine companies now provide about $1 million annually to the American Vineyard Foundation for research, and the U.S. Department of Agriculture spends an additional $2.5 million per year. That is a pittance compared with the A$50 million (US$39.5 million) per year that Australia's public authorities invest for an industry one-third the size. California's academic wine centers were literally being starved for research dollars.

The reputation of UC Davis also took a heavy blow in the 1980s after an unexpected reoccurrence of the dreaded phylloxera in Northern California's wine country. When experts began examining where the outbreak was happening and why, they learned that the affected vineyards had been planted with a rootstock known as AxR1. In the 1950s, some people at Davis had recommended it to grape growers even though French experts had been warning their farmers not to use it because it was subject to phylloxera. In an August 6, 1985, memo, the Phylloxera Task Force, made up of Davis academics and state officials, still called it "a highly productive and phylloxera resistant rootstock." But by 1991, the same group was warning viticulturists away from AxR1, and soon wineries all across California were pulling out vines killed by the nineteenth-century pest. Davis defenders say farmers misread the Davis reports, but the university research center undoubtedly lost tremendous credibility with the wine community. Lewis Perdue in his book *The Wrath of Grapes* entitled the chapter on that episode "The $4 Billion Disaster That Didn't Have to Happen" and placed the blame squarely on Davis.

Davis continues today to turn out a steady stream of smart and well-trained graduates who staff wineries not only in California but also around the world. But other institutions have replaced it as the research meccas for global wine research.

While the number of new UC Davis studies slowed down because of the paucity of funds, private research labs grew in importance in California. These were nonacademic companies conducting technical tests and sometimes offering consulting advice for wineries. The major difference between their work and that of UC Davis was that the information gathered in the studies was totally proprietary. Little of the data from private labs ever made its way into scholarly journals or was peer-reviewed. The private labs still have a great impact despite the charges from critics that their work is suspect because they are in the pay of clients.

On the ground floor of an unexciting but functional office complex on a quiet side street in St. Helena in the heart of the Napa Valley is ETS Laboratories, the most prominent of the California private research centers. Marjorie Groat, a UC Davis graduate, who had been a medical lab technician before studying enology, founded the company. After graduation, she worked in the cellars of the Robert Mondavi Winery and Spring Mountain, but quickly realized that winemakers didn't like to do wine analysis on such things as pH values and the measurement of acidity that are essential in winemaking. André Tchelistcheff, the longtime winemaker at Beaulieu Vineyard, had a lab and wine-consulting business in the 1940s also in St. Helena, but that was long gone and currently no one was providing those kinds of services. So Groat in 1978 founded ETS. At first, she held down three jobs—two in wineries and one in a medical lab—in addition to running her own company. She originally named it Enological Technical Service, but people kept massacring that title, so she simplified things by sticking to the initials.

The following year, she met Gordon Burns, who had just come back from a motorcycle tour of the world that had been interrupted for a time while he ran a construction company in Iran. Burns's father was an inventor who had many patents, including one for the first oxygen mask for commercial aircraft. Soon Burns and Groat married, and Gordon was working for the company.

ETS's first office was in the basement of the Burns home on Main Street in St. Helena, where Gordon laid down concrete over half of the dirt floor and built their first workbenches. The couple bought much of their early testing equipment from hospitals selling outdated items at auction. The business was soon successful, but stayed in the basement for eight years and with no outside employees.

While the couple was skimping on staff, they were investing heavily in new technology to run the complex tests winemakers wanted performed. With a clear vision of where he wanted to take the company, Gordon Burns knew he had to stay in the forefront of technology, and that meant having the latest and the best instruments, no matter what the cost. Today every academic research lab in the world envies ETS's mother lode of high-tech gear.

Over the years, ETS has moved beyond simple analyses of wine samples that determine such things as the level of free sulfur dioxide and now offers extremely advanced microbiology tools and services it has developed. The company is perhaps proudest of its genetic-based analytical tool known as Scorpions, which can help determine what ails a wine.

Gordon describes the work their company does as applied research, since the results go right into a winery's production. He has drawn a strict line, though, between analyzing a winery's problem and consulting with it to solve that trouble, so he keeps the testing and analysis separate from the consulting. Other private labs, such as one in Pomerol that the famous wine consultant Michel Rolland and his wife own, perform both functions. Winemakers, though, still ask Burns for informal advice since they know he is well-informed simply because so many wine problems go through the doors of ETS every day. When Dean Sylvester, the winemaker at nearby Whitehall Lane Winery, was puzzled over some issues with sulfides, he asked Burns about the problem and received useful suggestions.

Today ETS has more than forty employees as well as satellite offices in Oregon, Washington, and Monterey County. It does work for wineries mainly in the western hemisphere but also as far away as Australia and Eastern Europe. In 2003, ETS began a $50,000 research project for the American Vineyard Foundation on TCA, which is believed to be the first study the organization commissioned to a nonacademic institute.

As California's wine research was changing direction, Australian efforts in the 1980s were gathering strength thanks in large part to the unique cooperative working relationship among the nation's wine companies and government at the Australian Wine Research Institute and other research providers. AWRI was founded in 1955, when that country was almost invisible on the world wine map. That year 170 Australian producers exported only 383,994 liters (101,400 gallons) of table wine. Today more than 2,000 wineries annually ship abroad in excess of 1 billion liters (264 million gallons). The research budget of the AWRI in 1955 was A$20,700 (US$16,342). Currently it is some A$15 million (US$12 million) annually.

The key to AWRI's success is the funding mechanism for its studies. The money comes from a tax on both grape growers and wineries. The rate has risen over the years and is currently A$2 (US$1.58) per ton on grapes harvested, which grape growers pay, and A$5 (US$3.95) per ton on grapes crushed, which wineries pay. The Australian federal government then matches that dollar for dollar for money actually spent on research. The total amount is split primarily between two national bodies.

The first is the Commonwealth Scientific and Industrial Research Organization (CSIRO), Australia's national science agency, which does studies on viticultural issues through its Division of Plant Industry. The second is the Australian Wine Research Institute, which does studies on anything from when the grapes reach the cellar door to shipment of wine to customers. The CSIRO Division of Plant Industry and the AWRI are housed cheek by jowl in South Australia in the Adelaide suburb of Urrbrae on the Waite Campus of the University of Adelaide. The AWRI board of directors, which is made up of six wine-business representatives plus three ex officio representatives of government and academia, drives the research agenda and oversees the institute's management. While UC Davis has limited research dollars and is often at odds with the California wine industry, in particular, Gallo, the AWRI is run basically by its industry and has plenty of financial support to fund research into the subjects it deems important to the future of Australian wine. The AWRI also has a unit that does private analysis and research for clients on a proprietary basis much like California's ETS.

In the 1960s and 1970s, a large amount of the Australian research was focused on viticulture, improving the quality and quantity of grapes with work on such topics as clonal selection and machine harvesting and pruning. This helped bring the country's vineyards up to world quality quickly. In more recent times, AWRI studies have centered on various winemaking topics, in particular wine closures.

The current AWRI director, Isak (Sakkie) Pretorius, is a cautious scholar who sprinkles his conversation with allusions to his native South Africa: "In the early morning in the bush all the animals are running, but only the swiftest survive." Pretorius says AWRI research has both theoretical and practical applications. His model, he says, is not Nobel laureate

Niels Bohr, although he respects him, because he was only interested in the pursuit of fundamental understanding without any practical end in mind. Nor is it the equally admirable Thomas Edison, whose goal was practical solutions through trial and error. The model for Pretorius—and for AWRI—is Louis Pasteur, who integrated Bohr's search for fundamental understanding with Edison's drive for practical utility. "You can't just solve problems, because problems always keep coming," Pretorius says. "You must solve problems by understanding why they happen, and when unexpected issues arise, you must take off your lab coat and become the fire brigade to solve them."

Moreover, research itself is not the answer, he says. AWRI's goal is "information dissemination." The forum for that is what the institute's staff calls its "road shows," where they meet with winemakers around Australia. The sessions, which can go from one to three days, are two-way flows of information from winemakers to the AWRI staff about what issues are on their minds as well as from the AWRI researchers to the winemakers telling about their latest studies. It takes the AWRI staff about three years to make the rounds of the country's entire twenty-nine wine regions. At each stop, sixty or seventy winemakers show up for continuing education.

The Australian wine-research system on paper looks so logical and successful it's surprising that other winemaking countries around the world have not copied it. The Aussie model, though, is unique. A survey done by the Harvard Business School in 2003 of the world's leading wine regions concluded that the Adelaide Cluster, which is made up of AWRI, CSIRO, and the wine faculty at the University of Adelaide, is the world's most innovative and productive wine center.

The highest compliment that could be made to Australian wine research and the Adelaide Cluster took place in 1997, when Gallo hired away Terry Lee, who had been director of AWRI for fourteen years, to become the American company's new head of research. Twice early in his research career Lee spent time studying at Davis; now he was going back to teach the Americans something.

During his last years at the AWRI, Lee had been getting strong messages back from his board and from the road shows that the biggest issue facing the Australian industry was wine closures. For several years those problems had been the largest single topic of calls coming into the institute's Consultancy and Problem Solving Service. "After years of turning out great wines only to have them spoiled by a faulty cork, people were desperate for an alternative," says Lee. It was time for a major study on the subject of closures that would be patterned on earlier ones AWRI had done on processing aids such as bentonite, diatomaceous earth, and pectic enzymes. The goal was simply to identify which type of closure on the market met the expectations of the winemaker, the bottling-line operator, and the consumer. Before Lee could get the project started, however, he was off to California, leaving that as a top priority for his successor, Peter Høj.

MESSAGE IN A BOTTLE: MIAMI

Dorothy J. Gaiter and John Brecher write the "Tastings" column for the Friday Wall Street Journal. *Wine retailers say that they have the greatest impact of any wine critics. After they recommend a wine, it's hard to keep it in stock.*

The couple met while both were working for the Miami Herald, *where their love of wine and for each other first developed. On December 27, 1978, John prepared to propose to Dottie over a bottle of 1974 Roederer Cristal Champagne. He sat her down on a sofa and brought out Champagne glasses that his parents had been given for their wedding in 1945. His plan was to propose as soon as the cork popped. He took the gold metal off the neck of the bottle, unscrewed the basket, and twisted the cork. And nothing happened. It didn't budge. He pulled and twisted. Sweat was pouring off his face. But he was not going to propose until the cork came out. Then the phone rang. It was John's father. John told him what was happening.*

"Use pliers," said his father, who had rarely opened a bottle of Champagne in his life.

John told him that there was no way you should open a bottle of Cristal Champagne with pliers.

"Use pliers," his dad said again.

John thanked him for the advice and, still doubtful, hung up. Then he went and got the pliers.

With their help, the cork began to move, grudgingly. Finally, finally, out it popped. To the couple, the cork looked as big as a tree.

John finally proposed, and Dottie said yes. The couple still has the cork encased in a large piece of plastic that sits on their mantelpiece.

CHAPTER SEVEN

The French Cover-Up

*Pascal Chatonnet quietly helped
wineries uncover and solve their
cellar problems.*

The 1980s were a glorious decade for French wine, especially in Bordeaux, when nature blessed winemakers with several great vintages. The most famous was 1982, which brought American critic Robert M. Parker Jr. to world fame after he correctly called it one of the great vintages of the twentieth century in Bordeaux. Many American consumers were just discovering wine, and Franco-American relations were relatively good. With the help of Parker—an admitted Francophile—and a strong dollar, Americans were both drinking up and storing away lots of Bordeaux's best.

Since they were enjoying some of their highest profits ever, French winemakers planted new vineyards massively and installed shiny new equipment in their cellars. In this heady time, normally conservative vintners were investing like spendthrifts. New stainless steel fermenting tanks, once used only by the most famous First Growths, were installed at more modest wineries. Storage space was increased with new barrels and new cellars. As a symbol of the new prosperity, the barrels, walls, and ceilings of storage facilities were painted with a wood preservative that not only protected them but also was a shining symbol of success.

Wineries also installed new ventilation and air-conditioning systems in their cellars. Evaporation of wine through the sides of wooden barrels is a major problem, and by keeping the wines cool and the moisture level relatively high, wineries could lower the amount of evaporation. Cool underground caves used to be the way to reduce the problem, but now they added air-conditioning to eliminate it.

As the 1980s progressed, however, winemakers began noticing some strange smells emanating from their cellars and sometimes from their wines. This pervasive mousy smell was similar to the infamous cork taint that had been around for years. But it was also different. There was no denying it. The wives of Bordeaux winemakers complained to their husbands when they came home for dinner, that they smelled like cat urine. The winemakers were not as aware of the smell because TCA causes anosmia, the temporary loss of smell. In those distant times before the Internet, winemakers were writing letters to each other asking if they had the same trouble. When the letters were opened, the recipients would often pull back in shock because of the offensive smell drifting out of the envelope.

One of the worst cases of the problem was at Roederer, the famed Champagne house whose most prestigious product was Cristal, considered by many to be the world's best bubbly, which was already then selling for more than $100 a bottle. As early as 1982, Roederer began getting reports from the U.S. market about significant returns of bottles after complaints that they were corked.

Jérôme Quiot, president of the powerful Institut National des Appellations d'Origine, which regulates the top tier of the French wine business, admitted later that wineries were able to keep the troubles out of the press and away from the public through quiet gentlemen's agreements. Said he, "The consumer would say, 'Your wine isn't bad; it's just corked. If you replace the bottle, I won't say anything more about it.'" Wineries such as Roederer were only too happy to agree to the proposal, and so for nearly a decade vintners talked about the problem openly with each other in private and also with wine-research institutions but never with the general public or the press. It was just their little secret. There was a conspiracy of silence toward the outside world.

During the 1980s, the problem spread to some of the most famous wineries in France, included Château Latour, one of the Bordeaux First Growths, Château Ducru-Beaucaillou, a top Second Growth, and Château Canon, a well-respected wine from the St.-Émilion area. Since Bordeaux has the highest concentration of wineries in the world, the problem easily migrated from one location to another.

The same gas chromatography–mass spectrometry (GC-MS) technology Hans Tanner had used to identify first 2,4,6-TCA and then 2,3,4,6-TeCA in the early 1980s arrived in Bordeaux in the late 1980s. Professor Alain Bertrand, one of the stars of the University of Bordeaux's enology faculty, still remembers the enthusiasm with which he greeted new and more modern GC-MS equipment. For the first time, it was possible to make massive tests in search of cork taint or this still unknown problem troubling so many French wine cellars. And while previously an excellent researcher had to spend weeks, or even months to do just one analysis, now an average lab technician could do five or six a day. Previously the University of Bordeaux enology staff had to depend on sensory analysis and could only vaguely say that a wine seemed to have some off odor; now they could pinpoint that a specific wine had, for example, 5 parts per trillion of TCA.

Another person who also saw the potential of the equipment was Pascal Chatonnet, a graduate student whose thick eyebrows made him look like a young Charles Aznavour. At the time, Chatonnet was working on an advanced degree, which he received in 1991. His field of research was the influence of oak barrels in the composition of wine. He was one of the rising stars of French wine research, especially when it came to troubled wines, having done extensive original studies on such topics as *Brettanomyces,* a yeast sometimes found in barrels that can cause off-flavors.

Chatonnet came from a family of Bordeaux's right bank that had been in the wine business as far back as there were records and included links to such famed wineries as Château Ausone. His wife, Dominique Labadie, also earned a degree in enology at Bordeaux. She had several excellent internships, but winery owners were then reluctant to hire a woman winemaker, so she ended up back at the university labs doing studies on aromas and quality control.

Chatonnet was soon working almost full-time on the perplexing issue facing wineries in the Bordeaux area. The stinky problem was clearly not cork taint, because it was not isolated to a random bottle here or there.

It was usually found throughout most or all the wines at a location. One case involved one of the most famous producers in Sancerre, which had no less than 1 million contaminated bottles in inventory. Another winery in the Rhône's Châteauneuf-du-Pape region threw away its entire production for a year because of its pervasive problems with the vintage.

Even the Chatonnet family's Château L'Archange winery in St.-Émilion could not escape the problem. At first Pascal thought the trouble was in the barrels, since his father had been renovating the cellar. But the contamination was also found in wines that had been fermented in stainless steel tanks and had never been in contact with wood. The new winery, though, had new insulation made of wood particles. Chatonnet studied samples of that with the help of the new equipment and found the contamination was similar to TCA, but was not exactly the same. As he pondered the dilemma, Chatonnet concluded that the contamination occurred when the wines were being pumped from tank to tank, a common procedure in winemaking, and was caused by wayward chloroanisoles floating in the winery's air.

The young scientist dug into the known research looking for the answer. He soon found Tanner's two publications from the early 1980s and read with special interest the 1983 one on 2,3,4,6-tetrachloroanisole (TeCA). Chatonnet also uncovered German studies of similar contamination in potatoes stored in wooden cases and chickens raised in wooden cages.

Chatonnet concluded the cause of the problem was the chlorine-based pentachlorophenol, one of the compounds in the wood preservatives widely used around wineries. That was the first cousin of trichloroanisole and tetrachloroanisole, which also gave wines bad odors through corks and wood products. The pentachlorophenol preservative became pentachloroanisole, which is not as strong as the other two, but still gives off low levels of the same moldy, stinky smell. In some wineries, Chatonnet found all three compounds: trichloroanisole, tetrachloroanisole, and pentachloroanisole. Chatonnet and three Bordeaux University colleagues in 1994 published a paper, "Nature and Origin of Musty Odors in Wine Cellars and Their Influence on Wine Contamination," in the French wine review *Journal International des Sciences de la Vigne et du Vin,* but it attracted little attention outside the scientific community.

The Chatonnet work showed chloroanisoles were often found trapped in inert absorbent material such as porous plastics and even bentonite, a material used to remove fine particles from wines. Once they were in a gaseous form, they easily infiltrated an entire location. They could also be shipped throughout a facility via air-conditioning units, which often contained chlorinated water. The high humidity in cellars sent the process into overdrive. After several years of low-level contamination, the itinerant compounds were not just on the barrels, but also on walls, floors, and wooden pallets, where many wineries stored bottles of wine for years before they were shipped. Cork and plastic materials, in particular, just soak them up through the air. Studies showed that a flame-retardant chemical painted on wood was a major cause of the problem. In one cellar the wooden racks had 2,185 parts per trillion pentachloroanisole per gram of wood. Wine stored in year-old barrels had 38 parts per trillion. Léonard Humbrecht, a leading winemaker in Alsace, used to point out to visitors how he had his wine on beautiful oak pallets, little knowing that the treated wood was contaminating it.

Entrepreneur is a term originally coined by the French to describe people who start innovative, new companies, although French entrepreneurs are relatively rare since that society values security more highly than risk-taking. But Pascal Chatonnet looked at the crisis facing the French wine industry as a result of cellar contamination and recognized the opportunity to be an entrepreneur. He was familiar with California's ETS Laboratories and thought there might be a market for a similar private research lab in France.

From his current position at an academic research center, Chatonnet had also concluded that universities were not good places to do the type of work French wineries needed to clean up their cellars. The industry demanded fast turnarounds on analyses and concrete suggestions about how to solve problems. They didn't want theories; they wanted solutions. And they didn't want them the day after tomorrow; they wanted them the day before yesterday. The very survival of some French wineries was now in question. Since he had grown up in the wine business, Chatonnet instinctively understood the value people in that field place on confidentiality. An unflattering story in the press can devastate a winery's sales for years. The wineries facing cellar taint didn't want the world to know what was happening.

Chatonnet was also more interested in having an impact on the world than doing research that ended up perhaps forgotten in some scholarly journal, such as had happened with Tanner's groundbreaking work. "I'm not the one who identified TCA," Chatonnet says. "But I pointed to it and said it was like a bomb you could find anywhere." He wanted to see results.

"It's not sufficient to identify something. If you are just doing research at a university and identifying things, you are not changing anything. It's true with wine as well as with other areas. I wanted to change things. It's not by publishing a paper that you solve a problem in the real world."

Chatonnet understood that the key to being innovative in this field was new technology, in particular having access to GC-MS equipment to do the analyses. Bordeaux had some of the hardware, but not as much as it needed because of the internal battles to get research money in any academic institution. Success, he concluded, would only be guaranteed if he took the financial risk of buying the latest machines, which then cost more than $100,000 each. In addition, he recognized he would have to keep spending on technology to stay at the forefront of research. If he did, he could quickly overtake the Bordeaux University research center and become one of the leaders of international wine research.

When Pascal approached Dominique with the idea of their starting a business, she was skeptical because of the risk. They both had good, secure jobs with France's leading academic wine-research institution, which was already doing work on this exact topic for wineries. Was there really a place for an unknown, private lab?

Fortunately for Pascal's entrepreneurial dream, Dominique was bored with the repetitive and somewhat tedious research she was then doing at the university. Finally the two decided that she would start the company, while he stayed with Bordeaux University's enology faculty so they would continue to have a regular paycheck. After doing the basic studies in 1991 and 1992 to identify the cellar-taint problem, the following year the couple founded Excell, a private wine-research institute. It was located in a small office in Mérignac, a Bordeaux suburb. Much of the start-up money came from a contract with the barrel-making company Seguin Moreau, which was then investing heavily in research and young scientists working on the interactions of wood and wine. Excell at first had only one employee, Dominique. For the next eight years, Pascal spent his day doing research at the University of Bordeaux and then his evenings at his fledgling company. While still holding down two jobs, Pascal earned his Ph.D. in 1995, which was a continuation of his work on the role of oak barrels in wine development.

Excell was quickly doing a brisk business. Every winery in Bordeaux was concerned about the problem, whether it had contamination or not, and they all came to either the researchers at Bordeaux University or Excell for solutions. No one was any longer dismissing cellar taint, which was found in a growing number of wineries. Troubles were popping up in the most unexpected areas. In some wineries the wood used in the rafters had been treated with chlorine-based products. Says Bordeaux's Bertrand, "Wineries were willing to spend no matter what it took to get rid of the problem and no matter how small the problem. Places that had only two parts per trillion of taint in their wines, which is below the level that most people could identify, were terrified."

Slowly over five to six years from the early to late 1990s, the Bordeaux wineries quietly cleaned up their facilities—often with the help of Excell. In some cases it meant only a routine inspection of the cellar to make sure that no contamination was present. In extreme cases such as Château Latour it meant rebuilding the winery.

By that time, the problem had started to find its way into somewhat broader public attention. In the third edition of his Bordeaux wine guide, which was published in 1998, Robert M. Parker Jr. took note of it, although he didn't identify the cause or the extent of the problem. Consumers had to read between the lines to understand what had happened. In one section he wrote, "Château Ducru-Beaucaillou had a problem with bottles in 1988, 1989, and 1990. The question marks that accompany my tasting notes reflect the fact that many bottles from these vintages had a musty component in the aromatics, probably attributable to some noxious aromas given off by the insulation in the old *chai* at Ducru. This *chai* was completely rebuilt and the sources for the off smells eliminated."

Parker also gave poor marks to the wines of Château Canon, which had well-known taint problems. In his 1998 Bordeaux book, he wrote, "Contamination in the aging cellar caused many of the wines produced between 1992 and 1996 to smell and taste excessively musty." He wrote specifically of the 1993 vintage, "In addition to unpleasant severe, tough tannin, a moldy, wet dog/musty cardboard bouquet is present in this clipped, unattractive wine. Avoid." And he wrote of the 1994 one, "This wine is marred by damp wood, wet cardboard, musty, cork-like aromas."

Just before Christmas 1998, two French publications, the weekly newsmagazine *L'Express* and the consumer review *Que Choisir,* blew the top off the French cover-up. In their detailed joint exposés, the whole story was revealed, even though it had by then been solved. The story quoted the new director of Château Canon as saying that when the Chanel group of luxury products bought the property in 1993, it was aware of the problem and had to spend some $500,000 scrubbing down and in some cases replacing old equipment. The article quoted top French wine officials as saying that they had hidden the news of the cellar problems from the general public because "consumers would be a little lost" in the details of the issue. It quoted several sources saying the trouble was an "old story," which indeed it was.

L'Express accompanied its article with a table reporting on a test it had conducted on some of France's most famous wines. It had found in them some staggering amounts of all three troublemaking chloroanisoles: trichloroanisole, tetrachloroanisole, and pentachloroanisole. The 1994 Château Latour wine had a combined 360 parts per trillion, and in the 1996 vintage of the winery's second-label Château Forts de Latour it was 340. In the 1989 Château Ducru-Beaucaillou the level was 149. There were also lesser amounts in the 1994 Château Gazin (139) and the 1994 Château Gruaud-Larose (84).

The international wine press picked up the story from *L'Express,* and the "French Problem," as cellar tainting was soon dubbed, was finally known to serious wine consumers. But by then the wine collections of connoisseurs and leading restaurants around the world had a good supply of tainted bottles in their cellars.

Chatonnet still had one more source of wine off-odors to find. In 2002, he was called in to work for a winery in Argentina whose wines were having TCA-like aromas. He tracked the problem down to a wood treatment used in the winery's roof and its large oak vats that contained the chemical tribromophenol, which was transformed into 2,4,6-tribromoanisole. The chemical was then widely used in both Latin America and Europe as a flame retardant. In 2004, Chatonnet's work on 2,4,6-tribromoanisole was published in the *Journal of Agricultural and Food Chemistry.*

With this research, Chatonnet in a sense completed the work of Hans Tanner, who in the early 1980s discovered two sources of taint: 2,4,6-trichloroanisole (TCA) and 2,3,4,6-tetrachloroanisole (TeCA). Chatonnet added pentachloroanisole (PCA) and later 2,4,6-tribromoanisole (TBA). Most important, he also described the exact way the wine can easily be contaminated through indirect contact with those volatile compounds. He showed how storage or movement of wines in the atmosphere of a contaminated cellar is enough to change wine aromas quickly and significantly.

Chlorophenols—trichlorophenol, tetrachlorophenol, and pentachlorophenol—have a wide range of uses in modern society as cleaning agents and pesticides. As a result, they have become almost ubiquitous in the environment. Phenols are found in many organic substances, including wood products. When they come in contact with chlorine, the result is chlorophenols. When those interact with mold, they form the corresponding chloroanisoles—trichloroanisole, tetrachloroanisole, and pentachloroanisole.

Cork-manufacturing is particularly susceptible to TCA. An Australian study published in 1987 found TCA in the bark of nearly half the cork oak trees in a forest. But the main origin of contamination appears to be the heavy growth of fungi on the wet cork bark just after boiling under uncontrolled conditions and in contaminated storage centers. That, however, is not the only source. Wood preservatives and insecticides can also contain tetrachlorophenols, pentachlorophenols, or tribromophenols that can be turned into foul-smelling anisoles.

TCA and TBA are equally potent and can be detected by most people at about 5 parts per trillion, while the threshold for recognizing TeCA is about 10 ppt. The human nose, though, is simply not up to the job of differentiating between various taints, which can sometimes be found in combination in the same wine. As evidence of how people can jump to the wrong conclusions, Chatonnet points to a 2002 study by the Ontario Liquor Control Board that involved twenty-four hundred wines. While 49 percent of those with musty odors turned out to have more than 2 parts per trillion of TCA, the problem with 51 percent of the bad wines was other sources.

Although the general public and the wine press regularly refer to "corked wines" and knowledgeable people might blame it on TCA, the off-smells in wines could come from any one of several troublemakers, in particular the four Tanner and Chatonnet identified. The French problems in the 1980s had nothing to do with cork, yet the headline on the *Wine Spectator*'s story about the incident read "Wood Preservative Blamed for Corky French Wines."

News of noncork sources of wine taint offered some relief to Portuguese cork producers, and with only a small leap they began claiming that troubles beyond cork were a prime source of taint problems. That reaction, though, only infuriated researchers such as the University of Bordeaux's Bertrand, who felt that cork producers had been trying to bury their problems by denying they even existed. Says Bertrand, "Researchers in this field had been muzzled by the big cork producers into denying that there was cork taint. They were aware of their part of the problem and should have taken action."

CHAPTER EIGHT

Supreme Corq Breaks the Monopoly

Supreme Corq's Jerome Zech
soon had a smash-hit product.

In 1990, Dennis Burns, a Seattle plastics entrepreneur, was taking a wine tourism trip to California's Alexander Valley in Sonoma County. Going from winery to winery, he sampled wines and visited cellars where French oak barrels were stacked to the ceiling and guides explained the intricacies of turning grapes into wine. Burns, a liberal arts graduate from the University of Washington, had unexpectedly become a businessman. His entrepreneurial moment came in 1963 with a smack in the face. Burns, an avid amateur hockey player, was playing in the third period, and his team was down by one goal when an opponent whacked him in the face with a stick. Later he looked into buying a mask so that wouldn't happen again, but he couldn't find any because the National Hockey League at the time prohibited their use. So Burns made one for himself. After parents at hockey rinks started asking him where they could buy one for their children, he started a company called Pro-Tec to manufacture plastic hockey helmets, which was soon also making bicycling and skydiving headgear. In 1982, Burns turned the division that made sunglasses with impact-resistant lenses into a second company, Gargoyles.

As he was touring wine cellars, Burns noticed that wine barrels had white plastic plugs sticking out of the top. Winemakers called them bungs, and they provided easy access to the wine. Burns asked his guide why the barrels had plastic stoppers, while the bottles he had just seen in the tasting room had cork ones. The guide explained it was because natural cork sometimes caused something called cork taint that could ruin wines. The winery wanted to protect its precious product from that, the guide said, so the wine in the barrel had a plastic stopper. A logical enough answer for everyone on the tour except Burns, who thought to himself, "Boy, if you could do that with a wine bottle, you'd save a whole lot of grief." Why not a plastic cork? If plastic is good enough for a barrel, why not for a bottle?

When he returned to Seattle, Burns asked his patent attorney to check out if anyone had a patent on a plastic cork. Actually there were lots of them; eight had been filed just in the 1980s. In fact, two companies were already making plastic corks. One was the French company Novembal, which called its product Tage. The British company Metal Box also had a plastic cork, which was being made under license by New Jersey's Lermer Packaging and sold with the brand name Cellucork. When he looked at the patents and the two products, though, Burns saw a market opening. The existing synthetic corks were made using an old technology and an inexpensive plastic, ethyl vinyl acetate. Burns recognized that didn't have the elasticity needed to make the cork fit tightly into a bottleneck. He thought another type of plastic, thermo plastic elastomers, would do a better job. The attorney pointed out that they might be able to get a patent on a new product using a new material or a new process.

So with little more than an idea that he might be able to build a better plastic cork, Burns decided to give it a try. Since he was already tied up running two businesses, the entrepreneur hired Jerome Zech, a forty-one-year-old ex-IBM executive who was then working in the Seattle area for a start-up mobile-phone company, to run the new venture. Zech was a perfect candidate for the job. IBM's training program was known for producing excellent managers, but at the same time he also had experience working at a young, small company and was aware of the challenges and perils that involves. An added plus was that Zech knew his way around Seattle's venture-capital community, and raising capital would be an important part of the job. Burns basically told Zech to take his idea and see if he could turn it into a successful company. A Seattle advertising/design company came up with a catchy name. The new corporation would be called Supreme Corq (two words), but its product SupremeCorq (one word).

With no staff and a nebulous mandate, Zech set out to learn the plastics and wine businesses. He quickly realized several of the premises for starting the company were wrong. Both the raw material and the manufacturing process were not what Burns had originally envisaged. Many people in the plastics business, including a plastics broker, told Zech that what he was trying to accomplish couldn't be done. One pleasant discovery was that the wine industry was unhappy with both of the existing products because bottles closed with them tended to leak and the corks were hard to extract from the bottle.

Zech first hired an engineer, Chuck Roehm, to help him work through the issues of how to make the product. He found an Illinois company that sold a plastic compound made with Kraton, a medical-grade product that was a better raw material. It cost nearly three times more than the one used in the two existing plastic corks, but had many of the characteristics Zech and his engineer wanted. The material dated back to World War II, when there was a crash program to make rubber substitutes, and had been improved since then. It was currently being used in a variety of products ranging from roofing materials to surgical goods.

There are basically two ways to manufacture a plastic product. The first injects molten plastic that has the consistency of toothpaste into a mold that gives it a shape. This is called injection molding and is the same as the process used to make glass bottles. The other is to manufacture a long, continuous stream of plastic and then cut it to the desired length. This is similar to the way spaghetti or cookie dough is made and is called extrusion. Given Burns's background making hockey helmets and sunglasses with injection molding, Supreme Corq naturally went with that.

Working out of a corner in a warehouse filled with Gargoyles glasses, Zech and his staff of now three other people set out in early 1993 to make plastic corks. On May 5, 1993, Burns made an initial patent application for his new and improved cork, then followed that up with a formal one eleven months later. The application described the product as "a molded closure for a liquid container comprising a thermoplastic elastomer and a blowing agent." Although Burns's name was on the patent application, he was selling both of his other companies and paid little attention to what was going on with plastic corks.

With the patent application in hand, Zech hired an outside company to make product prototypes, which had to be done one at a time at a cost of $1 per cork, more than twice the price of the best natural corks. After spending a large part of his annual R&D budget in 1993 to get five thousand corks made, Zech set off with them for California's wine country. At wineries he demonstrated the product and asked winemakers if they thought it might work and what features were important for it to have. Says Zech, "We wanted to learn from them and to see if we were going in the right direction." He made no attempt to sell the plastic corks because he wasn't even sure that he could mass-manufacture them. Zech was careful to show winemakers only one cork at a time because a bag of them smelled like ammonia. That was a problem he figured they could solve later.

During his travels, Zech established strong and lasting relationships with several wineries that provided invaluable guidance in the product's development. Among them: Murphy-Goode in Sonoma County's Alexander Valley; St. Francis, also in Sonoma; Bonny Doon in Santa Cruz; and Chateau Ste. Michelle in Washington State. The main reason they were so helpful was that they were all having problems with tainted corks and didn't like either of the plastic alternatives then on the market.

The experience of St. Francis, a small but fairly high-end winery that was old by California standards, having been founded in 1973, was typical. In 1990, founder/president Joe Martin and winemaker Tom Mackey were on the road promoting their wines. They were about to make a presentation to a wine buyer at a resort in Tampa to show off their latest Chardonnay when they pulled the cork and smelled it. The bottle was obviously corked. Nonetheless, Mackey poured the wine and tasted it. The taint taste was terrible. So the two put the cork back in the bottle, apologized to the resort's wine buyer for wasting his time, and left. "We could have tried to explain what cork taint was all about, and he might have nodded if he were courteous," recalls Mackey. "But I wouldn't buy the wine, and he would have been a fool if he bought it."

During the 1980s, St. Francis was suffering from what Mackey calls a "pandemic" of bad cork. Despite buying from several suppliers to spread his risk and performing spot quality checks, he figured St. Francis was getting between 7 and 9 percent corked bottles.

A couple of days after the Tampa experience, a salesman for Cellucork made a call at St. Francis to present his plastic cork that promised to eliminate cork taint. Not surprisingly, he found Mackey interested in his product. Mackey decided to do an experiment to see how well the cork worked and started by bottling six cases of his 1989 Merlot. He then began periodically testing to see how they were doing. The winemaker says he had three questions: how would the wines perform in the short term; how would they do in the long term; and how would consumers react? The taste tests went well enough that St. Francis in 1992 bottled 15 percent of its production with Cellucork to have a consumer test. The market reaction was also good, and the following year the winery switched to 100 percent plastic, becoming the first to make such a move. That generated nonstop publicity, which only helped St. Francis's sales. Even though the winery was already using Cellucork, Mackey was always willing to listen to Zech and help him with the development of Supreme Corq.

When Zech went to wineries, one of the first questions he faced was whether his product could be used in existing bottling equipment, since they didn't want to have to install expensive new machinery. The answer was yes. But the first time the new corks went into a bottling machine at Murphy-Goode, it ripped the tops off. Zech also learned that he had to coat the corks with lubricants just as with natural corks, to make it easier for the bottling machine to get them in the bottle. Zech bought a small rock polisher, and working in his hotel, he put silicone on his corks. Dave Ready, one of the founders of Murphy-Goode and a marketer by background, suggested to Zech that the company make colored corks to show that this was not just a fake cork but a new product that could be part of innovative marketing campaigns.

After learning all that and more from the wineries, it was time by the spring of 1993 to take the next step and go into actual production. Supreme Corq took delivery in the fall of that year of its first mold from a Southern California company where Burns had connections.

As with any new product, the initial production was a nightmare. The liquid plastic squirted out of the top of the mold or didn't cool properly. Nonetheless Zech decided to go public with his plastic cork at a trade show to be held in San Jose in January 1994. So the company ran a large production batch, and then its four employees pawed through the collection of mostly bad corks to pick out the few good enough to display. At their show booth for all the world to see was a huge bowl of Supreme-Corqs in a multitude of colors. Recalls Zech, "People were ten deep at our booth; we couldn't keep up. They thought it was the coolest thing at the show."

The young company got a great boost soon after when the *Wall Street Journal* ran a front-page story that mentioned it by name. The subtitle:

"[Wineries] Plug Plastic as a Stopper of the Future." Soon several early adopters were trying out SupremeCorqs. Bridgeview Winery in Oregon launched Blue Moon Riesling with a range of colored plastic corks. While Supreme Corq was mainly giving away samples in 1993, the following year it sold four hundred thousand and the future was looking as rosy as one of its colored corks.

Meanwhile St. Francis, which had by then become the national poster child for plastic corks, was having trouble with its Cellucorks. Without telling its customers, the manufacturer had changed the product to make it tighter in hopes of reducing the problem it was having with leaking bottles. The change, however, also made it much more difficult to extract the plastic cork from the bottle. Customers were even complaining that they were breaking corkscrews trying to get the plastic stoppers out of bottles. "We had zero cork taint, but if you can't get the cork out of the bottle, what's the point?" asks Mackey. So in early 1995, after he had already bottled part of his production with Cellucorks, Mackey called Zech and said he wanted to talk about switching to Supreme Corq. Zech had been giving him samples for a year and half, so Mackey knew the product well. Since St. Francis was such a high-profile user of plastic corks and represented a great opportunity, Zech blew his marketing budget and paid $10,000 to lease a Learjet to bring Mackey and the winery's two owners to Seattle. It was money well spent. That summer St. Francis began bottling with SupremeCorqs.

Despite the success with St. Francis, Zech still faced the problem of getting plastic corks accepted by other American wineries. It wasn't a question of quality, but of perception. Perhaps an inferiority complex still existed among New World winemakers who believed the old European ways were better, but Zech continued to have trouble with what he called "the challenge to change mentality." When Chateau Ste. Michelle said it would switch from cork to plastic if a focus-group test went well, Zech staged one, which clearly showed consumers were more interested in the wine in the glass than the closure in the bottle.

Then quite unexpectedly, interest in Supreme Corq began developing abroad. In early 1995, Zech got a call from Richard Gibson, the technical director of Australia's Southcorp, a huge winemaker that owned brands such as Penfolds and Lindemans and made about 20 percent of the country's wine. An Australian on vacation had seen a SupremeCorq stopper and brought it back to show Gibson, who now wanted samples and asked Zech to fly to Australia to talk about some business. Zech jumped at the opportunity and extended his stay so he could see other Australian wineries. Sometimes he was welcomed; other times the door was slammed in his face. The meeting with Gibson, who was particularly interested in getting yellow corks, went well, and Supreme Corq soon received its first order.

A few months later, Zech was driving his blue Jeep Pioneer on his way to sales calls in eastern Washington when his cell phone rang. With a proper British accent, the caller said she was Liz Robertson and suggested Zech should fly to London to see her. A bit nonplussed by the call, he asked exactly who she was and how she had heard of him. Robertson replied that she was the wine buyer for Safeway, a supermarket chain like the American company of the same name but not related to it. She also said Richard Gibson had suggested that she give him a call. Before hanging up, Zech said he'd see if he could set up a trip and would call her back.

When he returned to his office, Zech called Gibson to find out more about Robertson and the British wine business. Gibson said she was a Master of Wine, a prestigious British title given to people who have passed a rigorous examination. She had seen the SupremeCorqs when she visited him recently in Australia. He also explained that chains such as Safeway, Tesco, and Oddbins sold about 85 percent of the wine consumed in Britain. They owned the whole market, with the exception of the still profitable high-end, where establishment firms such as Berry Bros & Rudd ruled. The chains sold many wines under their own brands and could therefore dictate the packaging, including the closure, to wineries. Gibson urged Zech to fly to London to see Robertson.

Unbeknownst to Zech, Robert Joseph, a wine writer, the editor of *Wine International,* and an organizer of London's International Wine Challenge show, had been waging a campaign against cork for several years. He felt that cork producers were throwing expensive public relations at anyone criticizing their product rather than trying to solve their problems. Joseph ran a site on the still relatively new Internet called corkwatch.com, which had declared unconditional warfare against cork and cork taint. Wherever Joseph had a forum, he relentlessly blasted the cork companies for not doing enough to solve their problem. It would have been hard for any British wine consumer not to hear from him about the cork problem, and the grocery chains had clearly gotten the message.

In October 1995, Zech flew to London. While there, he saw not just Safeway but also the other big wine retailers. He was totally unprepared for what awaited him. Says he, "I walked into a firestorm." The chains had previously been demanding that their winery suppliers use low-grade natural and agglomerate Portuguese corks, which were giving them about a 5 percent TCA rate. Some stores had policies of giving consumers as much as double their money back and then demanding the wineries give the stores even higher rebates for corked bottles. The chains were simply fed up with unhappy customers and the nuisance of returned bottles. At the same time, they were furious at what they considered to be unresponsive Portuguese cork companies, which were saying that it wasn't their problem and weren't willing to remedy the situation. The British chains were mad, and they were looking for someone—anyone—to liberate them from Portuguese cork.

For Zech the London trip was an "Aha" moment. At a stroke he realized that if he could get his product approved by the British chains, he would have an open door to wineries around the world, especially among New World producers. The original Supreme Corq business plan was to develop a nice little company serving wineries on the U.S. West Coast. But now Zech realized that the international market could play a much larger role. Almost overnight Supreme Corq had liftoff. Indeed, the company was soon doing some 85 percent of its rapidly growing business abroad.

The first British wine to use a plastic cork was a Safeway Semillon-Chardonnay packaged in a clear Bordeaux-shaped bottle with a blue label and a bright yellow cork showing through the glass. A year later, Robertson gave Zech a chart that showed sales going straight up after the new closure was introduced.

Soon so many people around the world were asking Zech to come see them about being his distributor that he had to come up with a system to separate the serious prospects from the tire-kickers. He decided that he would talk to anyone who was willing to fly to Seattle and see *him*. One of those who came was Italian Roberto Cassini, who wanted to become the Supreme Corq distributor in Italy. He was sure his design- and packaging-savvy compatriots would be attracted to colorful plastic corks. Cassini, though, was in the business of importing and distributing electrical components, and Zech was skeptical he was the right person to represent him since he wasn't even in the wine business. When the American voiced his doubts, Cassini replied, "But, Jerome, everyone in Italy is in the wine business." Zech was charmed by the response and said they could have a handshake deal and would see how it went. Cassini was right, and Italy turned out to be Supreme Corq's best European market. Over the next two years, Zech set up distribution in ten countries ranging from France to South Africa.

As Zech made the rounds of wine trade shows, he found a new respect for Supreme Corq. The combination of a prestige winery such as St. Francis using his product and the mass-market British supermarkets also endorsing it gave his plastic corks credibility. Unlike screwcaps, which failed in early tests in Australia and California because they were considered a cheap closure for cheap wines, SupremeCorqs were an interesting, new, colorful marketing tool that would eliminate cork taint in quality wines. It didn't hurt that it also cost a lot less than most natural corks. At his booths Zech served St. Francis wines to potential customers, and representatives of wineries stayed around to taste the wines and talk about the closures. Even though St. Francis came in only midway through 1995, sales that year went up sixfold to 2.5 million and would soar to 10 million the following year. Zech suddenly felt as if he were driving a Porsche at 180 miles an hour; his job was simply to keep it on the road.

Supreme Corq was growing so fast it had to lease a new manufacturing facility in Kent, Washington, and buy new machinery to keep up with demand. That required a new infusion of money, so Zech in 1997 went out to the Seattle venture-capital community looking for investors. The company was now hot, but it was still difficult to raise money for a manufacturing firm in the dot-com era. After it became known within the tight group that local billionaire Bill Gates was in, however, several wealthy people who had made money with other new technology businesses also wanted in. Eventually some twenty new investors put in several million dollars in a deal that closed in January 1998. The Gates involvement was supposed to be secret, but it became known after lawyers inadvertently put his name on some court documents filed with the State of Washington. That drew even more attention to Dennis Burns's little company.

Any business expanding that fast is certain to attract competitors, and they were already coming. One day in 1994, Bob Pedigo, a venture capitalist, was playing tennis in the Napa Valley with Peter Stern, a well-known winemaker who had worked for Gallo and Mondavi and had also been a distributor for Cellucork. During a break in play, Stern mentioned that he was interested in synthetic corks but was having trouble getting the technology right. He told Pedigo it was an admittedly weird question, but did he happen to know anyone who knew plastics, had experience with a start-up company, and also knew wine. Pedigo replied maybe the question wasn't so weird after all. He was on the board of a small company that had just gone public. Just such a person worked there, and he knew the guy was looking for something new now that the company had been sold. His name was Stuart Yaniger.

Yaniger studied chemistry in the early 1980s at the University of Utah, then did postgraduate work at the University of Pennsylvania. There he had worked with later Nobel laureate Alan MacDiarmid, who introduced him to the world of polymers. Yaniger went on to work for Lockheed, but left there to get into the high-tech boom with a start-up company called Interlink Electronics, which had its offices in a converted Mexican restaurant in Santa Barbara. The company made computer peripherals. Yaniger was the chief scientist, but in his spare time was an admitted wine geek.

Shortly after the tennis game, Yaniger got a phone call first from Pedigo and then one from Stern asking him if might be interested in working for a company that was going to make plastic corks. Yaniger had no experience with synthetic corks because all the wines he drank had natural ones, so he called Dan Berger, a friend and well-known wine writer, and asked him what he thought of both plastic corks and Stern. Berger said synthetics were interesting, but flawed, and that Stern had one of the best minds in California winemaking. With that as an endorsement, Yaniger agreed to have dinner with Stern. Part of the evening was a blind wine tasting in which Yaniger was asked to pick out the wine that had a synthetic cork. He nailed it and got a job offer.

In the spirit of the go-go 1990s, the founders wanted the business to be financed by venture-capital investors and also to be a virtual company that would outsource such operations as manufacturing. The first job was to raise money, and for the next year that was the focus of Stern, Yaniger, and a new partner, Andy Starr, who had worked for Stern as a winemaker and selling Cellucork. He also had an MBA degree, which would be helpful in launching a business. Following a common strategy for start-ups, they first went to companies that might be their potential clients. In this case, that meant California wineries. Owners of wineries were anxious to talk because they were unhappy with their natural cork suppliers and were looking for an alternative for two reasons. The first was cork taint, and the second was the steadily rising price for natural cork. They felt that if another potential supplier was out there, the cork companies might have a reason to improve their product and slow down the price hikes. Eventually five wineries—Clos du Bois, Beringer, Kendall-Jackson, Robert Mondavi, and Sebastiani—invested an initial $1 million to get the new company off the ground. That would be enough to keep it going for a year while the product was created. In addition to being investors, the wineries were also going to be development partners, telling Yaniger what they needed in the new product and then testing his prototypes.

In March 1996, Neocork Technologies was launched, and Yaniger got down to serious development work. No restrictions were put on him as he set out to design the new product, and he quickly decided to go a different route from Cellucork and Supreme Corq, which both had molded plastic stoppers. Yaniger proposed adopting the same technology used to manufacture thousands of miles of coaxial cable: extrusion. The material would come out of production as a long stream and then be cut into individual corks. The cost of production would be much less, while the quality could be much more carefully controlled since every inch of plastic cork material would be exactly the same.

Early plastic corks, including Cellucork and SupremeCorq, had two problems: oxidation and the difficulty extracting them from bottles. They did not form a tight enough seal, so air was getting in the bottle and causing oxidation, sometimes within only a few months of bottling. In addition, consumers still complained about troubles getting them out of bottles. Yaniger's solution for both problems: coextrusion. The corks would be made up of two parts. The first was a tight, but thin, outer core made of elastomer. That would provide a tight seal. The second was a softer, foamed inner core that would make it easier to get the cork both in and out of the bottle.

Working alone out of his two-car garage in Ventura, north of Los Angeles, Yaniger started developing prototypes. As he recalls, he worked flextime—any one hundred hours a week he wanted. Because of his experience at Lockheed and Interlink, Yaniger was able to get help from companies such as Dow Chemical that don't normally work with garage inventors. After he had a test cork, Yaniger would call around to the winery partners to see who had some free time in the bottling line so he could see how it worked. Not all the feedback was positive. Tim Mondavi, head of winemaking at the Robert Mondavi Winery, was quoted in the November 15, 1998, issue of *Wine Spectator* as saying, "We're on the inside of Neocork working to advance that front, but I've seen enough problems with synthetics to enter the arena carefully."

Early on in development, Neocork got together a focus group to get some feedback. The invited people were put in a room with some wine bottles and glasses but without any instructions about what they were supposed to be judging. They all pulled the corks and then began discussing the wines. "We knew we had something because they didn't notice the cork," says Yaniger. Sometimes the perfect product is the one no one notices.

It took nearly a year and more than one hundred prototypes to get the technology right, but eventually Yaniger got U.S. patent 6,085,932 to protect his invention. By then the company had to go out for more money, this time raising $1.5 million from a variety of backers including some of the original wineries.

Extrusion production can only be economically done in large and expensive operations, and the virtual company, even with the new money, could not afford to own that. So in 1997, Neocork began looking for a contract manufacturer to make its coextruded product. One of the companies it approached was Nomaco, a Belgian company that had started business in 1950 making sponges. In 1979, it opened a U.S. subsidiary that first made foam pipe insulation by extrusion and then spread out to other products including toys and packaging.

There is a disagreement about what happened next. According to Neocork, Nomaco stole its idea and decided to use Yaniger's process to make its own plastic cork. According to Nomaco, the company had in the 1970s began working on an R&D venture nicknamed Project Broomstick that used its existing technology to make a plastic cork. Neocork threatened to sue, but that never materialized, and in 1998 Nomaco launched its plastic cork, which it named Nomacorc. Neocork eventually found a manufacturer in North Carolina to produce its plastic corks and in February 1999 began selling its first product. Neocork was a quick success and struggled at first to produce enough corks to keep up with demand. The biggest client at first was Sebastiani, one of the original wineries that financed the company. Sales went from zero to 100 million corks in a year and a half, but Nomacorc grew even faster, becoming the dominant player in coextruded plastic corks. Since it does its own manufacturing, Nomacorc could be the low-cost producer.

Both Neocork and Nomacorc, though, had much smaller sales than Supreme Corq, which saw its business nearly triple from the year before to hit 80 million in 1998 and then 180 million in 1999. At the end of 1998, *Food & Wine* magazine awarded one of its Golden Grape Awards for achievement in the wine business jointly to Dennis Burns and Jerome Zech. Among the other honorees was Heidi Barrett, the winemaker of the cult Screaming Eagle Cabernet Sauvignon. The picture accompanying the story showed Zech chest-high in a giant container of brightly colored SupremeCorqs.

Natural corks still controlled more than 95 percent of the market for wine-bottle closures, but the Portuguese industry couldn't ignore the upstarts that were coming on so strong and were taking away the low-end business. Its initial reaction starting in 1998 was a massive public relations offensive that attacked plastic stoppers on a variety of fronts. Leading the campaign was Amorim, the largest cork producer, which turned out about a quarter of the 13 billion corks made annually. Amorim asked Len Evans, the dean of Australian wine, to become a public spokesman, and he was quoted as saying, "I like cork. I've always used cork for my own wines, and I like the wines I buy to be sealed with cork."

Cork manufacturers also charged that plastic corks, unlike natural ones, would end up in landfills since they couldn't be recycled. A campaign was started in Britain to recycle natural cork that was supported by wine writer Jancis Robinson and large chains such as Tesco, which had ironically given Supreme Corq its big push.

Environmentalists were also recruited to join the antiplastic campaign. They argued that if synthetics replaced natural corks, the cork forests of Spain and Portugal would be cut down and forty-two species of native birds and countless other animals would become extinct. Even Britain's Royal Society for the Protection of Birds flew in to lend its endorsement to natural corks as a way of protecting the forests.

A series of dubious scientific reports on the flaws of plastic corks soon appeared. An Amorim-sponsored newsletter reported that the Leatherhead Food Research Association had "called for more research on whether there is any chemical migration into wine which has been stoppered with synthetic corks." Another article in an Amorim newsletter reported that the Research Institute Geisenheim in Germany had "recommended that producers stick to cork stoppers" because of oxidation in bottles with synthetic ones. There were also reports that plastic corks caused cancer.

An unknown outfit called Clifton Consulting Services in Melbourne sent letters to people such as Randall Grahm, the owner of Bonny Doon Vineyard, which was using SupremeCorqs, warning of the dangers of using plastic corks. Said the letter to Grahm, "You may be interested to learn that a boutique North Eastern Victorian winemaker lost his entire US export order after his 1997 vintage white wines sealed under synthetic closures were totally oxidized. It cost him A$230,000 [$181,585] in lost sales."

The British business magazine *The Economist* picked up the story in its June 5, 1999, issue with a story headlined "A Corking Row." It said, "In Britain cork's defenders have unleashed a ferociously negative (and largely counterproductive) public-relations campaign."

At first, Zech was mildly amused that the giant Amorim empire, with all its billions and huge market share, was coming after his still small company in Kent, Washington. Later, though, Supreme Corq began putting out "Fact Sheets" contradicting the Amorim claims. One pointed out that Leatherhead Food Research had never said, "Synthetic corks cause a health risk." It also said no test results such as those Amorim reported had been published by Geisenheim. Another "Fact Sheet" stated, "Synthetic wine closures account for less than 1 percent of the market. Supreme Corq is simply providing an alternative to natural cork. Our product has very little impact on the market, or on the health of the cork industry and the forests that supply it."

The most dramatic encounter in the cork-vs.-plastic confrontation took place at the London Wine Trade Show in May 1999 in a panel that included Robert Joseph, Jerome Zech, a representative of the Royal Society for the Protection of Birds, and executives from Amorim and Sabaté, the world's two largest cork companies. With Amorim and the Royal Society leading the antiplastic attack, the discussion deteriorated into a debate over whether synthetics were going to cause the extinction of the Iberian eagle. Zech countered by saying the eagles actually died by flying into power lines. Finally Jancis Robinson from the back of the room pleaded, "Can't we get off the bird!" The audience roared with laughter.

After Gargoyles became a public company in 1997 and Dennis Burns sold his remaining share of the company, he began spending more and more time on a dream home he was building in central Oregon. Although he always attended Supreme Corq board meetings, he was now totally out of day-to-day management. Meanwhile a majority of the board wanted to dress up the company to sell it, which meant maximizing short-term profits in order to get the highest sale price. Part of that strategy involved putting off new investments on such things as research and development. Zech, who was focused on the company's long-term growth, soon found himself in conflict with his board. He, for example, wanted more R&D and to start a Supreme Corq line of extruded plastic corks to compete with Neocork and Nomacorc. Zech in February 2000 finally left the company he had built to join a small private-equity company in Seattle. He had enjoyed a fantastic ride at Supreme Corq, but it was time to move on.

Supreme Corq goes into history as the company that broke the natural-cork monopoly on wine closures. Before it came on the scene, there was no viable alternative to natural cork. Portuguese cork companies could do what they wanted and ignore the problems with their product because wineries or wine stores such as the British chains had no place else to go. A new generation of screwcaps would later come along to compete with both natural and synthetic corks, but they would not have enjoyed their success if Supreme Corq hadn't first broken the monopoly.

In addition to that achievement, Supreme Corq created greater public awareness of cork's problems by offering the wine world and its customers a credible solution to them. It's sometimes possible to appreciate a problem only when someone comes along with a solution. Cork taint had existed since cork was first used in wine bottles in the early seventeenth century. But like the crazy aunt in the attic who family members know is up there but no one wants to talk about, the trouble was ignored. Once Supreme Corq offered a credible answer to cork taint, that became one of the hottest topics in the wine business.

MESSAGE IN A BOTTLE: HOUSTON

California's Harlan Estate Cabernet Sauvignon is one of the rarest of cult wines. Harlan also produces a wine called Matriarch, which is only slightly easier to find. Denman Moody, a veteran Texas wine critic and proprietor of winewiththewedding.com, considered himself lucky when he got his hands on three bottles of Matriarch.

Being generous, Moody gave one to a charitable event, one to a friend, and kept one for his wife and him to share on some special occasion. After the wine had been in his cellar for a year, he couldn't stand it any longer, and in early 2006 he made reservations at one of downtown Houston's best restaurants, where bringing your own bottle is not allowed. But the manager, being a friend, said he would be happy to allow the bottle of Matriarch. Neither the manager nor his sommelier had seen a bottle, much less tasted one, and Moody promised each a sip.

When the great night arrived, Moody was filled with anticipation—after twenty-eight years of traveling the world and writing about wine, there weren't too many great wines he had not tasted. Shortly after sitting down, the sommelier arrived and opened the bottle. From the moldy cardboard smell that emanated from the bottle three or four feet away, Moody knew it was corked. This was the first time either he or the sommelier had experienced that with a Harlan wine, but after a confirmation sip, there was no doubt. Moody, his wife, the sommelier, and the manager sat in silence for a minute or two. Then the sommelier quietly left the table to pour out the wine, and a saddened Moody turned and opened the wine list.

CHAPTER NINE

From Perfect Cork
to Perfect Disaster

In January 1995, François Sabaté arrived in San Francisco on an Air France flight from Paris with excitement, optimism, and anticipation. He and his wife were embarking on a new life in a new country, and the future offered unlimited promise. The couple soon moved into the Marina district of San Francisco, where the city's young crowd lived in an idyllic setting of sunshine and sailboats. The area also offered an easy commute to California's wine country north of the city.

François was a member of the family that owned Sabaté, a cork producer that then ranked in the industry's top ten. His grandfather Modest Sabaté, a Spanish-born journalist who had escaped from Barcelona in the waning days of the Spanish Civil War, had founded the company in 1939. Modest had been the publisher of a successful daily newspaper in Barcelona during that bloody conflict and had encountered enough problems with anarchist and communist militias that he knew he had to get out of the country. Modest's uncle had been in the cork business in Catalonia, where a particularly high-quality, dense cork grew. The émigré settled in the Languedoc-Roussillon region of southern France, after hearing that Champagne producers in northern France were desperate to obtain a reliable supply of cork now that war and dictatorships had settled over the entire Iberian Peninsula. Since he had good connections to the Catalan manufacturers who could provide cork, Modest opened a business that bore his family name.

Over the next six decades, Sabaté grew and prospered, expanding beyond its Champagne roots to encompass the entire gamut of wine-bottle closures. As a French company in a field increasingly dominated by Portuguese firms, Sabaté was an outsider. But it was known as an innovative company in an industry where change came slowly, if at all. In the mid-1980s, Sabaté teamed up with researchers at the University of Perpignan in southern France to find an alternative to the chlorine washes that Switzerland's Hans Tanner had singled out as the primary cause of cork-taint contamination. Their new process used peroxide, rather than chlorine, which produced a clean white cork that was even better than the chlorine-treated one. Winemakers loved the product and the company began enjoying 25 percent annual growth. While most French cork companies got out of manufacturing and only sold cork, Sabaté maintained a production factory in Le Boulou, a village near Perpignan in the foothills of the Pyrenees. By now the company was being run by Modest's oldest son, Augustin, and his brothers.

Concerned by the growing complaints about cork taint, Sabaté in the 1980s set out to develop the next generation of cork stoppers for wine bottles. The driving concept was to optimize the benefits of cork by providing a good seal that would protect the wine from air, would be easy to extract from a bottle, and would dramatically reduce TCA. The goal was nothing less than a perfect cork.

From its work with peroxide, the company's research group had found that troublemaking phenols, which are part of the process that forms TCA, are located in the woody part of the cork called the lignin, which surrounds the lenticels, the minuscule pores in the cork. They concluded that if they ground the cork material into a fine granular substance, they could then separate the larger and heavier lignin by pushing all the material through a fine screen that blocked the dangerous material, while letting the rest fall through. That would remove much, but not all, of the potentially dangerous material from corks. The company then developed a process to reconstitute the material with the help of polymer microspheres, which were developed in conjunction with the Nobel Group, a global network of food, industrial, and energy companies. The plastic material, which partially replicated cork's features of elasticity and permeability, filled the gaps within the cork structure left by the removal of the lignin. The third ingredient was food-grade glue that held the two materials together. The corks were manufactured by individually molding them at an extremely high temperature to obtain a total integration of the three ingredients.

Just as the research phase was drawing to a close, François Sabaté joined the family company. His older brother Marc followed him a few months later as chief financial officer. François had studied at the European Business School in Paris, before working for a short time in the food industry prior to his inevitable entry into the company with his family name on the door. He naturally gravitated to the new product and helped develop the marketing strategy for it.

An important part of that was pricing. In addition to being an improvement on nature's nearly perfect product, Sabaté's manufactured cork would sell for far less than pure cork because there was no waste product. Unlike punched cork, where at least half of the cork material remains as remnants that have to be made into less expensive products, Sabaté turned all its cork material into its reconstituted stoppers. As a result, the price of the new product for a large winery was going to be less than ten cents a cork. It was a marketing person's dream: a far-superior product selling at a much reduced price.

Another part of the marketing campaign was to emphasize that the new product was almost indistinguishable from a natural cork for the average consumer. People opening a bottle don't normally spend a lot of time studying the cork, unless they have trouble getting it out. They simply pull it and throw it away, put it aside for later reuse, or add it to their collection of corks. Countless users of the new Sabaté product over the years have undoubtedly thought it was just another cork, rather than a manufactured product.

The company again broke with industry practices in how it launched the new product. Sabaté wanted to set it apart by giving it a brand name, which was something new for the cork industry. The company hired a consulting company to come up with a name that could be easily pronounced in French, Spanish, English, and German. The consultants proposed the name Alto, but Augustin and François didn't like it, thinking it was too musical and feminine. The company had recently moved near the river Tech, so father and son borrowed that name, added it to the consultants' suggestion, and called their new product Altec. François thought the name had the added advantage of sounding high-tech in the go-go tech times at the end of the millennium.

François then set out to do an intense analysis of the international cork market, with a particular emphasis on what the American market wanted. In contrast to European countries, where wine consumption was falling, in the United States wine sales—and the demand for cork—were booming. America was the great market opportunity, and that was where Sabaté wanted to concentrate its efforts. Studies showed him that the Americans wanted a more reliable cork that could be easily stored and sold at an attractive price. The company, though, was having trouble keeping good salespeople, so it decided to establish a subsidiary in California. And as often happens in family companies anywhere in the world, Sabaté placed a motivated family member in charge of that ambitious, but also risky, new venture. At age thirty, François went to California to run Sabaté USA.

Just before leaving, François orchestrated the launch of Altec in France. The market reaction was more than the company could have asked for. The product was an immediate and smashing success. Winemakers liked the look and the price, while to consumers it was just another cork. In fact, it was more attractive than natural cork because it was more regular and had no flaws. Sabaté sales soon soared.

The early and promising success of Altec was part of the story told just after the launch of Sabaté stock on the main Paris stock exchange. The step had been taken both to raise capital for investments in raw materials and production facilities and to allow the seven family members working at the company to diversify their financial holdings so they would not have everything tied up in Sabaté. Between 1995 and 2000, the family sold approximately half the company to outside investors. It was an ideal time to sell shares because of the hot world stock markets. Sabaté was not a dot-com company, but it was the dot-com era and share prices were high.

Once François and his wife had settled in their apartment in the Marina district, François began making sales trips north across the Golden Gate Bridge to the wine country of Napa, Sonoma, and Mendocino counties. One of the first wineries to sign up for the new product was Parducci Wine Cellars in Mendocino County, which had been started in 1932 and had been a jug-wine producer for many years but had been moving toward higher-quality products. Another early adopter was Barefoot Cellars in Sonoma, which attracted a youth audience to its 1.5-liter bottles with a logo showing a bare footprint on the label.

Soon U.S. demand for Altec exploded in the most successful product launch in cork history. Sabaté pushed production as fast as it could at its two plants in France and Spain, but it was hard to keep up with demand, which was now suddenly running at hundreds of millions of corks per year. Almost overnight Sabaté, the industry outsider, was the second-largest cork company in the world after Portugal's Amorim. Eric Mercier, a Canadian then working for the French company Pechiney but who left to join François in California on October 1, 1996, remembers those heady days when sales just wouldn't stop. Even after Amorim unveiled Twin Top, a somewhat similar brand-name product, Altec sales kept rising. "I joined the company just because of Altec," says Mercier.

In 2001, Sabaté sold 800 million Altec corks around the world, with nearly 100 million of them just in the U.S. market. The company had by then sold 2.5 billion of its new corks and was confidently looking forward to its first 1-billion-cork year. It seemed indeed to be the perfect product. In 2000, an occasional winery complained about strange smells that seemed to come from the Altec corks, but those were isolated cases, and news of any problems didn't get outside a small circle of wine-industry people.

With outsiders now owning half the shares, Sabaté was a different company from the one the family had totally controlled. After Augustin Sabaté died in 1998, Marc became president, but nonfamily investors were trying to push the company in new directions. At the end of 2000, Sabaté merged with Diosos, a French barrel manufacturer, and Marc Sabaté became co-CEO of the Sabaté-Diosos Group.

Everything changed on September 7, 2001, when François Sabaté received a phone call in his office outside the city of Napa from Daniel Sogg, a reporter for *Wine Spectator*. François was not expecting the call, but felt he had to take it because of the clout the publication had in the California wine business.

When Sogg got on the phone, he explained that he had heard from several wineries using Altec corks that they were causing cork-taint problems and wanted to know if Sabaté had any reaction to this. The two men then had an extended conversation about the Altec corks and the charges raised by the wineries. That same day a story was posted on *Wine Spectator*'s Web site under the title "Wineries Claim Alternative Cork Caused Widespread Taint Problems." The article, which was long for the Internet, going some one thousand words, was detailed about the charges, the TCA issue, and Sabaté's response. Ironically John Parducci, one of the first clients of Altec, who now owned the Zellerbach Winery in Mendocino County, was the first critic mentioned. He said Zellerbach was about to release its 1997 Mendotage at $35 a bottle when he discovered cork-taint problems. The story quoted Parducci as saying, "It's my first wine, and I'm not about to put that out [in the market] and get killed with it." The story quoted Zellerbach's attorney as saying Parducci was going to ask for compensation of $630,000, the cost of all fifteen hundred cases of Mendotage.

In addition, the story reported that Bogle Vineyards was also seeking compensation for wines bottled with bad Altecs between 1997 and 2000. The article further said the owner of Foppiano Vineyards in Sonoma County had gotten so many complaints about Altecs that he had stopped using them.

The story quoted François Sabaté in detail, saying, for example, that there was "a lack of accepted industry standards both on levels of TCA as well as how TCA occurs." He also said that his company had received only a few complaints out of the billions of corks that had been made, adding the problems seemed to be "traced to a few isolated production batches that occurred mid-2000." Sogg's article reported that outside research in Australia "found that Altec taint problems were not limited to a few batches produced last year." Sogg even gave the final word in the story to Sabaté: "Nobody has found the perfect closure, and I don't think it exists yet."

The news hit at a bad time. In addition to concerns about Altec, Sabaté's California sales were already declining because of the beginning of a downward cycle in the wine industry. The rest of the press then jumped on the story, and suddenly charges against the company were flooding in from other sources. Soon other reporters both in the United States and abroad were onto the story, and it was the talk of the wine world. Robert Joseph in Britain said he could always detect if an Altec cork had been used to seal the bottle. He speculated that it was due to the glue used to hold the cork material together. Larry Stone, a master sommelier and the wine buyer at the Rubicon restaurant in San Francisco, told wineries not to bother to offer him their wines if they had Altecs. Other wineries, including Carneros Creek in the Napa Valley and Van Duzer Vineyards in Oregon, also claimed to have had tainted Altec stoppers and demanded compensation.

Altec, the product that had been designed to bring to the wine world a superior closure, had to take the brunt of years of built-up, intense anger from wine writers as well as winemakers toward the cork industry. People were both outraged and frustrated, feeling cork companies had been unresponsive for years to what was perceived to be a pervasive and unacceptable incidence of cork taint. Now the longtime critics had a concrete target in Altec, and all their resentment came rushing out. "We were passionate about what we were doing, and suddenly we were accused of being the source of all the problems the wine industry faced with cork companies," François Sabaté recalls. "It turned into a nightmare."

After more than a month of steady attacks in the media and many canceled orders from wineries, François realized he needed some help in handling a corporate disaster that was rapidly spinning out of control. If left unchecked, the whole company, or at least the U.S. subsidiary, could come crashing down around him. So he turned to Michael Fineman, a San Francisco–based public relations man who specialized in crisis management. Five years earlier, he had handled the case of Odwalla, a California maker of fruit juices that was found to be the source of an *E. coli* outbreak. Fineman had also worked for Fresh Express, a producer of bagged salads that was charged with selling bacteria-laced products.

"I was impressed with his sincerity when François first came in," recalls Fineman. "He was clearly shaken, but he was genuine and sincere. He wanted to defend the reputation of an old family company, which was being killed in the media. The press was treating Sabaté as Darth Vader and the Evil Empire."

At Fineman's suggestion, the company took a more assertive posture to the media and sought out ways to tell its story. Within three weeks, a press event was arranged at the California Welcome Center in Sonoma County. Marc Sabaté and Michel de Tapole, the copresidents of Sabaté-Diosos, flew in from France for the event, which turned into a tense affair when two lawyers representing wineries showed up uninvited and tried to argue their clients' cases. After they were asked to leave, the press conference went on as scheduled.

During the next few months, Sabaté struggled to get its story out without ever fully explaining what may have happened to its product that allegedly caused TCA presence in wine. In early 2002, the company published an "Open Letter to Altec Customers" in several wine-industry publications. It stated that the company had "less than a dozen claims" against its product, which represented "less than half of one percent of all Altec closures produced and distributed in 2000 and 2001."

The letter then defended the product, stating, "Altec was designed to meet winemakers' demands for minimizing TCA-related taint in wines, eliminating random oxidation and inhibiting bottle leakage. Based on input since its introduction in 1995, and on its continued market popularity, Altec has consistently done all three."

Wine Spectator published a letter from François Sabaté defending Altec in its last issue of the year, and a long interview with him appeared in *Wine Business Monthly*. The company presented to the press its new quality-control system, which rejected stoppers with more than 3 parts per trillion of TCA. Earlier, 6 ppt or even higher had been considered an acceptable level, but winemakers and the wine press were increasingly saying that any level of TCA was unacceptable. Sabaté had correctly told *Wine Business Monthly* that 99.5 percent of his clients were "happy with the product," but his message was not getting across.

In a telephone press conference in late January 2002, François Sabaté took off the gloves at both his critics and wineries threatening to sue his company. Said he, "We can no longer permit our image to be sullied and our product to be demeaned by customers that are unwilling to allow us to come to a resolution. We won't succumb to bullying tactics."

While the public-relations offensive was under way, Sabaté was also active behind the scenes on its real problem. It began working with ETS Laboratories in St. Helena to help it get control of its troubles with Altec. The company also commissioned independent studies with wine experts in Britain and the United States about the amount of oxygen that various types of closures let into the bottle. In both studies, Sabaté had experts compare Altec with other wine closures including a prototype of a new composite cork it had in development. These showed that some oxygen improved the taste of even early-consumption wines. In addition, the research revealed vast differences among wine professionals in the perception of TCA. Some tasted it as low as 1 part per trillion, while others did not notice it until 5 or 10 ppt. There was even a relatively high degree of false positives, when testers thought there was TCA when in fact none was present.

After all the threats and counterthreats of legal action, four wineries—Parducci Wine Estates, Carneros Creek Winery, Sapphire Hill Vineyards, and Van Duzer Vineyards—eventually filed suit against Sabaté demanding major compensation. The four cases were consolidated into one trial, and jury selection was due to start in February 2003. But five days before that, all the parties agreed to settle out of court on conditions that have never been released. Obviously Sabaté realized enough damage had already been done in the press to its reputation and that a public trial would probably only make that worse.

Sabaté has never revealed what happened to Altec that caused a product that had seemingly performed well at first to suddenly go so bad. Cork industry insiders speculate that the company was probably a victim of its own success. Sabaté initially used high-quality cork to make the new stoppers and removed most of the TCA from the raw material, but after demand took off it couldn't keep up and began using lesser-quality cork. Some of it came from Morocco and Portugal and had much higher levels of TCA. Several industry insiders told me Sabaté essentially lost control of its basic raw material.

The company was also clearly unprepared for the crisis that started in the American market. Marc Sabaté admits today that like most old-world wine-industry suppliers, the company had plenty of experience amicably resolving cork issues with wineries by quietly making financial settlements, without having to hire lawyers and going to the press, as was the common practice in the United States. "We were a French company dealing mainly with Latin countries, and we were not ready for the Anglo-Saxon way of handling this kind of problem," he says. Marc Sabaté also notes that in 2001, when the problem was blowing up in the United States, the company didn't have similar troubles in France, its biggest market. "Why was that?" he asked me rhetorically.

Despite its troubles with Altec, Sabaté was still interested in the concept of turning cork material into granular material and then removing the offensive ingredients. Augustin Sabaté had in 1996 met the head of the French Atomic Energy Commission at a lunch of regional business leaders in Montpellier. The two men got to talking about a still new process that the agency, which was located nearby, had been working on called supercritical CO_2. It could extract flavors from products and was already being used to remove caffeine from coffee beans and fragrances from flowers. The commission was also looking to it as a new way to cleanse radioactive materials. At a relatively low temperature of 31.1°C (88°F) but high pressure (73 bars), CO_2 has the characteristics of both a liquid and a gas. By penetrating like a gas, but also dissolving things like a liquid, it would be an ideal way of removing unwanted elements from a material.

Augustin Sabaté thought supercritical CO_2 might be useful for getting rid of TCA, and scientists from the company and the agency began working on a joint project in 1997. Over the next two years they developed a process for extracting TCA from cork, patenting it in 1999. In July 2002, the company went public with the news that it was working on a new way of removing tainted material from cork that it thought was better than the method used with Altec. The extraction technology was named Diamond, or in French, *Diamant*. Prototypes had already received excellent reviews in the earlier testing.

By this time, though, the family firm of Sabaté was well down the road to moving beyond the family. In April 2002, Marc Sabaté left active management in the company and became just a consultant. In June 2003, Sabaté-Diosos changed its name to Oeneo, and Sabaté USA, the company François had started in 1995 with such enthusiasm, soon became Oeneo USA. In October 2003, François Sabaté left the company as well. At the end of the year, Oeneo USA stopped selling Altec in the American market, although a successor product that allows slightly more air permeability and a lower threshold for TCA now enjoys good sales under the brand name Reference. Altec, and consequently Sabaté, were clearly a damaged brand, and it was easier for the company going forward to market itself under a new name.

Did Altec kill the nearly seventy-year-old Sabaté family firm? Yes and no. Sabaté was going through the always difficult transformation from being a closely held company to a much bigger, public corporation still geared toward innovation. But Altec, a product born with such hope, had become a burden that was dragging down its new owners. They hoped to regain the company's former market position with new names for old products and one entirely new closure, Diam, which used the Diamond technology that Augustin Sabaté had launched. Diam appeared to have the potential to be the product the company had hoped Altec would be: a perfect cork.

Looking back on the Altec saga nearly a decade after it unfolded, Marc Sabaté reached for the title of the theme song of the famous French chanteuse Edith Piaf and told me, *"Je ne regrette rien."*

CHAPTER TEN

A New Generation at Amorim
Makes Big Changes

*António Amorim's task was nothing
less than to save his family's,
and his country's, heritage.*

Early in 2000, Américo Amorim, the chairman of Portugal's biggest conglomerate, a family-run collection of companies that had investments ranging from cork forests to gambling casinos, decided it was time for him to turn over the running of the cork operation to another manager. The Amorim Group has assets of some €1.5 billion ($2 billion), and half its annual revenue comes from cork. In 2006, the company had sales of €442.6 million ($584.2 million) and posted a net profit of €20.1 million ($27.5 million). Amorim makes some 3 billion cork stoppers a year, or about one-quarter of all corks manufactured. There are around five hundred cork-producing companies in the world, with the vast majority being Portuguese. But towering over the whole industry stands Amorim, five times bigger than its closest competitor.

Américo Amorim, who is a member of the select club of international billionaires, had been running the cork operation for nearly a half century after going to work at the company when he was eighteen. His other financial interests in banking, real estate, and elsewhere were, however, taking up more and more of his time, and it was also necessary to get a new generation in place in the cork business. The last and most important task of any CEO—but one that is often handled poorly—is to select and train a successor. Américo was determined to do that correctly.

The transition of a family-owned business from one generation to the next is especially difficult. Genes seem to thin out in family firms as heirs stretch out to children, grandchildren, and great-grandchildren. A few rare families such as the Rothschilds have successfully kept a company in the family and the family in the company. But the vast majority, including the Rockefellers and the Fords, lose control or the business has to carry the burden of incompetent managers whose only claim to lofty titles is their bloodline.

Exactly how a family business goes about picking the next generation of leadership is usually a mystery hidden behind closed doors. Some families follow strict primogeniture, with the oldest son inheriting the mantle of power. More often than not that fails because the son has grown up in the shadow of his father and lacks the independence or entrepreneurial spark that drove his parent. Other families take the more risky approach of trying to pick the best and brightest from the next generation at a young age and then grooming him or her to succeed in the fullness of time.

The Amorim family has followed the second solution more than the first. In 1870, António Alves Amorim started a cork-manufacturing business that employed three workers in Gaia, a city across the Douro River from Oporto, which was the center of the country's prosperous Port business. He launched the company with a wealthy partner, but after twenty years he discovered the investor was taking all the profits. So in 1908, at age seventy-six, António went out on his own and started a second cork company in the village of Santa Maria de Lamas, south of Oporto.

António died in 1922, shortly after he had established a new company owned by his nine surviving children. The company was called Amorim & Irmãos. Eventually five siblings came into the business, one started another company, and three emigrated to Brazil, a common career move for ambitious Portuguese. The Brazilian members eventually had to sell their shares back to the family at the outbreak of World War II, and ownership devolved to just five brothers. The company was run by collective management, with Henrique, the sixth son, the first among equals.

In the third generation, the family picked Américo Amorim to head the growing Amorim Group, which was already moving into other businesses such as real estate. He was the fifth of eight children in his generation. Born in 1934, he went to work in the company's cork factory fresh out of secondary school and was soon running the production plant and then began traveling the world selling cork.

After the company was almost nationalized following the 1974 revolution, Américo took advantage of Portugal's newly liberalized economy and its greater acceptance among Western European governments to dramatically expand the Amorim Group. He opened the Banco Comercial Português and also moved into textiles, real estate, and tourism. Cork, though, remained at the core of the company's history and its business.

For the leader of the fourth generation, the family again picked from the middle of the pack among a dozen siblings of his generation. Américo's brother António had three children, a boy and two girls. The boy was also named António, and at an early age was already on the fast track to the top. At his father's insistence, the younger António took a different road from his uncle. After graduating from secondary school, the boy planned to attend Portugal's historic Coimbra University to study law, but his father pushed him to go to Britain so he could master English and study business management. Américo speaks fluent French, the most important language in the wine world of his time. António, though, was going to learn English, a key communications skill for his era. Although the family money could have gotten him into one of the more prestigious British universities, António in 1986 entered the University of Birmingham because he felt more at ease there. He picked up a variety of certificates in both English and business before graduating in 1989. That same year he earned a degree in enology from the University of Bordeaux and in 1992 attended the Executive Business Management Program at Columbia University. He later also got a degree in international commerce from the French business school INSEAD. António had built a solid foundation for a high-level career of international business.

Young António was still in short pants when he started attending Amorim Group board meetings, and in 1990, at age twenty-three, he became a board member when his father retired. The previous year the young man had already started a rotation of high-level jobs around the firm

in preparation for moving on to the jewel in the Amorim crown: the cork
company. He first spent two years at the holding company before becoming CEO of the textile operation. Then in 1992, he moved to the tourism
group, where he was responsible for bringing the Ibis and Novotel hotel
chains into Portugal. He next moved to the real estate division and drove
development of what was then the country's largest shopping center and
a major office complex in Lisbon.

Finally in 1996, António landed where he had been destined almost
from birth. He was named CEO of the stopper division, which makes up
about half of Amorim's total cork output. The other half is split among all
the other uses of the material. Then five years later, in March 2001 and at
the age of thirty-four António succeeded his uncle as CEO of the entire
cork operation.

The young Amorim was not taking over a smoothly running engine
where all he had to do was count the money. The cork company was facing the most serious problems it had since the first António started the
company. "We were facing a crisis, and I was running a family business that
had been around for one hundred and twenty years," António recalls. "We
could have done nothing and just milked the cash cow, but we would have
been out of business in fifteen years. There was no doubt about it."

The new CEO was well aware of the company's serious and growing
problem around the world with cork taint. Amorim's customers were
unhappy, and the issue could no longer be ignored. He had heard the complaints firsthand from customers while acting as his uncle's translator. After
finishing his education in Birmingham and before going to work in the
company's cork operation, António traveled with his uncle on sales calls in
the English-speaking world and listened to unhappy customers tell his
uncle, often in passionate terms, about their problems with cork taint.

Despite his awareness of the TCA troubles, though, that was not the
young Amorim's top priority. He faced an even more pressing issue:
Álvaro and Joaquim Coelho, who had been running the cork business day-
to-day for Américo for thirty years, had just left the company and taken
a phalanx of middle managers with them. Not only had they gone, but
they had also started Álvaro Coelho & Irmãos, a rival cork company that
was going to be Amorim's toughest competitor. "For eighteen to twenty
months, I couldn't even think about TCA," says António. "I had to keep
up the morale of the people who remained and keep them focused on the
company's future."

When he finally came up for air, Amorim's cork business was facing new and serious competitors in the closure marketplace from synthetic corks and agglomerated corks in the form of Altec, which had just taken off. "My competition now was no longer in Portugal," says António. For the first time in nearly four hundred years there were credible alternatives to cork. It didn't matter that the market share of plastic corks and Altec were still minuscule; the challengers were there and growing rapidly. The entire closure market was growing fast thanks to wine producers in New World countries, but the threat was serious.

During most of 1997, the cork company's board of directors wrestled with the challenges Amorim faced from plastic corks and Altec. Tradition was one of the biggest hurdles to overcome. Up to this point, Amorim had always been strictly a natural-cork company. Some board members feared that if it went in the direction of either new alternative, it would be cannibalizing its existing business. If it began selling a much less expensive product, wouldn't it be putting at risk the annual sales of 3 billion higher-priced natural corks?

The solution was a new, inexpensive closure called Twin Top that could compete with both alternatives on price and perhaps help solve the taint problem. The technology was nothing new; an Italian company had first developed it during the 1970s and sold it under the generic name One plus One. The industry called them technical corks because they are made with natural cork through a manufacturing process. The move was a major break from Amorim's past. With Twin Tops, the central part of the closure was made from ground-up granules of natural cork held together by glue much like the Altec, but at the two ends were disks of natural cork. By using cork waste for the central part, the company's overall cost of production would be significantly reduced. The two high-quality natural-cork ends, one of which would be in contact with the wine in the bottle, should help in the fight against TCA. The board still worried about the danger of losing its existing business, but it had to act.

The gamble worked. Twin Tops were immediately a huge market success, even soon surpassing the takeoff of Altec. Says António, "We lost three hundred million sales of natural cork, but we gained eight hundred million sales of Twin Tops." A big user of Twin Tops was a wildly popular new California wine named Charles Shaw that sold for $1.99 a bottle and was known to its thousands of fans as Two Buck Chuck. The California producer Bronco Wine Co. concluded that its inexpensive wine couldn't afford to go out with a cheap closure such as a plastic cork or a screwcap. It needed the prestige of cork to be successful, and it chose the Twin Top.

The second part of the Amorim survival strategy was greater vertical integration and major new investments. António concluded the company had "to get control of our entire supply chain." A new European study into the origins of TCA had taken the problem all the way back to the cork-oak forests and showed that it could develop at many places along the production line. Portugal's old decentralized system of many small cork operators and a few large exporting companies meant it was difficult, if not impossible, to have reputable quality-control procedures. There were simply too many stops along the way with weak standards where something could go wrong. Amorim had to move more aggressively into cork production, starting in the forests with more company-owned properties. In addition, it had to introduce new technologies to an ancient process.

Part of the answer was to open two major new production facilities, one in Ponte-de-Sôr and the other in Coruche, with the latest equipment. In a break with the past, they would be built in the south, rather than in the north near Oporto, to be closer to the Alentejo cork forests and reduce the delays and dangers of shipping all the raw material north. Both facilities had expensive stainless equipment for washing raw cork bark that also circulated the water to keep it at a uniform high temperature of about 200°F and changed the water more frequently. In the north the company also constructed a new three-hundred-thousand-square-feet storage facility with concrete floors, so that freshly harvested cork would no longer sit on the ground where mold could form.

All of this cost money—big money. Between 1998 and 2000, Amorim invested €43 million ($56.8 million), largely in new equipment. In 2001, the cork business lost money for the first year in its history largely because of that investment. The company, however, didn't have an option if it was going to have a future. The cost for just the washing equipment at Ponte-de-Sôr was ten times more than the company had ever before paid for such machinery. Each new plant cost €12 million ($15.8 million). Says Amorim, "There could be no limit on spending to save the company. That was the only way I could sell it to the board to spend ten times more for a new boiling system. You can't put that into a spreadsheet."

A final part of Amorim's vertical integration was to start selectively buying up small Portuguese companies and to get tighter control over its Spanish operation. More than one hundred Portuguese cork companies had been shutting their doors annually, unable to keep up with the spending on new equipment that the industry was demanding, and Amorim bought some of the better firms. Meanwhile in Spain it stopped buying Spanish raw cork material through middlemen and opened two companies that would purchase raw material directly from farmers.

By the time all the initiatives had been taken, Amorim had dramatically changed the structure of its cork business. In 1990, some 75 percent of the cork Amorim sold came from outside suppliers; in 2006, about 95 percent of it came from the company's own production. "Only vertically integrated companies will be successful," says António, "because only they can control their whole production. You can't depend on small- and medium-sized companies that don't comply with basic quality-control procedures."

Despite the new investments and changed internal procedures, Amorim still faced a hostile market. In March 1999, Geoff Linton, the longtime technical manager at Australia's Yalumba, traveled to Portugal for a tour of Amorim's facilities that included a stop at the new Ponte-de-Sôr factory. The cork company regularly brought in winemakers for schmooze visits like that where the Port wine flowed freely. António Amorim decided to spend three days personally with Linton on the trip. Day after day, Linton pummeled him with questions about the nature of TCA, how it developed, how it could be eradicated, when the company was going to solve all its problems—and on, and on, and on. Linton was relentless. Recalls Amorim, "Geoff is a very practical person, and he was asking me very tough pragmatic questions. He was asking the toughest questions I had ever heard, and I didn't have any answers. All I could do was say that was a good suggestion and that we'll have an answer in a year—or three years—or two years. I never felt so pressed up against the wall in my life. I felt terrible that I couldn't give real answers to any of his questions."

Linton went back to Australia unsatisfied, but António Amorim left the visit with a determination to build up a new research-and-development operation that could come up with answers to the questions of Linton— and the wine industry. The future of cork, if it had a future, had to be anchored on solid scientific research. The cork industry had to stop blowing smoke at winemakers or blaming them for its problems. Only unchallenged scientific facts could provide the solution for what ailed the cork industry.

António soon went on a search for a director of research. In December 1999, he hired Miguel Cabral, a Ph.D. microbiologist who was a professor in the pharmacy faculty at the University of Oporto and was head of the quality-control lab for the Vinho Verde Commission, which oversees production of that lightly effervescent white wine. Cabral had a solid research background and had published extensively in scholarly reviews. He also spoke good English, which Amorim thought was important because the toughest markets they faced were Britain, Australia, the United States, and New Zealand. Cabral was given an annual budget of €6 million ($7.9 million) and told to get to work understanding cork taint and other cork problems and coming up with the solution—or solutions—for solving them.

Cabral had only been on staff two months when António took him on a trip into the belly of the beast for cork producers: Australia. The company's public-relations firm set up a dinner at the Stamford Plaza Hotel in Adelaide with the six toughest cork critics from the local wine industry and from the Australian Wine Research Institute. Cork had no friends among the guests. The group included Linton, who was still looking for answers. The dinner started at 6:00 p.m. with all-out attacks on the quality of Portuguese corks in general and those from Amorim in particular. António at first let Cabral handle the questions to show that the company now had a top researcher working on the issues. But after less than thirty minutes, the scientist looked like a fighter who had just gone fifteen rounds against a world heavyweight champion.

António then jumped in and took the attacks for the next four hours. It was well past 10:00 p.m. and his mouth was getting dry from all the talking, so António asked a waiter for a glass of water. Adelaide is known for its low-quality water, and when he took a taste of it, the cork maker realized the water had TCA. Amorim passed the glass around the table for the rest of the group to smell, and they all recognized the taint. Then he said, "I know there is a lot of work for the cork industry and for Amorim to solve our problems. I won't dispute that for one single moment. But I think it's time for your water to stop contaminating my cork!"

That ended the night on a lighter note with lots of laughs around the table. But on the way out of the restaurant, António took Cabral aside and whispered, "I don't ever want to go through a meeting like that again in my life. I don't care what it costs; just fix this problem! We have to come up with answers for those guys. Again, I don't care what it costs." Then António added that if Cabral solved the TCA problem, the company would erect a statue of him at the entrance to its headquarters in Santa Maria de Lamas.

MESSAGE IN A BOTTLE: LAS VEGAS

APCOR, the Portuguese Cork Association, in 2006 sponsored a contest in the United States for the best cork story. The winner was Shalom Stella, who received $1,000 worth of wine for this entry:

> While working in a Las Vegas restaurant with a view of The Strip that made every evening glamorous, one small cork influenced my love for wine. I was only twenty-four and had moved to Las Vegas two years prior to work as a sommelier. One evening in May of 2003, I approached a table of two gentlemen. Their reservation had an asterisk next to it, meaning that this was a VIP table sent by the casino.
>
> After a brief discussion of favorite wines, dinner was to include a bottle of 1961 Château Margaux. I located the prized bottle and wheeled it over on my decanting cart. While cutting away the foil, I got to thinking that the cork had been placed in the bottle more than forty years before. I extracted the cork and presented it to the host on a silver coaster. It was soiled with wine that had been waiting for just this occasion for four decades. I was elated to see the cork in outstanding condition, resilient yet soaked about halfway up and without any seepage.
>
> It took about two hours for the wine to open up in the glass, a sizable glass poured for me by the host. To this day, that glass still represents my favorite for many reasons, but mostly due to the longevity and youthfulness that it held even though it began as just fragile grapes ripening in the sun forty-two years prior, held together by a cork and bottle.

CHAPTER ELEVEN

California Looks
for a High-Tech Solution

To the wine-consuming public, a cork is a cork is a cork. There is no way even the most knowledgeable connoisseur can see the difference between a cork coming from a well-respected company that adheres to industry best practices and one from a fly-by-night firm manufacturing poor-quality corks out of a backstreet sweatshop outside Oporto. In the late 1980s, Bruce Scott, a California importer of Portuguese cork through his company Scott Laboratories, became concerned about the lack of international standards or guidelines for selling corks. He felt that the shady producers were dragging down the whole industry, and some wineries were buying strictly on cost without looking at all to quality.

In an attempt to separate quality companies from the shoddy ones as well as respond to the challenge posed by synthetic stoppers, seven cork-importing companies—two American firms, plus four Portuguese, and one Italian—in 1991 established the Cork Quality Council. It was the first national organization of its kind in the world, and its goal was to promote cork by educating both wineries and consumers about cork. The group hired Napa's Balzac Communications to handle public relations, and its owner, Paul Wagner, came on as the head of the council.

The Portuguese companies had lots of complaints of their own against their American customers. They were tired of getting shipments rejected because of cork taint. Many exporters established sensory panels in Portugal, which were groups of wine experts with particularly good senses of smell and taste who sampled wines looking for problems. They were not finding particularly high incidences of bad cork, but the Americans were still rejecting a large number of ten-thousand-cork bales. The cost of shipping all that cork back to Portugal was mounting up, and companies wanted a more reliable way to verify that the cork was clean.

It became clear that the cork industry had to do more in the United States than just sprinkle a little public relations pixie dust around. So the council in 1996 hired Peter Weber to head up an expanded effort to redeem its reputation by enlisting high technology to get a better handle on the incidence of taint in the corks sent to American wineries. After graduating from Yale, Weber spent a short time on Wall Street, then moved to California, where he got into the wine business. After being offered the job, he checked with some of his winery friends about their views on cork vs. plastic closures. They told him that the synthetics didn't work because they caused rapid oxidation. Weber was also personally skeptical about the seriousness of the taint problem. One of his previous jobs had been running the direct-mail business for Windsor Winery. It sold two hundred thousand cases of wine a year that were delivered by UPS, and he rarely got any complaints about corkiness. So Weber decided to take the job, thinking it was a no-brainer to defend cork against synthetics, which apparently didn't work, and perhaps the cork-taint problem wasn't so bad after all.

Although he had been a history major in college, Weber had to begin digging into science to understand what had already been done in the field and how taint moved from the cork to wine. His research eventually took him to ETS, the private research lab, to see what it had done on the topic. Weber explained to co-owner Gordon Burns that the cork companies wanted to come up with a scientific and reliable way of measuring TCA.

The sensory panels the cork companies were using were simply too arbitrary. There was also disagreement over the threshold level at which TCA could be detected. Some said it was as low as 2 parts per trillion, while others maintained it was as high as 40 parts per trillion. One early Cork Quality Council study showed that trained panel members picked up taint smell and taste at 6 parts per trillion. Another problem was that members of sensory panels quickly lost their sensitivity to TCA. Just as French winemakers in the 1980s didn't realize they reeked of it until they went home and their wives told them they smelled, testers soon suffered from anosmia and had to take a break to regain their sensitivity to the taint. The CQC wanted to remove the human factor and come up with an acceptable and independent way to measure TCA.

Burns and ETS were familiar with Tanner's research, and a recent graduate student from UC Davis had worked at the lab on a TCA project. But ETS had not yet done any comprehensive studies on the subject.

Burns, though, was aware of the potential of using solid-phase micro-extraction in conjunction with gas chromatography and mass spectrometry, or GC-MS as it was called, to tackle the problem. The technology had progressed dramatically since Tanner had used it in the early 1980s and had become a major tool of forensic police work. GC-MS was about to become a star in the TV series *CSI: Crime Scene Investigation,* where high-tech sleuths use the technology to solve crimes. If GC-MS was replacing sniffing dogs at crime scenes, maybe it could also replace TCA-sniffing humans in wineries. Burns explained to Weber that gas chromatography separates the different molecules in any matrix such as a sample of wine. Then the mass spectrometry identifies and quantifies the strength of specific molecules such as TCA. "It's like pulling needles out of an immense haystack," Burns explained. After Burns showed Weber and the Cork Quality Council members the potential of gas chromatography and mass spectrometry, the group agreed to finance a major research project to confirm that the technology would help solve its problems.

The equipment, however, wasn't worth anything without a trained chemist to run it. Luckily, soon after the machinery was bought, Burns met Pascal Chatonnet at a wine symposium and asked him if he knew someone experienced with the use of GC-MS on wines. As it so happened, Chatonnet had the perfect candidate. His name was Éric Hervé. He had just gotten his Ph.D. at the University of Bordeaux and had used GC-MS in doing his thesis on the aroma compounds in Cognac and Armagnac, but he hadn't found a job to use his talents in France. After a brief telephone interview, Burns invited Hervé to come to the United States for a three-month internship. This sounded like a great opportunity to the Frenchman, but it was also a bit terrifying because he had never been to the United States and had little experience speaking English, although he could read it well. Nonetheless, Hervé jumped at the opportunity and arrived in August 1997 to begin work.

For the next two years, Hervé bounced back and forth between Bordeaux and Napa every three months, working on narrowly focused projects with detailed goals and tight deadlines. In the first period, for example, he became familiar with the new equipment ETS had. This was all heady stuff for the young wine scientist. When the electronics company Hewlett-Packard told ETS about a new GC-MS system it was about to put on the market, Burns flew Hervé in his private plane to Palo Alto with some samples to test the equipment for a day. Burns immediately bought the instrument, and two weeks later it was operational at ETS. At the Bordeaux University lab, the French scientist had been able to do five or six TCA analyses per day working full-time. With the new equipment, he was doing twenty-four a day working part-time.

Christian Butzke, an instructor at UC Davis, had done research that got the detection of TCA down to 5 parts per trillion, but Hervé knew that was not good enough. His target was 1 part per trillion or less. To give visitors a sense of the magnitude of the challenge, Gordon Burns said 1 part per trillion was comparable to one step on a walk to the sun. A breakthrough came when researchers in Germany developed a method of measuring a single ion, which permitted recognition down to levels significantly below that of any taster's nose.

After becoming comfortable with the GC-MS equipment at ETS, Hervé began a series of tests with corks soaked in wine, usually Franzia Chablis from a five-liter box. That wine had never been exposed to cork and also had a mild smell so any taint readily stood out. An initial project was to find out what happens when a tainted cork comes in contact with wine. Hervé found that TCA is at first quickly released, then comes out much more slowly until equilibrium is established between the TCA level in the wine and the level in the cork. The researcher determined that if tainted corks had no paraffin or silicone coating and were soaked in white wine, the wine reached a maximum taint level in twenty-four hours. If the corks were coated, the wine reached the maximum level in forty-eight hours. When the cork was in a bottle, the taint transfer rate was much slower, but it eventually reached an equilibrium level and then went no higher. That was a major breakthrough in solving the TCA puzzle.

Further tests showed there was a poor correlation between the amount of TCA released into the wine during the soaking and the total amount present in the cork. Hervé did that by registering the level during a soak and comparing that to the amount in the cork particles after he ground them up.

Perhaps the most surprising conclusion of Hervé's research was that the amount of TCA released by the cork was the same even if it was soaked several times. If the wine reached a taint level of 10 parts per trillion in the first test, for example, it attained that same amount every other time the cork was tested. He proved that by soaking the same tainted cork repeatedly in different batches of wine.

Hervé also determined that the alcohol level of wine strongly affected the amount of TCA extracted from the cork. Higher-alcohol wines might have more TCA, but that was offset because the TCA was less volatile and not as easy to smell. Red wines with 14 or 15 percent alcohol might have greater levels of TCA, but the taint was not as apparent. Hervé concluded that the maximum recognition of TCA takes place in a wine that has about 10 percent alcohol. At that level it is much easier to smell and analyze the TCA, which is why he used 10 percent wines in his testing. That is also the reason relatively low alcohol wines such as Champagne, Vinho Verde, and Riesling have a high incidence of TCA.

All of his preliminary work led Hervé to come up with a new concept in the discussion of cork taint, which he called releasable TCA—the amount of taint the cork releases into the wine when it reaches equilibrium. Other scientists had been measuring the level of TCA by grinding up corks. Hervé was interested in the amount of TCA the cork released and whether there was a correlation between that and the level of TCA in the bottle.

This was where the GC-MS equipment came into play since it would allow the ETS staff to measure the level of releasable TCA. As a result, ETS was able to deliver to the Cork Quality Council a totally objective method of measuring TCA. Cork producers were no longer dependent on the vagaries of the human nose, and the tests for TCA levels could be repeated using the same equipment and the same standards in Oporto, Bordeaux, California, or anywhere.

It would be impractical, of course, to inspect every single one of the some 13 billion corks produced each year to determine which were tainted. Weber talked with NASA officials about their deep-space technology and whether that could be used to inspect each cork and kick out the bad ones, but the discussions never got far. The more realistic approach was to take a random sampling of corks that would be representative of a much bigger lot. In 1997, Butzke of UC Davis developed a sampling protocol to address exactly that issue. Weber looked at this work but decided not to use it because he felt Butzke's program would require larger lot sizes than were realistically available.

At the same time, though, Weber was concerned that his sampling method stand up to outside scrutiny. So he decided to use the most widely used sampling method in the world: the Pentagon's Defense Standard procedure. This is the system the U.S. Defense Department uses to make sure the products the military buys, ranging from bullets to folding chairs, meet detailed government specifications. When the army buys one thousand jeeps, it doesn't inspect each one to make sure it's acceptable. Officials consult the Defense Department handbook and inspect a random number of jeeps based on the total size of the purchase. The Pentagon's long use of the system gave it great credibility. The only thing the cork companies had to do was follow specific instructions in the handbook.

With the sample procedure in place, Hervé had to determine whether he could test the samples in large batches or if he had to examine each cork individually. He did that by doing a composite soak of one hundred corks from fourteen bales in a 10 percent alcohol solution and compared the results to what he got when he tested the one hundred corks individually. He found only a minor difference between the two approaches and concluded he could use large soaks.

Finally it was time to do a bottling experiment to determine if the whole system worked, in particular the relationship between releasable TCA and the level of it in the bottle. For the test, Napa Valley's Beringer Vineyards donated four hundred bottles of white Zinfandel, which had a 10 percent alcohol level. Hervé then selected four hundred corks at random from three bales that had already been identified as having a high incidence of TCA. He coded and soaked the corks, then measured the level of releasable TCA. The corks were finally dried, coated with the normal paraffin and silicone, and inserted into bottles on the Beringer production line.

Bottles of the Beringer wine were opened at one, three, eight, and fourteen months and tested for TCA. The conclusion on Hervé's final report: "Analysis of bottled wine for TCA shows a high correlation of the releasable TCA measured in the individual corks prior to bottling." After fourteen months in the bottle, the TCA was at about half the level of releasable TCA, and it was continuing to increase toward the equilibrium level. The system worked.

It had taken two years to develop the program for testing cork being imported into the United States, but by the end of 1999, the Cork Quality Council and ETS had all the pieces together. If the member companies adopted the procedure, they would be sampling some 75 percent of American cork imports and would be able to reject batches where the TCA level was above an acceptable standard.

The trips back and forth from Bordeaux to Napa for a year and a half had been a heavy burden on Hervé's private life. His wife, Isabelle, was also a Ph.D. wine scientist with a Bordeaux degree and was the lab manager for the winemakers' council of Bergerac, a region east of Bordeaux. At a meeting in December 1997, she proposed to the council's former and current presidents that the organization adopt some of the quality-control mechanisms being developed in California. The two men, almost in unison, said, "But, mademoiselle, there are no cork-taint problems with

Bergerac wines." After that encounter, Isabelle began to think about working in the Napa Valley.

At the end of 1998, Éric told Gordon Burns that he and Isabelle couldn't keep up the commuting life indefinitely. Either he or his wife would have to give up a job, so they could be together. Burns immediately offered Isabelle a position at ETS. By the time she arrived in the United States, Éric Hervé had taken the French accents off his name and became Eric Herve. Americans had no problem pronouncing it correctly.

Isabelle reached the United States just in time for Eric to unveil the ETS research in a presentation at the 1999 meeting of the American Society for Enology and Viticulture in Reno, Nevada. The immediate reaction from the group was polite, and Herve at first wasn't sure the Americans had comprehended what this meant. Only later did he get calls from both U.S. researchers and from Sabaté indicating they had understood. There was some lingering skepticism in France and Australia about both the ETS's sampling method and its batch soaks, but those questions faded over time. Today the ETS procedure is the generally accepted way to sample the quality of corks worldwide. The entire study cost the Cork Quality Council members $500,000.

Scott Laboratories was the first member of the Cork Quality Council to use the ETS system, starting on December 1, 1999. Other members began a pilot project in March 2000. For the first year, most of the cork importers had bales tested both by their sensory panels and by the new ETS method, but they later eliminated the noses.

The testing system was straightforward. Imported corks arrived in bales of various sizes, and the importers had a list of how many corks were to be randomly selected and then sent to ETS for testing. The batches faced a strict pass/fail system. If the taint level was below the set standard, the bale could be released to a winery. If it failed, the bale was tested again. If it flunked two tests, the bale was shipped back to Portugal. Importers got the results of testing in two to five working days. To keep up with all that testing of corks, ETS today has a dozen of the $150,000 GC-MS machines.

At the beginning of the testing in March 2000, the mandatory rejection level was set at 6 parts per trillion, since that is the point that had been determined by earlier human experiments at which TCA is clearly evident. Despite that high level, however, the rejection rate was running about 30 percent.

In May 2000, Gordon Burns and Peter Weber flew to Oporto to make a presentation of their new quality-control system to a meeting in the Costa

Verde Room of the Solverde Hotel in Espinho, on the Atlantic coast near the epicenter of the world's cork industry. Present were the patriarchs of most of Portugal's leading cork families, often with their heirs in tow. As the Americans ran through their PowerPoint presentations, the audience sat in stunned silence as the high—and consistent—level of cork taint in shipments to the United States flashed on the screen. When Burns and Weber said TCA levels would initially have to get down to 6 parts per trillion and then even lower later, the producers complained that simply couldn't be done. They were already doing their best. The goal was impossible!

By the end of the meeting, however, it was clear that the Portuguese cork industry as a result of the ETS work had entered a new and much more rigorous era. The old ways of human testing and blaming tainted cork on improper handling or dirty cellars in wineries were finished. For the first time, the industry had equipment and a methodology that were accurate and independent. The producers would have to live by that in the future; cork taint was no longer going to be determined by someone's nose. There was finally an easy and an internationally accepted objective way to calculate it. Said António Amorim after the Espinho meeting, "Either we get rid of TCA, or we don't have a future. Gordon Burns is an independent researcher, and a person of integrity. We have to listen to him."

Amorim soon ordered its own GC-MS machine. The company now has nine, almost as many as ETS. They work six days a week, twenty-four hours a day, using the same methodology Eric Herve developed. Amorim realized there was no use sending all those bad corks to the United States only to have them shipped back. It was both wiser and cheaper to test them in Portugal before they left to eliminate ones that would fail the test in California. Sure enough, soon after the GC-MS equipment went into use in Portugal, the rejection rate fell precipitously in California.

CHAPTER TWELVE

Australia Blazes New Paths

Jeffrey Grosset led the Clare Valley winemakers who "took a fly" with screwcaps.

Pat Williams, the acting director of the Australian Wine Research Institute, in late June 1997, interviewed Peter Godden, a British immigrant to Australia, for the position of head of Technical Services at the institute. Godden had moved to Australia nearly a decade before to study economics after working in London in the financial markets. Once in Australia, though, he discovered a new passion for wine, and after teaching himself enough science to pass the state test required to get into Roseworthy Agricultural College, he entered its enology program. Godden graduated in 1991 and then spent the next six years working at wineries in Australia, France, and Italy. After returning home, he began making plans to start a small, high-end winery that was going to make a wine using the Italian

Nebbiolo grape. A job in wine research and his own small winery seemed like a good combination.

During the interview, Williams asked Godden what he thought were the most important issues facing the Australian wine industry. In his response Godden hedged his bet a little by saying that although it wasn't the only issue, he thought the biggest single one was "clearly closures." Williams agreed, since Terry Lee, when he'd left AWRI only two months before to go to Gallo, had suggested that a closure study be one of the institute's top priorities. Godden looked like the perfect candidate to put together such a study and was hired for the job. He was told that although he had to work on some other projects, the key performance indicator for how his work would be measured would be his success in getting a closure study up and going as soon as possible.

Working out of a cramped office in the badly overcrowded AWRI complex, Godden spent most of 1998 putting together the elements of a study. He knew instinctively that if he did it right, the research would have a major impact on the wine industry not only in Australia but also around the world. Although closure tests had been done recently in Germany and France, this one would be the most comprehensive, long-term study ever done looking at the broad spectrum of products currently being offered. As a result, the AWRI research had to be bulletproof because Godden was sure that some people in the wine industry would soon be shooting at it, no matter what the results.

Godden first pulled together the organizational details on how to staff and run the study, and also how much it would cost since this would be one of the most extensive, and expensive, studies AWRI had ever undertaken. The cost during the first eight years would reach about A$600,000 (US$473,700), with most of that going to pay for the salaries of the people in charge of the testing, rather than for bottling or storing the wine.

Godden first visited six of Australia's largest wineries, which produced about 80 percent of the country's output, to hear the views of winemakers and production managers. They became an industry working group that advised him during the tests. He also worked closely with Leigh Francis, the head of AWRI sensory programs that stage wine tastings. In addition, Godden solicited the help of a statistician from the Commonwealth Scientific and Industrial Research Organization (CSIRO), AWRI's frequent collaborator, to get through the land mine of details that go into designing a test that would meet rigorous international standards.

While TCA was the main issue in the study, it was decided early in the planning stage to play close attention also to variability between different bottles sealed with the same closure in order to identify the cause of random oxidation. Australia's winemakers had been complaining that an unusually high number of bottles under cork seemed to suffer from premature oxidation.

With the help of his advisers, Godden decided the wine for the trial would be a mid- to upper-quality Semillon that had not been either made or stored in oak vats so it would not have oak flavors that could easily be confused with those of cork. They chose that wine because it would last ten years, the likely outer limit of the study, but would still develop quickly because there was great pressure to have the results from the test published quickly. In addition, and most important, Semillon is light in taste and color, so any problems would easily show up.

The next issue was the number of closures to include in the trial. It was impossible to test all the closures on the market, but AWRI wanted to have a reputable representation of the various types being used at wineries at the time. Originally the plan was to have thirteen different closures, but at the last minute an extra synthetic cork was added to make it fourteen. They included one screwcap, two types of natural cork each with a different length, two technical corks, and nine synthetic stoppers. AWRI obtained many of the closures from the companies that produced them. The screwcap came from Auscap, an Australian firm that manufactures a wide range of closures. The two natural corks came from wineries that used them and were randomly selected from different batches.

The names and types of the fourteen closures:

Name	Type
Aegis	Synthetic molded
Altec	Technical cork
Auscork	Synthetic molded
Betacorque	Synthetic molded
ECORC	Synthetic extruded
Integra	Synthetic molded
Nomacorc	Synthetic extruded
NuKorc	Synthetic extruded
One plus One	Technical cork
Cork 2, 44 mm (1.7 in.)	Natural cork

Name	Type
Cork 3, 38 mm (1.5 in.)	Natural cork
Auscap	Screwcap
Supreme Corq	Synthetic molded
Tage	Synthetic molded

The planners set out in advance a series of tests that would be performed beginning the day after bottling. The objective was to examine the wine on the basis of three criteria: physical, chemical, and sensory. Physical tests were made of the closures prior to bottling to get a statistical baseline and then after extraction of closures from the bottle to determine how they had changed. Researchers kept records of the extraction force needed to open a bottle under various closures, and the speed and extent that closures recovered to their original shape after extraction. Chemical tests analyzed the wine compounds over time. Sensory tests judged how the wine smelled and tasted.

The original plan was to taste the wines at six-month intervals starting at six months for up to two years and then annually after that. Additional tests were later added at fifteen months and twenty-one months. Before each tasting, the tasters determined the terms for rating the wines, which ranged from the good (citrus or spicy) to the bad (plastic or musty). These varied somewhat from tasting to tasting depending on the Semillon's natural development. In addition, GC-MS analysis was done on wines along the way.

All the tasting was done at AWRI. With only a few exceptions, the same members of the AWRI technical staff did all the chemical testing. Ten people participated in every tasting, nine from the staff of AWRI plus Patrick Iland from the University of Adelaide wine program. The goal was to have the exact same judges for each event, but there must have been something in the wine because several judges became pregnant and substitutes had to be found. Most of the judges, though, remained the same throughout the first five years of testing.

The format for the tasting was spelled out in writing and in incredible detail. Judges sat in isolated booths and examined only one wine at a time. The room had sodium lighting, so judges could not see color differences in the wine since they were only to rate taste and smell. When a tester wanted another wine to taste, he or she flicked on a light. An AWRI staffer then brought a standard-size, white wineglass to the cubicle and took away the last one. The judges tasted every wine in the program four times a day and for four days in a row until they had run through all the wines. Just to keep the tasters on their toes, an occasional duplicate wine was intro-duced from time to time.

The intention from early in the planning was to bottle the wine as soon as the 1999 Semillon was available in the spring, and the bottling took place on May 26. The AWRI revealed only that the wine was produced in the Clare Valley north of Adelaide by an unnamed, commercial winery. It was soon learned in the industry, however, that Leasingham, a part of the Hardy group, made the wine. Vinpac, the leading contract bottler in the region, handled the bottling. The order of bottling was determined by hav-ing Rae Blair, the AWRI manager of communications and information services, pull closure names out of a hat. Two closures, the screwcap and one synthetic, required special bottling equipment, so they had to be handled separately. In most cases a company representative of that closure was pres-ent during the bottling and determined when they had three hundred acceptable bottles with a particular seal. Godden had determined that many were needed for the long-term study. Usually many more ran through the bottling line before they got three hundred. The bottling lasted fifteen hours and thirty-eight minutes, and Godden collected a mind-boggling amount of detail ranging from the temperature of the wine (between 14.7°C and 20.1°C or 58.5°F and 68.2°F) to the amount of tartaric acid in the wine prior to bottling (3.8 grams per liter).

After bottling, the AWRI staff stored the wine upright in cartons at the Vinpac plant for twenty-four hours, then trucked them to the AWRI offices outside Adelaide, where the eight thousand bottles were first taken out of boxes and placed in a large, empty room in the student winery. Finally at the statistician's advice, the staff put random tracking numbers on the bot-tles that he had selected and placed them back in arbitrary cartons with the necks down to totally level the playing field among the closures.

One thing not clearly spelled out before the test started was when the first results would be announced. Godden and company wanted to have some clear conclusions before they went public. So although they tested the wines at the predetermined times, none of the results were being made known.

Behind closed doors, though, the test team was beginning to see some interesting developments. "At about fifteen months, we started to realize that we already had fourteen different wines," recalls Godden. "They were heading off on different trajectories. The changes that occurred after bottling were profound. The most important thing that came out of the trial for me was the realization that by changing the closure, you created different wines." For the moment, though, such views were held inside AWRI in strictest secret. As far as the world knew, the test was simply under way.

Winemakers up in the Clare Valley, however, weren't sitting around waiting for AWRI to tell them what to do. They were making plans of their own even without the AWRI results. Andrew Hardy, the winemaker at Knappstein, which is owned by Petaluma, was the current president of the Clare Valley Winemakers Association and was guiding their search for an alternative to cork. The group earlier had great hope in the new closure from the DELFIN-Alliance, a European coalition of cork makers, whose product claimed to eliminate TCA by subjecting corks to microwaves, but the results had been disappointing. In mid-1999, Hardy telephoned a few fellow winemakers and asked them if they might be interested in having another look at screwcaps as a way to seal wine bottles.

The use of screwcaps had not totally died after the earlier attempt in the 1970s and early 1980s. In the late 1990s, a few isolated wineries were doing some experiments with screwcaps. Yalumba put its top-end Pewsey Vale The Contours Riesling under screwcap in 1995 and planned to age it for five years before releasing it. Henschke also did a 1996 Riesling that way, and Richmond Grove used screwcaps in 1998, also with a Riesling. Andrew Hardy, though, was proposing something different. He was suggesting that a large number of Riesling producers do it together and make it a major event.

Hardy received an enthusiastic response from Jeffrey Grosset, the region's most famous vintner, whose Polish Hill and Watervale Rieslings are regularly on lists of international best wines. In the world of superego winemakers, Grosset is a rare modest one, although he is not shy about voicing strong opinions. He first tasted wine at home at the age of fifteen in 1969, when his parents started drinking it with meals. After a family friend who worked for Leo Buring, a Riesling specialist, told him there might be a great future in Australian wine, he entered Roseworthy and five years later left with degrees in agriculture and enology. After eighteen months of working for Seppelt at Great Western, he made the Australian winemaker's almost obligatory trip to Europe to see how wine was made there. Unlike most of his colleagues, Grosset went to Germany, rather than France. He ended up in the minor wine area of Baden, but traveled all around the country, falling in love with Riesling along the way.

After returning to Australia, Grosset worked for several large wine companies that drummed into him the basics of hygiene, fruit management, and organization. "Because of our hot climate inland, things happen a lot faster and can go wrong quickly," he says. "As a result, you learn fast." Grosset, though, wanted out of the big-company environment so he could make quality wines, particularly Rieslings. The Clare Valley had been spotted as a good place for that grape in the late nineteenth century, and so he started looking there for property. He found a butter-and-ice factory, with a milk depot thrown in, for sale at auction. The minimum bid was A$20,000 (US$15,790), which was more than he could borrow, but he got it for less. Grosset in 1981 bought Riesling grapes that grew at a place called Polish Hill River and gave that name to his wine. The first year he made only eight hundred cases.

Success came quickly, and soon Grosset was buying his own land and planting vineyards as his annual production headed toward nine thousand cases. In addition to the Rieslings, he also makes Gaia, a classic Bordeaux-style blend of Cabernet Sauvignon, Cabernet Franc, and Merlot.

Grosset was anxious to try a new closure because of his bad experiences with cork. "I was apprehensive every time I opened a bottle," he recalls. He and his partner, Stephanie Toole, the winemaker at Mount Horrocks also in the Clare Valley, were repeatedly experiencing corked wines. "Stephanie has an incredible sensitivity to TCA, as some people do, and I was good at spotting oxidation. Between us we were getting ten percent to fifteen percent failures. Each night we were pouring at least one bottle in ten down the drain."

Since Andrew Hardy worked for a big company, it was hard for him to take the leadership role in the growing movement. So that task fell to Grosset. Eventually Toole and Andrew Mitchell, who owned a winery bearing his name, joined with Grosset and Hardy to form the four-person nucleus of the movement. With the exception of Hardy, they were all owners and in their forties. "It was easier for us to take the gamble because we answered only to ourselves," says Grosset. "Also, when you're young, sometimes you just take a fly even if you don't have all the things together. That's what it was here." By October 1999, the group, with absolutely no test-marketing and no focus groups, agreed to bottle some of their Riesling from the 2000 vintage in screwcaps.

It still helps when you're "taking a fly" to have the support of others, so the four began calling other Clare Valley winemakers to enlist them in the cause. Eventually they got just over half of those making Riesling, thirteen of twenty-five. "We felt that if we were jumping off a cliff, we'd do better if we jumped together," says Grosset. "But we were never really aware of the danger or of anything else that should have stopped us."

Time was short before they'd be bottling in July and August 2000, so the members of the group got cracking on getting everything together. A primary objective from the beginning was the aesthetics. They wanted the bottle, in particular, to look good. ACI, the glassmaker, showed little interest in doing a screwcap bottle, perhaps because of their experience in the late 1970s, so the Clare Valley group commissioned Saverglass in Cognac, France, to design a new one. It had a so-called Bague Verre Stelvin finish, which provided extra protection against nicking the capsule, and had a neck that reduced the headspace between the seal and the wine where oxygen could be trapped during bottling. The group also wanted a longer cap than was currently available in Australia, so again they turned to France and decided to use 60 mm Stelvin caps.

The group reinforced its decision by tasting wines left over from the failed earlier experience. Grosset told the others of a 1982 Hungerford Hill Riesling under screwcap that he had tasted years later and had been excellent. They got their friends at Yalumba to open some wines from the earlier experiment. They also talked with Stuart Langton, who ran Australia's leading wine auction house, about those early screwcap wines. He said the old Yalumba Rieslings were still "absolutely brilliant."

While some vintners using screwcaps would later say that they had to make some adjustments in their winemaking because the wine would be closed with an airtight seal rather than a cork, which lets in a little oxygen, Grosset maintains that good winemaking procedures don't change because of what's in the neck of the bottle. He says he made no alterations because of "our attention to detail," adding, "I'm not suggesting that people are sloppy in their winemaking; but if someone is lax, he or she will need to smarten up. The average cork can be very forgiving of bad practices, but a screwcap is not."

Bottling took place in mid-July and started with a somewhat ominous event for Grosset. On the first day, lightning struck the bottling plant, causing a loss of power. Was someone up in heaven unhappy with screwcaps? If so, he or she didn't strike a second time, and the bottling was completed without a hitch.

After all their study of the 1970s experiment, the Clare Valley winemakers had concluded that it had been a technical success but a market failure because the companies had not properly prepared the public for the alternative closure. To ensure that mistake was not repeated, the winemakers came up with a few rules on how to handle the expected inquiries from the Australian wine press. First, no marketing people were going to be involved. If a press person called for comment, one of the four winemakers, not a press spokesman, would answer the questions. Second, nothing they put out in writing would be more than a page in length. Third, they would all explain that the switch to screwcaps was not being done to save money but to protect the wines from problems caused by cork. The one-page press release announcing the Clare Valley Riesling Initiative was sent out in August 2000, and the thirteen wineries began selling the wines on September 1. The press release stated that the decision "had nothing to do with convenience" but was "a quality issue driven by winemakers."

Mount Horrocks and Mitchell did 100 percent of their Rieslings with screwcaps the first year, but Grosset hedged his bet. He put only 80 percent under screwcap, with the rest in cork. He shouldn't have bothered. He sold out of the screwcaps first and later had to tell customers he only had bottles with corks. The next year 100 percent of Grosset Rieslings were in screwcap. In May 2002, he released the 2000 Gaia, which sells for about A$50 (US$39.50), with only 30 percent in screwcaps and the rest in cork. The screwcap bottles sold out in two weeks.

The Clare Valley winemakers anticipated that the wine press and connoisseurs would hit them hard with one issue: don't top wines, in particular reds, need oxygen to age and reach their peak of perfection? Remembering their enology studies, they were ready with the answer: leading University of Bordeaux professors such as Jean Ribéreau-Gayon and Émile Peynaud had long said that wine does not need air to age. Although Pasteur in the nineteenth century said, "It is oxygen that makes the wine," those two giants in the twentieth century claimed just the opposite. Ribéreau-Gayon wrote in *Traité d'Oenologie—Sciences et Techniques du Vin, Tome 3*, a 1976 book he wrote with three other scientists, "The quantities of oxygen that normally penetrate into bottles are infinitesimal if not zero. Oxygen is not the agent of normal bottle maturation." Peynaud in his 1981 book *Knowing and Making Wine*, which was a popular treatment of Ribéreau-Gayon's scholarly work, wrote, "It is the opposite of oxidation, a process of reduction or asphyxia, by which wine develops in the bottle."

Preparing their response in detail, the Clare Valley group argued that a screwcap, just like the very best cork, provides a nearly airtight environment in which the wine can age. Peynaud in that same book wrote, "The quantity of oxygen that normally penetrates bottles corked and laid down, a position in which the cork is soaked and swollen, is negligible, if not entirely nonexistent."

The Clare Valley Rieslings under screwcap had been in the market nearly eight months and were enjoying good consumer acceptance when Peter Godden submitted the first report on the AWRI closure study on April 20, 2001, to the *Australian Journal of Grape and Wine Research,* the official publication of the Australian Society of Viticulture and Oenology. The report covered the performance of the wines under the fourteen closures up to twenty months after bottling. The title: "Wine Bottle Closures: Physical characteristics and effect on composition and sensory properties of a Semillon wine." The byline gave credit to eight AWRI staffers, starting with Godden and Francis but also including the institute's director, Peter Høj, and five others working on the project. The dense, forty-one-page report took up an entire issue and was heavy with statistics, graphs, and charts. The picture on the yellow cover showed a cork being pulled out of a wine bottle, but the contents of the report might have led some readers to conclude that cork was just about the last thing someone should be pulling out of a bottle of wine.

The authors reported that already at six months, tasters had serious problems with two closures. The Betacorque, a molded synthetic stopper, showed high levels of oxidized and styrene aromas and much lower citrus/lime aromas. It was obviously a product failure, and the closure was dropped from the tasting. Altec, the Sabaté agglomerated cork, even at six months scored much higher on TCA aroma than any other closure. A later test of all Altec bottles showed that all but one had a significant level of TCA taint.

Already at six months, the closures were also starting to form clusters based on type. The respective scores for the corks, technical corks, and synthetics all came in closely bunched together but with significant disparity among the three groups.

The twelve-month tasting was poor for the Tage closure, another molded synthetic. It showed unusually high levels of aldehyde and signs of oxidation. Judges also got gluelike aromas from the ECORC, an extruded plastic cork. TCA levels for both natural corks were starting to go up, in particular for the longer cork. The shorter one was also showing high levels of unattractive corkwood odors.

At eighteen months, the last full testing in the first report, the Altec cork again had a high TCA score, while Tage and ECORC showed oxidation.

The synthetics as a group were showing significant problems with oxidation, a charge made against many of them since they were first invented.

The eighteen-month tasting also showed the first indication that something unexpected might be happening in the bottles under screwcap. The report stated they were "exhibiting a reduced or sulfide/rubbery aroma." Noted the report, "This character is considered a negative attribute by the panel, and could be indicative that an extended period of close-to-anaerobic storage may not be desirable." Wine scientists call this reduction, and the authors gave several possible explanations for what might be taking place. The bottles could have been filled too high or the wine should perhaps have been treated before bottling to eliminate sulfur compounds.

The report's abstract gave the broad-brush conclusions of the AWRI study at twenty months. TCA, the original stimulus for the research, was found not to be a problem for screwcaps or plastic corks, but a significant one for both natural corks and technical ones. On random oxidation, the second most pressing concern, the screwcaps clearly performed best, while the technical corks did reasonably well. Synthetics did worst on that criterion, and natural corks also did poorly. Wines with high levels of retained SO_2, such as those under screwcap, scored well on retaining fruit flavors. The abstract stated that the synthetic corks, as a group, were "least consumer-friendly" because of problems getting the closures out of bottles and then back in. According to the judges, the ECORC stopper was "practically impossible" to get back in the bottle thirty minutes after it was extracted.

Overall, the twenty-month study clearly favored screwcaps. The scientists doing the chemical analyses said that wines under that closure had the most retained total and free SO_2, the most retained ascorbic acid, the lowest amount of browning, and the least bottle variation. At the same time, the tasters said those wines had the highest fruit aroma and taste, the least oxidation, and no TCA.

The testing would continue, and there was that nagging concern about the problem of reduction with screwcaps, but the initial conclusions were unmistakable.

MESSAGE IN A BOTTLE:

PASO ROBLES, CALIFORNIA

Jay Selman is one of the founders of GrapeRadio, *the most successful wine-talk show on the Internet. It operates out of Tustin, California, and reaches wine lovers everywhere. He's also an avid wine collector and travels the world in search of great wines and interesting guests for his show.*

Selman in May 2005 attended the Hospice du Rhône, a celebration of Rhône Valley wines held each year in Paso Robles, California. Accompanying him was a magnum of 1990 Beaucastel, which some consider to be the greatest Châteauneuf-du-Pape. When Selman opened it at the Paris Restaurant, however, he was devastated. It was corked! Asks Selman painfully, "How could a bottle that I had known for more than twelve years be corked?"

He tried to tell himself it was something else. Perhaps it was Brettanomyces? *Lots of people get the two compounds mixed up. Selman thought at first that the foul smell might just go away, but it didn't, and he began to think he was personally responsible for the taint. "I envisioned a huge purple 'T' on my forehead, announcing my transgression of bringing a corked bottle to the Hospice du Rhône!"*

Fast-forward to 2006—same time, same place. To atone for his past transgression, Selman returned to Paso Robles with another 1990 Beaucastel, but this one was a regular 750 ml bottle. This time he was prepared with a backup of the same wine just in case the first bottle turned out to be another corked disaster. He even brought a backup to the backup, so he now had three bottles of 1990 Beaucastel. Despite having the elaborate safety net in place, Selman still suffered through a few sweaty nights of worry. What if all the bottles came from the same lot, then they might all be bad!

When he opened the first bottle at a picnic celebrating the end of the Rhône celebration, he smelled it and his heart stopped. Then he realized it was beautiful. "There were tons of aromas, and none of them were TCA," Selman recalls. Then he opened his backup bottle, and it too was wonderful.

CHAPTER THIRTEEN

PlumpJack Makes a Bold Gamble

In 1998, Gordon Getty, the heir of oil billionaire John Paul Getty, was having a dinner for the top five executives from his new winery in the Napa Valley. They were dining in an elegant private room in the back of the PlumpJack Café in San Francisco. The main course was a simple pasta, but the wine was special, having come from his father's cellar, which had only recently been moved from New York City to San Francisco, where the younger Getty lived. The wine was a prized Bordeaux First Growth, but after it was opened, the sommelier sadly informed the group that the wine was corked. More puzzled than outraged, Getty asked the assembled group, "Why is this acceptable?" No one, however, had a good answer for him.

The PlumpJack group of companies is a conglomerate of thirteen independent luxury businesses that includes resorts, wine stores, restaurants, and boutiques founded by Getty and his wealthy West Coast friends. The company gets its name from one of Shakespeare's most endearing characters, the rotund reprobate Sir John Falstaff, who calls himself "plump Jack" in the play *Henry IV, Part 1*. Queen Elizabeth I was a great fan of Falstaff's and asked Shakespeare to write another play that would include him. The result was *The Merry Wives of Windsor*. Gordon Getty was also a fan, and he wrote a two-act opera entitled *PlumpJack,* which was first performed in 1989.

Gavin Newsom, a young man about San Francisco who was later elected the city's mayor, and Gordon's son Billy gave the name PlumpJack to their first venture, a San Francisco wine store that opened in 1992. Other upscale ventures followed, with different investors in each enterprise. The PlumpJack winery was financed primarily by Gordon Getty and Newsom and from the beginning set out to produce an ultrapremium Cabernet Sauvignon Reserve just like that of its neighbor across the road,

Screaming Eagle. The first PlumpJack vintage was in 1995 and garnered a 95+ rating from critic Robert Parker. PlumpJack was then making only one thousand cases a year, all of it bottled under cork, but was getting everything in place to ramp up annual production to ten thousand cases.

John Conover, a veteran of the California wine business who had previously been at Grgich Hills and Monticello, was brought in as general manager in 1998. "Gordon and Gavin had other interests and needed someone to run the winery," says Conover. "They handed me the keys to the Ferrari and said, 'Just don't wreck it.'"

PlumpJack did not produce a Reserve Cabernet in 1996 because difficult growing conditions made it impossible to get the quality of grapes the owners demanded. At the same time, Gordon Getty, Newsom, and Conover were trying to come up with an answer to Getty's question about why it was okay for an expensive bottle of wine to be corked.

Along with thousands of other American businesses, PlumpJack gives out a monthly award for an employee's best new idea. At the same time, though, it also has one for the best failure. Says Conover, "We feel that you can't succeed unless you're willing to fail." Aware that he might be putting himself in the running for the failure award, Conover set out to investigate the world of cork alternatives.

He first looked at synthetic corks, but quickly decided not to go there. Conover had seen too many embarrassed sommeliers have difficulties getting the plastic stopper out of a bottle—or get it back in. In addition, he was hearing from winemakers around the valley that synthetics seemed to give wines unexpected and unpleasant tastes. "So that was strike one, two, and three for synthetics," he says.

Then Conover turned to screwcaps and began calling experts at research institutions at the University of California, the Australian Wine Research Institute, and the University of Bordeaux. Getty and Newsom also made trips to Australia and France to talk personally with people there about new ways to seal a bottle. They quickly focused in on Stelvin screwcaps since at the time that was virtually the only brand in the field. Conover asked Stelvin executives in Paris if they had any research on the long-term aging of reds under their closures. He knew that the Australians and New Zealanders were bottling white wines—designed to be drunk quickly—in screwcaps, but what about reds? Conover was surprised to learn that there was little information on the subject. Stelvin executives, though, said they had a few samples of red wines that had been aged for ten years with both screwcaps and corks. They offered to send him some for tasting. Conover and his winemaker tried the two wines three times and concluded that they had aged identically. They couldn't tell the difference.

Even though the winery was young, Conover had a good fix on his market, which made the decision to try screwcaps easier. The company tracked every single case sold and knew that 80 percent of sales were in restaurants. That led him to conclude that most of the wine is consumed within six months of release. "Only about three to five percent of our wines are going into cellars to be aged for years and years," he says. "So in some ways we were putting corks in our bottles and taking the risk of taint for only 3 to 5 percent of our customers."

With Getty's personal endorsement, Conover decided to put half of the three hundred cases of 1997 PlumpJack Reserve in bottles with corks and half in bottles with screwcaps. Although the skeptical wine business never believed Conover, the move was not done to save money. In fact, the screwcap venture cost the company a lot of money, even for a Getty. Screwcaps required a special bottle, which was designed in California and then had to be made in Italy by an artisan glass producer that would turn out a small quantity. In addition, Stelvin's minimum order was sixty thousand caps, even though PlumpJack was going to use only a few hundred the first year. In total, the additional cost to produce the bottles and screwcaps came to nearly $130,000.

In May 2000, PlumpJack released the news to a stunned wine world. It also said the wine would be sold to consumers only in pairs, a screwcap bottle and a cork one, and be delivered in a wooden box. In a masterful stoke of in-your-face marketing, the screwcap bottles would be more expensive: $135 as compared with $125 for the bottle with a cork. The commercial trade could buy the Reserve in six-pack wooden boxes with three bottles of each.

Shortly after the announcement, Conover went on the road for what he calls a "preemptive strike" to talk with key accounts, such as restaurants, and to the media about why the winery was bottling part of its wine in screwcaps. "Everyone I talked with acknowledged that there was a TCA problem and really embraced what we were doing," he says.

In June, the first six bottles of 1997 Reserve (three screwcaps and three corks) were sold for $50,000 at the Napa Auction, the annual bash that raises money for local charities.

Today PlumpJack continues to sell the Reserve Cabernet half in screwcap and half in cork with a minimum purchase of two bottles, one of each. The 2006 price for two bottles: $320. Quips Conover, "You can do whatever gyrations you want with the math to see what each bottle costs." In addition, the winery sells its less expensive Estate Cabernet Sauvignon with either cork or screwcap for $46 a bottle. The winery also asked UC Davis to study how the wines developed over time under both closures.

Although PlumpJack's management seems more committed to screwcaps than to corks, the winery remains careful about its choice of corks. It pays top price to get the best and buys from five separate suppliers to spread its risk. The average price is now pushing $1 a cork. It tests bales of corks from each company by soaking samples in either Chardonnay or vodka to see if there are any problems with taste or color. Winemaker Anthony Biagi then taste-tests to see if he can spot any cork taint. Every year the winery rejects some cork bales.

Along with many American wine consumers, PlumpJack co-owner Gavin Newsom continues to have psychological difficulties with screwcaps. In the November 15, 2006, issue of *Wine Spectator,* he was quoted saying, "We're in the middle of this great experiment. As a restaurateur, I will admit a hard time when I order a bottle of a wine and the guy comes out and just twists [the cap] off."

CHAPTER FOURTEEN

New Zealand's Rebels with a Cause

*A parson joined the four upstart Marlborough
winery owners for the burial of cork.*

In January 2001, John Stichbury, the owner of Jackson Estate, and Ross Lawson, the owner of Lawson's Dry Hills, were attending the New Zealand Pinot Noir conference in Wellington. Neither of the local winemakers was in the best of moods since they had both just had to throw out several of their bottles because they were corked. In the back of the room and out of public sight were some eighty bottles of New Zealand Pinot Noir that been rejected due to suspected cork taint.

After commiserating about their shared problem with corks, Lawson asked Stichbury with deep exasperation, "It's just not good enough is it, Stich?"

To which Stichbury replied, "No, it's not. And I'm going to go broke if this continues."

Lawson was something of a legend around the Marlborough region at the top of the country's South Island. By the time he started growing grapes there in 1980 at the beginning of New Zealand's wine boom, he had already had a colorful career that included being a champion sheep shearer (three hundred in a day), labor union leader, swimming pool contractor, and opossum hunter. He switched from growing grapes to making wine in 1992, when he realized there was more money in the final product. Lawson was a maverick and man of action who didn't spend a lot of time agonizing over decisions. He was now fed up with his "gutful of cork."

The previous November, Lawson had read in an Australian wine magazine that Clare Valley Riesling producers were bottling part of their production in screwcaps. As was his wont, Lawson went directly to Jeffrey Grosset, who the article said was the leader of the Clare Valley group, and asked him how it was going, especially the market reaction. Grosset told him that he had already sold out of his Riesling under screwcap and was now having a little trouble getting rid of his bottles with corks. Lawson tucked that conversation in the back of his mind during the year-end holidays, but when he ran into the corked bottles at the conference in January, he thought it was time to do something about it.

Screwcaps had an almost inherent appeal in New Zealand, a geographically isolated country that only broke free of Britain in 1907. New Zealanders aren't weighed down by a lot of tradition because they don't have much. They came late to the international wine business, having for many years made undistinguished white wines largely from the Müller-Thurgau grape variety. The Kiwis, though, have long been early adopters of technology. For example, New Zealand in the 1980s had the highest per capita use of ATMs, and debit cards could be used for the most minor purchases. New Zealanders have a can-do mentality born of their frontier history. It's a national article of faith that any problem can be fixed with a little #8 wire, an all-purpose product originally used for fencing. The country likewise has a strong spirit of solidarity. Rugby, the national sport and the national passion, is a game where any player can score but depends on teamwork and having "mates" around watching your back.

The Clare Valley's cooperative strategy toward screwcaps appealed to Lawson because it seemed like a rugby-team approach to a problem. After the Wellington meeting, he got on the phone and asked other New Zealand winemakers, particularly those in Marlborough, if they'd like to meet to talk about doing something together to attack their common cork problems. The report of the Australian Wine Research Institute, which had strongly backed screwcaps, was then the talk of the business and made his job easier. Lawson also called Bob Campbell, a Master of Wine and the country's leading wine critic, who responded quickly that if a group of winemakers wanted to go with screwcaps, he'd support them.

In February, a meeting of the Marlborough Winegrowers Association discussed Lawson's initiative. It quickly became clear, however, that not all members of the association were ready to join an anticork crusade, but at the same time winemakers in other parts of the country would sign on. So Lawson and a few other winemakers decided to go ahead with a coalition of the willing regardless of where they were located. A technical committee composed of three winemakers was asked to do a quick study on three specific issues: closures, bottles, and bottling equipment.

The following month the owners of some twenty wineries agreed to set up a steering committee composed of the owners of four Marlborough wineries: Ross Lawson, John Stichbury, John Forrest of Forrest Estate, and John Belsham of Foxes Island Wines. At the end of the meeting, each winery contributed NZ$1,000 (US$705) to get the venture going. They also agreed that they wanted to roll out the first wines under a new closure, if possible, for the 2001 vintage, which meant they would be bottled in only about four months. It was an ambitious goal and a tight schedule, but with a little #8 wire they could achieve it.

The group of three Johns and a Ross shared a lot in common, although they had not previously been close personal friends. They were all predominantly Sauvignon Blanc producers, and corkiness often adversely affected that wine, just as it did Riesling. Along with the winemakers who drove the Clare Valley movement, the New Zealanders were all entrepreneurial owners who had the power to take action and were used to facing bet-the-company decisions. They didn't have to worry about corporate politics that would invariably delay matters. All four also ran small wineries at the premium end of the wine spectrum. Lawson produced some forty-five thousand cases annually, and Jackson Estate did sixty-five thousand. They all had at least one cork horror story. Stichbury, for example, had to write off two thousand cases of his 1999 Sauvignon Blanc because of failed corks. Perhaps it was because they had so much in common that in the months that followed, the steering committee members never took a vote. The four talked their way through issues until they reached a consensus without a show of hands.

Notably absent from the New Zealand closure group at the beginning were the country's biggest and best-known wineries. Montana, which then made half the country's wine, was nowhere to be seen. Cloudy Bay, New Zealand's most famous winery, which was owned by the French luxury conglomerate LVMH, gave the group moral and financial support from the beginning, but stayed out of the public eye. Villa Maria, another major player, showed interest but initially backed away because of strong opposition from its marketing department.

The twenty founding wineries were just as happy not to have the big companies, which made lots of inexpensive wines, join them out of fear that they would be tagged as cheap winemakers out to save money by putting a less expensive closure on inferior wines. The other overriding fear in the early days was that some loose-cannon winery would go off on its own and make a mess of the new closure execution, thus ruining it for the rest of them.

The steering committee began meeting every Monday morning. It was easy to get together because they were all based in Marlborough. None of the four were committed to anything at this point. They looked briefly at plastic corks, but quickly dismissed them because several had already had bad experiences with them.

The four realized this was going to be what New Zealanders call a big punt, or what Americans would call a big gamble. But they were going to watch developments closely and react quickly if necessary. Unlike American and most European wineries, New Zealanders bottle several times a year in response to market demand, so they could pull back quickly if things started going bad. Says John Forrest, "If it had been a disaster during the first year, I could have taken my losses, jumped in my hole, and gone back to cork, while I looked around for another solution to my cork problem."

One of the steering committee's first decisions was to recruit Michael Brajkovich, the winemaker of Kumeu River, to be the still unnamed group's chair. His family ran a winery outside Auckland that had been started in 1944 by his Croatian-born grandfather. Michael Brajkovich stands tall in New Zealand wine and not just because he is towering at six feet six inches and built like a rugby player. He graduated at the top of his enology class at Australia's Roseworthy Agricultural College and then worked in France for Établissements Jean-Pierre Moueix, which owns Château Pétrus and many other properties. He made wine at its Château Magdelaine in St.-Émilion. Inspired by top Burgundy producers he met in France, Brajkovich began concentrating on Chardonnay, and his Kumeu River Chardonnay quickly attained world-class status. Brajkovich was New Zealand's first Master of Wine, and with a scholarly, distinguished presence he gave the new group instant credibility both within New Zealand and around the world.

Brajkovich was interested in alternative closures because he had spent more than a decade banging his head against cork problems. His first experience had been with his 1989 vintage, when about 10 percent of the wines were corked. That spurred him to start searching for an alternative. He first looked at a cork from the German company Gültig Corks, which had a material barrier on the ends that was supposed to block taint. Initially it performed well, but after a year Brajkovich noticed the coating flaking off into the wine. Then he tried Cellucork plastic stoppers, but they leaked after a year and his wines oxidized. He then switched to Supreme Corq, which showed oxidation after only a few months and he thought gave a slight plastic taste to his wines. He also looked at Altec as well as natural corks that had been zapped with gamma or micro radiation, but nothing seemed to eliminate all problems.

In frustration, Brajkovich turned back to cork more out of desperation than conviction. But another disaster hit his 1998 vintage, when half of some shipments were corked. His American distributor told Brajkovich the wine could not be sold in the U.S. market, and a full container of Kumeu River Chardonnay was sent back across the Pacific to New Zealand.

With the 1999 vintage, Brajkovich was determined to control his corks by importing only the best quality and then inspecting them rigorously prior to bottling. He originally planned to accept only bales where samples had a 2 percent failure rate, but eventually had to raise the level to 4 percent because he was rejecting so many. Brajkovich in the end accepted only twenty-two batches of sixty-three tested. One bale had a failure rate of 30 percent. Despite those precautions, a quarter of the 1999 Maté's Vineyard, the winery's top Chardonnay, was corked.

Once in the early 1990s at a tasting of his red wines in Hong Kong, Brajkovich had to reject one-third of the bottles he had brought with him because of cork taint. "That's embarrassing and makes you angry," he told me in his slow, calm style that belied an underlying fury.

Shortly after the formation of the screwcap steering committee in March, the group hosted a seminar to educate winemakers about the issues that a technical committee had studied. The speakers included executives from companies that supplied screwcap products and equipment. One was Stephan Jelicich, the local salesperson for Stelvin. Up to that point, he had only sold a few screwcaps in New Zealand, to Villa Maria, which used them for the small wine bottles served on airlines.

Jelicich had been talking with Auckland's Kim Crawford Wines, which started as a virtual winery with no vineyards, no cellars, and no bottling plant. Nonetheless, it began winning wine competitions and slowly bought vineyards and built a winery. Founder and owner Kim Crawford was known above all for his creative marketing. Over the years, he tried a variety of bottle closures. Crawford switched from natural cork to Supreme Corq in 1999 because of taint problems, but saw that as only an interim solution because he was worried about oxidation. He liked screwcaps but was holding back because he thought the available bottles for them looked cheap.

At the Marlborough meeting Jelicich handed out a ten-page manual he had written about the technical details of screwcap bottling and stressed to the group that this was much more demanding than cork bottling. Following the meeting, Jelicich sent a young engineer on a quick trip to France and Switzerland to study screwcap bottling machinery and procedures. Although Auscap, the leading closure company in Australia and New Zealand, also spoke to the group and tried to interest the members in its shorter capsule, the New Zealand winemakers wanted the longer and more attractive Stelvin cap, the same one the Clare Valley Riesling producers used.

Andrew Sharp, the New Zealand representative of ACI Glass Packaging, the local subsidiary of the Australian company, also made a presentation. While his parent company hadn't given the Clare Valley winemakers any help when they came looking for bottles the year before, Sharp said he would work with the Kiwi group to get a screwcap bottle manufactured in New Zealand. That was a great relief to the winemakers because they were concerned about the high cost of the French bottles, which would have had to be airfreighted if they were going to arrive in time for bottling.

After the meeting with key suppliers, the technical issues seemed to be under control, and the New Zealanders made plans to press ahead with bottling under screwcap. While the task force was working on the technical issues, the steering committee was considering marketing questions. They were worried especially about what were called the gatekeepers who stood between them and the wine-consuming public. The winemakers concluded it was crucial to develop information material for distributors, the New Zealand wine press, and other key people that would clearly explain their reasons for making the move. In addition, they needed answers to objections skeptics would be making. Michael Brajkovich became the group's most visible spokesman and was repeatedly quoted saying that he was making the switch to screwcap not to save money but "because it will make my wines better." The full-scale media push, however, was put off until after bottling.

In May 2001, the New Zealand Screwcap Wine Seal Initiative was officially launched in Marlborough. Membership included thirty-two wineries from all the country's major production regions.

During the spring harvest and fermentation, winemakers freely

exchanged information about how they were adjusting their enology procedures to reflect that the wine was going to be in an airtight container. Surprisingly there were no secrets among companies that in a couple of
months would be competing fiercely with each other on wine-store shelves
and in regional wine tastings. The winemakers didn't solve all the problems
in the first year, but they started to get their hands around such topics as
the appropriate amount of sulfur dioxide, bottling levels, and using copper sulfate to protect wines from reduction, which had become an early
issue after it was highlighted in the first AWRI report on its Semillon study.
At one meeting in Stichbury's home, the four-man steering committee was
discussing reduction in a wine they had tasted when John Forrest, who had
a Ph.D. in molecular neuroscience, asked his host if he had a piece of copper. Stichbury, a former marine engineer, went out to his shop and came
back with a small piece of copper pipe. After Forrest put it in the wine, the
smell magically disappeared. Forrest then explained that they could solve
reductive problems by copper fining, the adding of small amounts of a copper sulfate solution to wine after fermentation but before bottling. This
would remove the hydrogen sulfide causing the problems. Once rarely used,
copper fining soon became standard practice.

The Marlborough winemakers were set to bottle in June and launch in
September, but the always competitive Kim Crawford beat them to market. In early May, and after months of delaying a decision, he told Stephan
Jelicich, the Stelvin representative, he wanted to bottle his 2001 Riesling
as soon as possible with screwcap. Jelicich replied that he couldn't get the
caps for about forty-five days, but Crawford agreed to pay to airfreight forty
thousand capsules from France. He also got bottles from Saverglass in
France. Bottling took place on May 15. Crawford and his wife, Erica, had
built a successful business by promoting sales of their wines by the glass to
upscale restaurants. Getting sommeliers behind them was crucial to that
strategy, and they used to hold parties for them at midnight after they finished work at their restaurants. Kim Crawford unveiled the first New
Zealand screwcap during such a midnight event at Auckland's Spy Bar.
Each sommelier was given a bottle of the Riesling that had attached to it
a condom and a note that said that the screwcap was there to protect the
wine from TCA and the condom was to protect the sommelier.

The Screwcap Initiative's first bottling took place at Lawson's Dry Hills
Winery in July. Assembled to watch the event was a host of other New
Zealand winemakers as well as representatives of Stelvin and ACI Glass
Packaging. Lawson and Stichbury were again standing next to each other

as the bottling began, when Lawson in disappointment said, "I've made a terrible mistake. I don't have enough glass bottles to bottle my Pinot."

Stichbury responded, "Well, I was thinking of perhaps doing some of my Pinot in Stelvin. If you bottle your Pinot, I'll do mine as well." The two wineries then ordered additional bottles from ACI and did both part of their Sauvignon Blanc and some Pinot Noir under screwcaps.

None of the members of the Screwcap Initiative were throwing caution to the wind and bottling all of their wines in screwcaps; in 2001 they all did a mix of screwcaps and cork. Lawson the next year became the first winery to go 100 percent screwcap.

On August 16, 2001, two weeks before the wines would be released into the local market, the New Zealand Screwcap Wine Seal Initiative put on a media event in the boardroom of the Selaks winery in Blenheim. Assembled were all of New Zealand's leading wine writers as well as representatives of the now twenty-five wineries in the group. Jeffrey Grosset was also there to show support for the New Zealanders and to talk about the experience in the Clare Valley. The highlight of the event, however, was tasting a number of old wines in screwcap bottles that Initiative members had found by searching high and low in Australia and New Zealand. Grosset helped them out by bringing two cases of old screwcap bottles with him. The star of the event was a magnum of 1982 Nobilo Müller-Thurgau under screwcap. It had never been a great wine, but the seal had held, and it was still delightfully fresh.

At the press conference, several Initiative wineries set up displays of their wines under both screwcaps and corks and invited journalists to see for themselves which they liked better. Michael Brajkovich gave a solid endorsement to the new closure, and Bob Campbell also added his voice to the chorus of supporters. Instead of normally combative journalists posing gotcha questions and trying to find fault with the presentations, the press conference turned into a celebration of antipodean innovation. One journalist questioned the aesthetics of a capsule with screw threads showing, and another asked about reduction, but they were the sole dissenters and were overwhelmed by the supporters.

The following weekend the headline on the top editorial in the *New Zealand Herald,* one of the country's leading national papers, read, "Don't Screw Around with Our Wine." With an almost uncontrollable enthusiasm, the writer piled one cork problem on top of another from its being hard to get out of a bottle to its crumbling, while gushingly praising the benefits of screwcaps. The editorial concluded, though, with a warning: "In their quest for improvement, winemakers are at risk of sacrificing some of the magic of their product. They may find that the genie, like the cork, will not go back in the bottle."

The initial focus of the Screwcap Initiative wineries was the domestic market, where they all sold at least half of their production. The target for year two was Britain, the destination for 80 percent of the country's wine exports. John Stichbury also argued that London was the center of the international wine media. British writers already followed New Zealand wines and also influenced their counterparts in the United States. Since the winemakers were after the market and the media, the place to reach both was the annual London International Wine & Spirits Fair in May.

A dozen wineries from the Screwcap Initiative agreed to go together to get a joint booth at the 2002 show, and Bob Campbell came along to help promote the new closure. Just as at the August 2001 press launch, the wineries set out bottles of Sauvignon Blanc under screwcaps and corks and invited visitors to compare the wines themselves. Winemakers were happily pouring their own wines as well as those of their competitors. That day, selling the screwcap concept was more important than the name on the label.

The secret weapons to drive traffic to the booth were five women, including John Stichbury's wife, Jo; Rosemary Marris, the wife of Brent Marris, the owner of Wither Hills Vineyards; and a Frenchwoman who worked for Stelvin. They met crowds coming to the show who got off the London subway at the Docklands stop and gave them invitations to come to Stand F25, where they could "sample a comparative tasting of fine New Zealand wines." The elegant and attractive ladies got lots of attention thanks to their white T-shirts, which on the front carried the slogan "We've Screwed 'Em" and on the back read "New Zealand's Guaranteed Click of Quality." The women, the T-shirts, and the comparative tastings were all huge hits, and Stand F25 became one of the most popular spots at the show.

John Forrest's British distributor had been worried about the acceptance of the new closure and wanted only 15 percent of his allotment in screwcaps. But after the London wine show, those quickly sold out, and he tried to change his order to get less cork and more screwcap, but the wine had already been bottled. With strong support also from British supermarkets, the country's prime method of mass wine distribution, New Zealand screwcaps were an immediate market hit.

The takeoff of screwcap sales turned out to be faster and stronger than even the most passionate supporters ever anticipated. In 2001, Stelvin's Jelicich sold 2 million screwcaps in New Zealand; in 2002, 11 million; and in 2003, 25 million. The first year 1.6 percent of New Zealand wines were in screwcap, but in the third year the number had jumped to 34.5 percent. Stelvin officials in France had never believed they would have that kind of success and couldn't keep up with demand. Stelvin soon had a six-month delay on deliveries, and other closure producers began anxiously eyeing the Kiwi market.

It was clearly time to celebrate the success of the New Zealand Screwcap Wine Seal Initiative, and that took place in November 2004 at the International Screwcap Symposium in Marlborough. Speakers at the two-day event came from Britain, France, and the United States as well as from Australia and New Zealand. All of them were prepared to pledge their loyalty to the new closure.

The night before the event, speakers gathered at John Stichbury's house on Jackson Road for dinner and to preview what they were going to say the next day. An extra table had to be brought into the dining room in the hundred-year-old house to handle the overflow crowd. The New Zealand hosts pulled out all stops for the foreign guests, and the menu included such Kiwi specials as whitebait, salmon soaked in vodka, and lamb shanks marinated in Pinot Noir. John Belsham was in charge of getting the wines. He collected more old ones under screwcap, this time from the Auckland storage rooms of Air New Zealand, which had served them on flights in the 1970s and 1980s. He also provided new vintages made by the founders of the Screwcap Initiative.

After host John Stichbury heard Michel Laroche of France's Domaine Laroche tell Michael Brajkovich that he was going to announce in his speech the next day that he was 100 percent behind screwcaps and was moving his wines that way, Stichbury went into the kitchen to see if he could be of any help. Several of the wives were dishing up plates on a rich, dark red-brown table made of matai, a New Zealand hardwood. It had recently been rescued from a sheep-sheering shed. Ross Lawson and a few other men were off to the side, talking about the next day's program.

Stichbury walked over to Lawson and said, "Well, it was a bloody big punt, but I think we're there. If we get the kind of enthusiasm at the meeting tomorrow that is out there in that room tonight, I think we will have achieved what we set out to do three years ago."

Lawson nonchalantly replied, "It was a big one, but I'm pretty relaxed about it."

"We're there, Ross," concurred Stichbury. "We've won the battle, but not the war."

MESSAGE IN A BOTTLE:

RINGOES, NEW JERSEY

Philip Ward got into the wine business in 1982 after spending ten years as a chef. He has worked since then for a variety of distributors in the Middle Atlantic states and currently is the Eastern U.S. sales director for Bernard Magrez, a major Bordeaux producer. Along the way, Ward has picked up some of the world's greatest wines, which he's carefully transported as he's moved from location to location in Pennsylvania, Virginia, and New Jersey.

Like many other serious wine drinkers who can remember exactly when and where they purchased specific wines, Ward recalls buying a 1970 Château Lafite Rothschild in 1974 at Welsh's Wines in Lambertville, New Jersey. At the time, he was living in Philadelphia, which has state liquor stores that did not then carry prestigious products. The wine cost only about $15, but it was still a lot for him at the time. Ward, though, knew it was worth the price. After all, some wine experts consider Lafite Bordeaux's best.

The bottle moved with loving care from Philadelphia to Virginia and then to Chatham, New Jersey, and Sergeantsville, New Jersey, and finally to a farmhouse in the horse country of Ringoes, New Jersey.

Ward was sure that an event would someday come along that would merit opening the 1970 Lafite. In the winter of 2003, that special moment finally arrived. Halsey Blake-Scott, an old friend and former colleague in the wine trade in Virginia, was coming with his wife to visit Ward and his wife in Ringoes. Blake-Scott really knew his wine and would appreciate the magic of that bottle. "I had thirty years of investment in that wine, but Halsey was worth it," recalls Ward.

The day before his guests were to arrive, Ward went down to his cellar, brought up the bottle of Lafite, and placed it on a table in the dining room so any sediment in the bottle could gently fall to the bottom before dinner the next night. The following day he got out a crystal decanter and candle. Just as sommeliers at the most expensive restaurants do with very old wines, Ward poured the wine into the decanter, holding the candle in back of the bottleneck to make sure that no sediment slipped out. When he was finished, Ward put his nose into the decanter to savor the experience of a wonderful, aged Bordeaux First Growth. "It was corked beyond belief," says Ward. "It was a very sad experience."

A special friend was still coming to dinner, so Ward went back to his cellar and brought back a 1989 Château Faugères from St.-Émilion. It was a fine wine from a good year and well aged, but not a 1970 Lafite.

The following day Ward thought back on the experience. The worst thing was, he had no recourse. "I couldn't go back to Dick Welsh, who had sold it to me thirty years before." But then and "just for fun," Ward sent an e-mail to Château Lafite explaining that he had opened a bottle of its 1970 wine for "some very dear friends" and found it was corked. He didn't ask for his money back or make any recriminations. A week later, he received a response from a woman at the winery, stating politely that what he had really tasted was the richness of a very old wine, not a corked one.

Ward sent back an equally polite response saying that he had been in the wine business for twenty years and knew the difference between an old wine and a corked one. He never received a response to his second e-mail.

CHAPTER FIFTEEN

Funeral for the Cork

"This heartfelt wake for the old stinker."

After a four-hundred-year history of colorful chaos and quixotic characters, New York City is a hard place to either shock or impress. Yet it had never seen anything quite like the Funeral for the Cork held there on October 2, 2002. Shortly after noon, a gray 1937 Buick hearse pulled up to the Vanderbilt Avenue entrance of the majestic Grand Central Terminal in midtown Manhattan. Out of the vehicle stepped four pallbearers, three wearing black suits and one sporting a dark purple tuxedo and a light purple, ruffled shirt. After the steel-gray casket was removed from the hearse, a trumpeter playing taps led the pallbearers and the casket through the railroad terminal and up to the Campbell Apartment on the southwest corner of the station's balcony. The apartment had been the office of the 1920s tycoon John W. Campbell, the chairman of Commerce Clearing House, a credit-reference firm to the city's important garment industry. Campbell decorated his fifty-eight-feet-long and twenty-five-feet-wide office in a grand European style with a painted beamed ceiling, a massive stone fireplace, and elaborate tapestries. By 2002, it had been turned into a bar, although most of the furnishings and the grandeur remained.

The pallbearers solemnly placed the casket in front of the fireplace and then opened it. Inside was a figure made of corks that had been crafted by the California sculptor Wes Modes. This was the corpse of Thierry Bouchon. For those who enjoyed—or understood—the pun, the corpse's name is a play on the French word for corkscrew.

Before dinner, Randall Grahm, the chief pallbearer in the purple tuxedo and founder of California's Bonny Doon Vineyard, stood in front of the casket and first thanked his "fellow mourners" for coming to "this heartfelt wake for the old stinker." Then he invited British wine writer Jancis Robinson to give the eulogy. Dressed in black with only a modest gold brooch for decoration, Robinson began in mock solemnity, "Oh, Cork. Oh, Cork. Oh, Corky, Corky, Cork." She went on to pay tribute to cork's many excellent qualities as a way to seal a bottle, adding, "You've had a jolly good run, Monsieur Bouchon." But then she denounced his "barky majesty," saying, "The great big supertanker SS *Screwcap* has set sail, and there will be no turning back."

After the eulogies, the guests sat down to dinner, which proved once again that nothing succeeds like excess. The candlelit evening included an eleven-course dinner accompanied by no less than thirty-four Bonny Doon wines. All through the evening Grahm hovered over diners pouring more and more of his wines.

Inspiration for the dinner came from an obscure, spade-bearded French intellectual named J. K. Huysmans, whose most famous work, *À rebours* (Against the Grain), is a tale of a decadent and ailing aristocrat in Paris who celebrated the temporary loss of his virility with an all-in-black party. Everything for his affair was black, from the food to the naked female servants who presented the food and drink. Mourner-in-chief Grahm copied Huysmans in as many details as possible, although—respectfully—there were no naked black servants. Main courses included a Black Squid Ink Risotto and Black Mole-Roasted Venison. For dessert there were diverse dark trifles and black nectarines as well as a chocolate tortoise with faux jewels in tribute to the "jeweled tortoise" at the Huysmans dinner.

For those unable to join the New York City fun, the *Wine Spectator* in its next issue carried a tombstone advertisement duly noting that M. Thierry Bouchon (1585–2002), "known to his close friends as Corky," had died after a long illness with "toxin 2,4,6-trichloroanisole implicated in his demise."

The New York City Funeral for the Cork and the obituary did not surprise the California wine community. Nothing that Randall Grahm could ever do—perhaps not even if he had used naked black servants—would shock them. In a business that had lost its sense of humor somewhere in the early 1980s, the Bonny Doon founder was California wine's resident iconoclast.

Born in Los Angeles and raised in Beverly Hills, Grahm was an unfocused professional student when he discovered wine. After graduating from high school in 1970, he traveled north to the University of California campus at Santa Cruz, aka Uncle Charlie's Summer Camp. It was the right place for his free spirit. There were no letter grades, only pass or fail, and the nearby beach was considered more important than any classroom. The students, Grahm says today, were "very smart, highly sensitive, socially retarded, and lazier than shit." After two years as a premed student, Grahm switched his major to philosophy. His senior thesis was going to be on *Dasein*, the phenomenological analysis of human existence that Martin Heidegger, the controversial early-twentieth-century philosopher, outlined in his book *Being and Time*.

While working on his thesis, Grahm got a job sweeping floors at the Wine Merchant, a retail store near his parents' home in Beverly Hills. There he had the opportunity to taste daily some of the world's great wines. Soon the thesis on *Dasein* was history. He applied to enter the wine program at the University of California, Davis, but was first turned down. He was finally accepted on the condition that he retake all the science courses that he had first had as a premed. Once in the Davis program, Graham was older than most of the students and something of a troublemaker, challenging professors in a way younger students dared not. Before graduating in 1979, he tasted a magnum of 1949 Musigny Comte de Vogüé and became a Pinot Noir fanatic. "It was about as great a wine experience as one can have in this lifetime," he recalls.

Grahm first went to Oregon to investigate Pinot there and met David Lett, who had pioneered cold-climate wine in that state. Then he traveled to the Santa Cruz Mountains after hearing that Ken Burnap at Santa Cruz Mountain Vineyard had made some outstanding Pinot. With financial help from his parents, Grahm planted a twenty-eight-acre vineyard in Bonny Doon, a hamlet north of Santa Cruz, after studying temperature data collected in the 1930s that indicated it would be a great place to grow his favorite grape. The experiment, though, failed. Later he discovered the information he was using to make the decision was wrong. Temperatures had been registered at a research station located below a temperature inversion layer, while his property was above it. In addition, the soil was sandy loam, while Pinot does best in limestone. Finally, he probably irrigated the vines too much instead of forcing the roots to go deeper to find water. Fortunately, though, more studies led Grahm to conclude that the area might be good for warmer-weather Rhône Valley–style grapes.

Kermit Lynch, a California wine importer and Rhône champion, had introduced Grahm to those wines. He first looked into planting Syrah, the grape that forms the backbone for Rhône's great Hermitage wines. At the time, though, there were only two Syrah vineyards in all of California, one in the Napa Valley and one in Paso Robles southeast of San Francisco. Then he investigated Grenache, the world's second most widely planted variety, which grows abundantly in southern France and Spain. In California there was lots of it in the San Joaquin Valley, but little in the cooler, coastal areas where Grahm's vineyard was located. While reading *The Wines of the Rhône* by John Livingstone-Learmonth, Grahm learned about the magic and mystery of Châteauneuf-du-Pape, a wine made of up to thirteen different grapes, but primarily Grenache and Mourvèdre, a vine known in California as Mataro.

In 1984, Grahm made the first vintage of Le Cigare Volant, a wine that he proudly calls "a tribute to a European wine without being a poor imitation." From the Livingstone-Learmonth book he also learned that the village fathers of Châteauneuf-du-Pape had in 1954 outlawed the landing in local vineyards of flying saucers, which were also called flying cigars. So Grahm called his new wine The Flying Cigar or Le Cigare Volant. The wine's label showed a spacecraft hovering menacingly over a vineyard, seemingly about to land. When the wine was released in 1986, the wacky name and the unusual grapes were enough to get a small story in the *Wine Spectator*. Bonny Doon Vineyard was then selling only thirty thousand cases a year, but business soon took off. Robert Parker's *Wine Advocate* also gave Le Cigare Volant scores in the 90s.

Three years later, Grahm was on the cover of the *Wine Spectator* with the headline "The Rhône Ranger." When the magazine editors told him they wanted to take his picture sitting on a horse just so no one missed the connection to television's Lone Ranger, he replied that he had a neighbor who had the appropriate white horse. The only problem was that the animal had a small patch of black hair on its head unlike the Lone Ranger's horse, Silver, which was pure white. A touch-up with white shoe polish, however, took care of that.

Although his Davis degree was in plant science, Grahm's talents are more as a vintner than a viticulturist. And when it comes to winemaking, he's a relentless experimenter. Each year he produces a dozen unusual wines that he sells to the winery's club, which is called DEWN (Distinctive Esoteric Wine Network). The Bonny Doon Web site calls the wines "adventurous and highly sought after acts of the viticultural high wire." Grahm is an advocate of controversial micro-oxygenation, a technique developed in France in the 1990s that adds small amounts of oxygen to wine in tanks to soften harsh tannins. He opposes high-alcohol wines and scrupulously works to stop fruit from getting "grotesquely overripe." Perhaps Grahm's most unusual experiment was in 2000, when he put rocks in barrels of wines to see how that would influence the flavor. After all, winemakers have for centuries been praising the mineral flavors in some wines. He put different rocks in five barrels, then threw a few pebbles into test bottles before he sealed them. Some experiments, he says, turned out "quite obnoxious" but others were "interesting." He never introduced the practice in his regular wines, and none of the bottles were ever released for sale.

While much of the international wine establishment makes local versions of such noble grapes as Cabernet Sauvignon, Chardonnay, Merlot, and Pinot Noir, Grahm is the champion of what he calls the "ugly-duckling grape varietals." That includes not only Rhône grapes but also Italian ones. "The world is a better place for all the oddball grapes that grow in Italy," he says. In 1990, he bought a vineyard in the nearby prison town of Soledad and began making Italian-style wines that are sold under the Ca' del Solo Big House label, a play on the term for solitary confinement in the prison.

Bonny Doon's top two wines, Le Cigare Volant and Old Telegram, a takeoff on the Rhône's famous Vieux Télégraphe, sell for only about $30, far less than most California producers charge. Ever the maverick, Grahm says that many California wines are overpriced and consumers can often find better values with European ones. Such outrageous, although accurate, opinions have only solidified Grahm's reputation as the Peck's Bad Boy of California wine.

Grahm also fostered a unique brand of marketing. He claims that this style is due to his inherent shyness, although not many people would describe him that way. The winery's labels are known for their over-the-top designs that mix up type fonts with stream-of-consciousness writing and unusual illustrations. The Bonny Doon Web site is also an eclectic mix of fun and games.

Grahm's impishness is best on display in the company's newsletter. From spring 2005 through spring 2006 he wrote a three-part series entitled *Da Vino Commedia* patterned after Dante's *Divina Commedia*. Grahm has never met a pun he didn't like, and his satire is chockablock with jokes in English, French, German, Italian, Latin, and Yiddish. He skewers everyone in the wine business with equal disdain. In a move guaranteed to lose him any remaining support from 100-point wine reviewers such as Robert Parker and *Wine Spectator*, he attacked their "quasi-mystical numerology," writing, "Wine criticism has taken on the emotional tonality of a football game. Our wines, winemakers and wine critics are becoming even more competitive, bigger, brawnier, tougher and macho." Grahm has so far done only the first part of Dante's great work, the *Inferno*—or as he calls it the *Vinferno*. He has no plans, for now, to parody the *Purgatorio* or the *Paradiso*.

For many years before the Funeral for the Cork, Grahm struggled with different closures. When his winery was first opened, he used corks along with everyone else. He had just enough personal experiences with tainted corks, however, to be uneasy about them. In the early 1990s, he tried the Sabaté Altec in hopes that it would remove the danger of contamination on his line of Rieslings, but found it gave wines an off taste that he thought came from the glue that held the agglomerated cork together.

After that unhappy episode, Grahm used Supreme Corq from 1995 to 1998. The first two years, only part of Bonny Doon's production had them, but in 1997 and 1998 the entire bottling, including Cigare Volant, was under plastic. That experience was "a big mistake," he now says. "The wines didn't last." Grahm is still not sure exactly what happened. He doesn't think the seal failed and suspects that something in the plastic cork's material leached into the wine in trace amounts and caused oxidation. "That's my theory, but it is not based on science," he says.

After plastic, Grahm reluctantly went back to natural corks, but immediately began searching for a better closure. Almost by default, Stelvin screwcaps looked like the most attractive alternative. That the technology had been around for a long time and was well understood also attracted him. By 1999, Grahm had concluded that Stelvin screwcaps were the answer to his long-nagging problem of what to put in the neck of wine bottles.

Some issues, though, were holding him back. One was cost. The new bottling equipment needed for the screwcaps was going to run $80,000, not an insignificant sum for a modest winery. But Grahm was willing to make the investment.

In addition, there was the perennial question of whether the American market was ready for screwcaps. During endless hours of meetings, the Bonny Doon staff struggled with how to introduce wines with this new closure. Grahm's staff unanimously favored testing Stelvins in a small, but significant, market such as a single state. "We don't want the company to crash and burn over this, so let's test it in a state or one market or two," said David Amadia, the company's sales manager.

"Don't you think the big companies have already done studies that show customers don't want this?" replied Grahm. "Otherwise they would have adopted them. But I think we can change history. It won't help just to prove that we can sell screwcaps in Kansas." Grahm argued they needed to do it nationally and make a big bang. The company, however, should only do it with one wine—and not repeat the mistake of Supreme Corq, when it did its whole line. "We need to do this on a big enough scale that we'll get national attention . . . that will get us national buzz."

After several more meetings, the Bonny Doon staff reluctantly came over to Grahm's side. After all, it was his business, and if he wanted to bet the company on screwcaps, it was his decision. The group finally decided to bottle the company's Big House line of wines with Stelvin screwcaps. That would mean seventy thousand cases of Big House Red and ten thousand of Big House White. The wines sold for about $10 a bottle and made up some 35 percent of the company's total production. Grahm ended the meeting when the decision was taken by telling the group, "But we can't fail at this. We're putting all our chips on red. This can't fail."

On May 15, 2002, Bonny Doon announced it would be bottling its Big House line in screwcaps. It would be the largest commitment an American winery had ever made to the new technology.

As Bonny Doon's top executives were struggling with how to make sure the screwcap launch wouldn't fail, Grahm remembered that "funny, strange book" by J. K. Huysmans and the all-in-black party. Maybe that was just the high-profile event they needed to capture the public's attention.

CHAPTER SIXTEEN

Back to the Future with a Glass Solution

The glass stopper

Karl Matheis is a German medical doctor specializing in homeopathy; he's also a veteran tinkerer. After first starting his university studies in economics, he switched to medicine after meeting his wife, who was then studying that subject. Armed with a medical degree, Matheis worked in eighteen factories looking into the illnesses caused by the modern industrial society. Out of that came his invention of a worker's safety shoe, which made him financially independent. He and his wife still practice medicine together.

One morning in the fall of 2001, Matheis visited Hans Marx, the owner and winemaker at Weingut Marx, a neighbor just down the street on Hauptstrasse in Azey/Weinheim, a wine village near the historic town of Worms, where Martin Luther was tried for heresy and declared an outlaw. The vintner got to complaining about problems he was having with corks, which had ruined a good part of the previous year's Riesling and Sylvaner production. Marx said he was going to switch to a plastic cork. He wasn't totally happy with it, however, because a fellow winemaker from the

Franken region, who had been using plastic corks for three years, told him they caused oxidation. Marx lamented he just had to get away from cork.

A few days later, Dr. Matheis was in his home office when he noticed a bottle he used frequently in his practice. It was a variation on an airtight glass ampoule and was used for blood transfusions and other medical situations that demanded perfectly sanitary conditions. The glass bottle had a glass stopper and was topped with an aluminum cap. The doctor then remembered the conversation with Hans Marx and filed both ideas in the back of his mind.

Less than a month later, on December 5, Matheis was celebrating his father's eightieth birthday party with several local winemakers also in attendance. Just on a whim, the doctor asked the winemakers why they didn't use a glass stopper like the one on his transfusion bottles to seal their wine bottles.

"They looked at me like I was silly," Matheis recalls. "They said it wasn't possible."

Undeterred by that response, the doctor asked, "But if you could do it, would it be a good way to seal the bottle?"

"Oh, yes. It would be the best way," Matheis remembers them saying. "It would solve our problems with cork taint and with the oxidation of our wines."

That was enough for the tinkering doctor to begin looking into the possibility of inventing a glass stopper as a way to close wine bottles. Only twelve days after that first discussion at his father's birthday party, Matheis contacted the German Patent Office in Munich to start protecting his rights as the inventor of the glass stopper.

The idea of a glass closure for wine bottles was actually nothing new. Glass stopples, as they were then called, were used for years in England. In his 1676 *Treatise of Cider,* John Worlidge warned that defective corks could ruin drinks and "therefore are glass stopples to be preferred." According to Hugh Johnson's *Story of Wine,* "As late as 1825, the ultimate luxury bottle stopper was still, at least in some eyes, a ground-glass one." Johnson wrote that between 1820 and 1825, bottles of France's Château Lafite had glass stopples. The stopple was ground with emery powder specifically to fit a designated bottle and tied down with a string to a button on the neck. The only trouble was that the glass stopples were almost impossible to get out of the bottle without breaking it, so their use was discontinued. I asked Charles Chevallier, the winemaker at the winery now called Château Lafite Rothschild, if any of those bottles still existed. Although he has six bottles of Lafite with corks dating from 1797, he has none with glass stopples or even any records of them. It is assumed that the Lafite wine had been shipped to England in barrels and bottled there, which was common.

After some tinkering at his home office, Matheis took his primitive efforts at a glass stopper to a few of Germany's large glass companies in hopes of getting some prototypes made. None of them were interested, but finally a small, family-owned factory near Nuremberg made the test stoppers for him.

Matheis decided early on that to be successful he needed to partner with a big company that had the financial resources, marketing clout, and experience with closures to turn his prototype into a mass-market product. Although it did not make anything out of glass, Alcoa seemed like the right company. It was already the world's largest producer of screwcaps, making some 70 billion annually. Most of those went onto bottles of water and carbonated soft drinks, but the company also made screwcaps for wine bottles. It helped that Alcoa's German subsidiary was located in nearby Worms.

So in February 2002, the doctor, who by then had twenty patents on the glass stopper, knocked on the door of the Alcoa technical department, where he was quickly told this wasn't in the company's line of business. Not someone easily discouraged, Matheis got similar runarounds at three other departments of the company until he finally obtained a meeting with Siegfried Landskrone, the head of Alcoa's German subsidiary, who was always looking for new products and was intrigued with this one. Without asking for permission from company headquarters in Pittsburgh, Landskrone started what is known in business as a skunk-works project. Often used in high-technology fields where a premium is placed on innovation and cutting through corporate bureaucracies, these are small ventures involving only a few employees that operate outside the normal company structure. The Apple Macintosh computer, for example, was born in a skunk works. In March, Alcoa assigned three engineers to work on the glass-stopper project.

According to Matheis, six months later in the fall of 2002, Landskrone told him Alcoa had by then spent €250,000 (US$330,000) on his product, and it was time to tell headquarters and draw up a contract between Matheis and the company. The doctor was more than happy to sign an agreement that gave Alcoa rights to market the product, but still afforded him a financial stake in its success.

At the March 2003 ProWein show, the major international German wine event, Alcoa and Matheis presented the research project they were now calling Vino-Lok. By then, the engineers had done fifty prototypes. Alcoa had developed the glass stopper based on Matheis's concept and then identified an outside company to manufacture the product to strict specifications. The glass, for example, had to be so strong that it could be dropped several stories to a concrete floor without breaking. The stopper also had an Alcoa aluminum capsule on top that helped keep it securely in the bottle.

After Alcoa announced it was ready to test the new product, wineries started lining up to participate. Rather than experimenting with just one of them, the company decided to go with fifty in Germany, Austria, France, and Italy. The plan for the supersecret project was to send a bottling unit housed in a small truck to each winery, where it would spend two days sealing several hundred bottles. At the first stop, Weingut Becker in Rheinhessen, the truck was met with two television crews and dozens of other winemakers curious to see the new product. So much for secrecy.

Not surprisingly, there were bumps along the development road. After all, that's what tests are for. At the wine research institute at Geisenheim, students studied the tightness of the seal. One former student still remembers the sound the glass closures made as they popped off, much like corks exploding out of Champagne bottles. That was particularly a problem when the bottles warmed up.

Schloss Vollrads, a major Riesling producer in the Rheingau area, had not been part of the original fifty wineries, but it soon became the center of Alcoa's development project. The winery can document its winemaking back to 1211, when it sold four barrels of wine to a church in Mainz. It produced its first bottles with corks in 1820, and in 1920 discontinued the sale of wine in barrels and offered only bottles with corks. The winery started moving away from cork in 1993, however, by introducing Alcoa's short screwcaps for liter bottles. Winemaker Rolf Herke was anxious to get a better closure for the nearly seventy-five thousand cases of high-quality Rieslings he produced annually. He had looked at a few alternatives, such as plastic corks, crown caps, and Stelvins, but concluded that they were only good for "barbecue wines, not for wines to put on the table."

Although Schloss Vollrads was not included in the initial Alcoa test, Herke knew the winemaker at Weingut Becker and got a few glass stoppers from him. Those went onto a 2003 Riesling that won a prize at a 2004 London wine show. Alcoa officials couldn't at first understand how the Schloss Vollrads wine had a glass stopper until they noticed it had the Becker coding.

Schloss Vollrads was soon working closely with Alcoa on the development and testing of improved Vino-Lok models. The mission-critical part of the glass stopper is the O-ring that slips onto it just under the top to create the seal. While Vino-Lok proponents call it a glass-on-glass closure, the point of contact between the bottle and the closure is actually the O-ring, which is made of plastic material approved by American and European regulators. The side of the ring fits snugly against the inside neck of the bottle, and the bottom touches the wine when the bottle is lying down. Alcoa's consumer-product group, which has extensive experience with food products with its aluminum foil Reynolds Wrap, also lent its expertise to developing the O-ring. After some forceful prodding from Herke, Alcoa developed a new and superior ring. This one was made with a Du Pont product called Elvax, which is an ethylene vinyl acetate. After it was announced, the trade publication *New Materials International* was almost breathless about it, writing, "The highly-elastic, durable, halogen-free and plasticizer-free polymer is insoluble in alcohol and resistant to weak acids and other wine constituents. Furthermore, Elvax is absolutely without aftertaste."

Independently, the Schloss Vollrads staff put Vino-Lok bottles through the toughest tests winemakers could imagine. They sent bottles to friends in the United States, Denmark, and Sweden without any explanation just to see how people would react or whether without instructions they could figure out how to open the containers. Everyone got the bottles open, and some sent back messages saying they liked the wine. Company masochists packed a dozen bottles into an already beaten-up case and sent it to Chicago with instructions to send it back in the same container. The bottles survived this torture by transportation. The winery also put bottles into a heater and raised the temperature to 80°C (176°F).

The technical requirements for bottles used with Vino-Lok are both different and more detailed than those for a cork or a screwcap. The bottleneck's first five millimeters (.2 inch) have to be perfectly straight down. If the neck is at all concave, the stopper will pop out of the bottle; if it is even a little bit convex, it is very difficult to extract the stopper. With those kinds of specifications in hand, Schloss Vollrads ordered 1 million specially designed tall, green bottles to be used with the Vino-Loks.

Then, to have a consumer face-off between the old closure and the new one, the winery in January 2005 bottled half a tank of Riesling with corks and half with Vino-Loks. The two products went on sale at exactly the same price in its winery shop and through its direct mail. In February, the first month on the market, the split in sales was 80 percent Vino-Lok to 20 percent cork; in March it was 90–10; in May it was 95–5. Consumers had clearly spoken.

In December 2004, after a $5 million investment and major input from Schloss Vollrads and other wineries, Alcoa began full-scale, automated production of Vino-Lok at the Alcoa plant in Worms. In a daring strategic move, Alcoa decided to focus on the high-end closure market, setting the price of its product at about fifty cents per stopper, roughly the same as that of a premium cork. It was not going to repeat the Stelvin mistake of going down-market and getting stuck with a cheap image. As Alcoa officials told winemakers, they were producing the Porsche 911 Turbo of wine closures, so it was naturally a little more expensive. For wineries asking for a less costly alternative, the company also had an acrylic version that sells for about half the price. Sales of those, though, have been slow.

In 2005, the first full year of production, Alcoa sold 10 million Vino-Loks. In 2006, sales doubled, with 20 million going to 450 largely European wineries. Working from its Worms offices, the company's sales group concentrated at first on the nearby German and Austrian markets, but they were soon selling the new product to wineries in Italy and as far away as Australia. Manincor was the initial Italian client, while Henschke was the first in Australia.

One of Alcoa's most visible and biggest customers was Lufthansa, the German national airline, which immediately adopted them. In an in-flight video promotion, Thierry Antinori, a member of the Lufthansa board of directors, explained that the airline switched to Vino-Lok because of the declining quality of cork. The new closure, he said, was part of Lufthansa's "search for perfect service."

After nearly two centuries of using corks, Schloss Vollrads in 2006 entered a postcork era, bottling 90 percent of its production in Vino-Loks and 10 percent in screwcaps. Its most expensive wine, Riesling Trockenbeerenauslese, comes in a a half bottle with a Vino-Lok and sells for €174 ($230). When Rowald Hepp, the winery's CEO, was asked why he was breaking with tradition, he replied simply, "Our tradition is good wine."

In California's Napa Valley, Tom Leonardini, owner of Whitehall Lane Winery, also had his frustrations with cork. A successful businessman in San Francisco, Leonardini had an extensive private wine collection and had experienced plenty of corked wines before buying the winery in 1993.

Leonardini encouraged General Manager Mike McLoughlin to look at alternatives. One big issue was how Whitehall Lane's Cabernet Sauvignon would do under a noncork closure. Starting in 1995, McLoughlin and winemaker Dean Sylvester studied synthetic closures as well as technical corks. They were quickly turned off by plastic, thinking the seal was not tight enough and also, as McLoughlin says, "You can get a hernia trying to get them out of the bottle with a corkscrew."

After Leonardini suggested they also consider screwcaps, the winery in 2001 put some of its half bottles of Cabernet in screwcaps. The smaller-sized bottles, which are usually drunk young and often consumed in informal settings such as picnics, seemed well suited to a screwcap. The following year the winery did full bottles of Sauvignon Blanc in screwcaps, partly because New Zealand had already paved the way for using that closure with that wine. It also put its less expensive Bommarito Cabernet under screwcap. McLoughlin, however, still wasn't ready to put full bottles of his top-of-the-line Cabernet Sauvignons in a screwcap bottle.

Based on its encouraging trials in Germany, Alcoa officials in the United States were by 2003 looking to work with a prestigious California winery. They found it at Whitehall Lane. Early that year, when a salesman showed McLoughlin the glass stopper, he saw it as an "elegant alternative to cork" that Leonardini would also like. McLoughlin later showed the closure to customers in the winery's tasting room, where it got rave reviews.

Alcoa officials in Indianapolis and the staff at Whitehall Lane began developing what was soon dubbed the Gen Two, or Generation Two, Vino-Lok. One thing that had to change was the product name because California's Sutter Home Winery had earlier used a Stelvin screwcap that it called Vinloc. So for the U.S. market, the Vino-Lok became Vino-Seal.

From experience with other products, Alcoa officials knew American companies don't usually like to just pick up something made for a foreign market. And sure enough, after examining the German Vino-Lok bottles, Leonardini, McLoughlin, and Sylvester decided they wanted a slightly different look for their bottle. Their main objection with the German version was what they considered to be the clumsy aluminum overcap. The German one also had a small notch in the neck that let the consumer break open the overcap. The Americans wanted a traditional capsule, like one they might see on a bottle with a cork, to hold the glass stopper in place. That required a new bottle, and Alcoa and Whitehall Lane began actively working on that in early 2004.

Alcoa executives were in no rush to market. They had heard about problems Cellucork and other plastic-cork companies had encountered when they launched products that were not totally developed and tested. Alcoa wanted to get it right the first time. Endless testing was at times frustrating for Whitehall Lane. Says McLoughlin, "They are engineers and wanted to test every test—twice." A top Alcoa executive on the project admits that his group "tests the bejesus" out of new products but says that's the company culture.

In addition to removing the notch from the bottleneck, the neck was made slightly shorter to reduce the amount of airspace between the stopper and the wine. Encore Glass, an American company, made the bottle, which is virtually identical with a traditional Bordeaux one, in Mexico.

After two years of testing, Whitehall Lane in April 2006 finally announced it would be releasing its 2003 Reserve Cabernet Sauvignon (price: $75) as well as its 2003 Leonardini Vineyard Cabernet Sauvignon (price: $100) with Vino-Seal stoppers. The first bottles went to its wine-club members and were sold at the tasting room. At the time and with perhaps a hint of more to come, Leonardini said, "We aren't a cork-free winery—yet."

In the winter of 2006, Karl Matheis was skiing in the small village of Gargellen in the Montafon Valley of Austria. While dining at a small restaurant, he noticed it was serving local wines in Vino-Lok bottles and asked the proprietor what he thought of them. He replied enthusiastically that he loved them because they were so easy to use. "They're the best," said the owner with élan. Matheis then told him that he had invented them, but the innkeeper wouldn't believe him. Who would believe some skier boastfully claiming to have invented the glass stopper?

Never mind, Matheis thought. He left the restaurant with a confident shrug since he knew the whole story.

MESSAGE IN A BOTTLE:

HATTENHEIM, GERMANY

Every year in the late fall and just after harvest and winemaking, an intense period when workdays are long and sleep is short, Rolf Herke, the winemaker at Schloss Vollrads, and some of his fellow winemakers from the Rheingau get together to share outstanding wines. All their production by then is in the cellar, and fermentations are finished. So it's time to relax and have some fun. The wines for the celebration come from all over the world, and the only rule is that a winemaker can't bring his or her own wine.

In November 2003, Stefan Gerhard of Weingut Gerhard, whose family had been making wine since 1442, hosted the annual get-together at his winery in Hattenheim. Four winemakers brought twenty-two bottles from top producers in France, New Zealand, Chile, and other countries. Herke had hunted around his personal cellar and selected six prized bottles. One of his most favored was a 1993 Zind-Humbrecht Riesling from France. After he got to the party, though, Herke was devastated when he opened the bottle and smelled it. The Zind-Humbrecht wine was corked. In fact, four of the twenty-two bottles at the celebration turned out to be corked.

The end-of-harvest celebration went on with the eighteen good bottles, but the experience encouraged Herke in his quest to find an alternative to cork.

CHAPTER SEVENTEEN

The Bottle That Wears a Crown

For ten generations, the Kühn family was a bulk-wine producer in the Rheingau area of Germany. Some 80 percent of its output was sold before bottling, and much of that ended up in the sparkling wine Germans call Sekt. Peter Jakob Kühn, of the eleventh generation, took over Weingut Kühn from his father in the late 1970s. A quiet man with a stocky build and ruddy face earned during a lifetime of working in the vineyards, Peter decided to take the winery in a different direction. He wasn't interested in producing commodity wines; his goal was to turn out prize-winning quality ones. While Peter worked the vines and made the wines, his wife, Angela, handled business matters. "The wine market was different," says Angela. "The days of selling bulk wine were coming to an end. We had to break down barriers that existed only in our minds. That was the only way to lead the company for another generation." Reflecting the changes he was making, the name of the winery was changed to Weingut Peter Jakob Kühn.

Over the next two decades, Peter and Angela changed almost everything his father had done. They started by building a new winery and replanting their vineyards. They grew different grapes and altered cultivation. Peter was a believer in biodynamic farming and tried to keep everything in close relationship with nature, eschewing chemical fertilizers. In 2006, he planted two hundred birdhouses in his fields to attract the fowl. Birds might eat some of the grapes near harvest, but they would also eat bugs and were a natural way to have a pest-free vineyard. As someone who liked natural things, Peter was happy sealing his bottles with cork. Synthetics might be okay for others, but not for Weingut Peter Jakob Kühn.

During the 1990s, Peter and Angela began to reap the rewards of their minor revolution. The young winemaker and his wines started getting attention around Germany and soon abroad. While he made some Pinot Noir called Spätburgunder, a little Sekt, and some elegant sweet wines such as Beerenauslese Riesling, Kühn was most noted for his dry Rieslings. A German wine magazine in 1992 named his 1991 vintage the country's best. British wine writers such as Jancis Robinson took note, and the winery built sales in Holland and Spain. In 1998, the wine magazine *Alles Über Wein* named Kühn the Rheingau's winegrower of the year. The future for Peter and Angela plus their three children looked bright. Daughter Sandra was already enrolled in the winemaking program at the nearby Research Institute Geisenheim, ensuring that there would soon be a twelfth generation of Kühn vintners.

All of that success came crashing down in the spring of 2000, when Peter and Angela were on the annual trip around Germany promoting their 1999 vintage in presentations at leading hotels in such cities as Bremen, Hamburg, and Berlin. The products being tasted were the winery's top wines, which sold at its highest prices, ranging from €20 (US$26) for a dry Riesling up to €50 (US$66) for a half bottle of the sweet Beerenauslese. As part of those presentations, the owners opened several hundred bottles of wines but were horrified to discover that they had to reject a large number because they were corked. "No one had to tell us we had a problem," says Angela. "We recognized it ourselves. Once you have tasted a corked wine, you never forget it." The corking was totally random. In some six-bottle boxes, five bottles would be tainted, while other cartons would be fine. Overall, the couple estimated that 30 percent of their wines from that vintage were bad. That included some nine thousand bottles of normal-quality wines, and fifteen hundred of their most expensive ones. The estimated loss of some €120,000 (US$158,400) was devastating for a small producer. Kühn later sold off the wine to a distiller for very little and received some insurance compensation, but the financial hit was still severe. Just as Kühn was becoming known as a high-quality producer, his still nascent reputation also took a hard hit.

As a result of his problems, Peter Jakob Kühn decided to get away from cork. He would start bottling his 2000 wines in the spring of 2001, which left him little time to research various closures. Moreover, he didn't like any of the options he had. He considered synthetic stoppers but thought they would be good for only a couple of years, while his best wines lasted much longer. He didn't like the look of the short screwcaps, which were mainly used on low-quality wines in liter bottles. In addition, he was concerned about storage problems. Along with most German wineries, Kühn kept bottles for long periods in large steel cages before labeling, where the screwcaps could easily be nicked or dented and the seal broken.

Shortly before the 2001 bottling, Peter and Angela reluctantly decided to go with a one-year solution while he searched for a longer-term strategy. For 70 percent of his production, he went with plastic corks from two producers, Nomacorc and Integra. The other 30 percent would still have corks, but these would be the red wines, since the threshold of TCA recognition for them was higher, and some late-harvest wines, where tradition is more important. It helped that the 2000 vintage was not a great one in the Rheingau, so the wines were going to be drunk early.

While doing their research, Angela had heard that a young neighboring winemaker named Peter Querbach had invented an interesting new closure that he called StainlessCap. It wasn't really new. After William Painter invented the crown cap in 1892, it went on to become the world's most widely used closure. It was inexpensive, resilient, easy to install, and provided an extremely tight seal. Crown caps have been used in the wine business for more than a half century, although consumers never see them. Champagne and other sparkling wines are fermented twice, first in barrels or tanks and then in bottles. During the second fermentation, when the wine gets its fizzy carbonated style, the wine is under a crown cap because the pressure being built up in the bottle is so strong that it would pop a natural cork. Most Champagne thus spends more than a year of its production life—the most important part—under crown cap. After the so-called disgorgement and dosage, when unwanted deposits are removed and the bottle is topped up, a technical cork is put in the bottle, then wire is placed over that to hold down the cork. While Champagne companies had enjoyed extensive and successful experience with crown caps, still-wine makers have had almost none, even though many of them are quick to say that it provides the best seal.

Weingut Querbach was founded in 1650, and Wilfried and Resi Querbach and their son Peter now run the family firm. Nearly 90 percent of its production is Riesling, and it too has had problems with cork taint. Peter got the idea of using crown caps for still wine in 1995, when he was still in his twenties, and noticed that the best German bottled water was closed with a stainless steel crown cap. That was the classy closure for sparkling water, while plastic or aluminum caps were used on less prestigious ones.

For the next four years, Peter Querbach tried to put together the elements that would make a wine crown cap work. There was no need to reinvent the closure since they were being used daily by millions of German beer drinkers. The challenge was to come up with an attractive-looking package. Doing virtually all the work himself, young Querbach found a glass company to produce the double-lipped bottle needed for the seal. He also lined up a distributor.

The final product looked quite elegant. The bottle had a traditional tin capsule at the top, which was cut to expose a black plastic cap that fit over the familiar crimped crown cap. On the inside of the closure was a plastic liner, the same one used with many screwcaps. Querbach also developed an attractive, although heavy, stainless steel tool to take the cap off without bending it, which happens with a regular bottle opener. If all the wine was not drunk, the original cap could easily be placed back on the bottle for a tight reseal.

At first, Querbach called his product the Stainless Steel Cap, but an American friend suggested that Stainless Cap would be an easier name to remember, so he obtained the registered trademark StainlessCap and launched a Web site. The Querbach winery in 1999 did about one-third of its twelve-thousand-case production with StainlessCap, and the following year all its wine had that closure.

By the following spring, when Weingut Peter Jakob Kühn was ready to bottle its 2001 vintage, Querbach's StainlessCap looked like a more attractive alternative than using plastic corks for a second year, so the winery did 70 percent of its wine with StainlessCap and the remaining 30 percent with natural cork. Its highest-quality wines were equally split between cork and crown cap. Kühn felt some comfort in that Querbach had now been using its new closure for three vintages and seemed to be getting good market acceptance. By then, about a half dozen other German wineries were enthusiastically using StainlessCap.

When Kühn's customers saw the crown cap, however, they were confused. To them crown cap meant beer, and why was such a prestigious winery sealing its great wines with a beer cap? Sandra Kühn recalls trying to answer a myriad of questions in the patio area where drop-in customers try her family's wines. "I wanted to talk about the vintage, and all they wanted to talk about was the beer cap," she remembers. The German wine press was also filled with stories about Kühn that dealt in detail with the new closure, but reported little about the quality of its wines. Only after two years did the questioning begin to abate. "It was horrible for us," Angela says.

An experience I had while visiting the Rheingau to research this book reflected the attitude of sommeliers and waiters toward the crown cap. While ordering a meal in a restaurant, I saw a Kühn Riesling on the wine list that I knew by the vintage had been sealed with a StainlessCap, so I ordered it. The waitress brought the wine to the table with the capsule still on the bottle, and it looked exactly like any bottle with a capsule covering the cork. The waitress then took the bottle away and brought it back with the crown cap off and an attractive, clean bottleneck showing. Obviously, the waitress didn't want to show the closure or go through the opening of the crown cap in front of a customer. That scene may have been repeated in other German restaurants.

By the 2005 vintage, the StainlessCap was in trouble. The project had from the beginning been undercapitalized because the Querbachs lacked the money needed to launch a new entry into a highly competitive market. In addition, Peter Querbach had troubles with the bottle manufacturer and the distributor, who were not excited about making a product for only a few wineries. Kühn couldn't get as many bottles as it wanted or at the right time to do its bottling. Finally, in desperation, the winery turned to Stelvin, which was getting more and more market acceptance in Germany. "We still needed a special bottle for Stelvin," says Angela Kühn. "But so many companies are now making the bottles that it was almost as easy to buy those as it was to buy a pound of butter in a grocery store." After several years of switching closures, Kühn now hopes to stay with Stelvin for a long time.

In late June 2006, Peter Querbach told me he was trying to sell his patents to a company that would have the money to get the product into the market. "You need a big international name to get the financing and marketing support for the system to be accepted worldwide." One industry insider told me that it's unlikely that any such company would step forward to do that. So the StainlessCap system will likely slowly fade away.

At the same time Peter Querbach was trying to launch StainlessCap, a British expatriate in Italy was attempting to start a similar product that he called CrownCap. Robin Woodhouse had been in wine retailing in Britain before going to Italy in 1990 to get into importing. As he was traveling around the country visiting local winemakers, he heard not only about their problems with cork but also their praise for the crown cap as the best available closure.

Just as Querbach, Woodhouse had limited funding, but in 2000 and 2001 he bottled two vintages of Italian wines in crown caps. He went down the same path as the German and had a special bottle made. Woodhouse, though, made no attempt to hide the crimped cap on the bottle, hoping to win over consumers with what he called "the shock of the new." The Robin Woodhouse Collection wines got some excellent reviews, but they died in stores and on wine lists. After the second vintage, he discontinued his efforts and went back to his business of exporting Italian wines to Britain, Canada, and Scandinavia.

Woodhouse blamed his failure on "the people in the middle—restaurateurs, retailers, importers, distributors." He says those people, whom he calls "gatekeepers," have no interest in promoting crown caps, which are a small part of the closure market and only show up the problems of corks. Woodhouse says he remains "anticork" and is using Stelvin on a new line of wines. Yet he still thinks crown caps provide a better seal. "I was just ahead of my time," he says.

Crown caps may still find a role in the world of wine as a seal for sparkling wines. Several makers of Italian Prosecco are bottling their bubbly with crown caps, and three national subsidiaries of France's Moët & Chandon—Australia, Argentina, and the United States—are now selling some of their sparkling wines that way. The Australian one went on sale in 2003 as Chandon ZD, and the Argentine one the following year as Chandon Eternum.

In June 2006, at the Aspen Food & Wine Classic, California's Domaine Chandon launched its crown cap with much fanfare and a jazzy-looking gold-colored bottle opener. Sparkling winemaker Tom Tiburzi says his company decided to go with crown caps for its top-of-the-line Étoile brand, which sells for about $40 retail, because it was getting a 4–5 percent cork-taint level on the wine, as compared with less than 1 percent for its lower-priced sparklers. He says the winery concluded that since the leading product is particularly light and sensitive, any flaws stand out more than they do in its other brands.

The first release of Étoile under crown cap was a 1999 wine that had been bottled in 2000. It had a production crown cap for five years until that was removed just before it went on sale. Then a new brown cap plus a seal and ribbon were put on the bottle. Although the actual crown cap costs less than the cork it replaced, all the handwork makes the new closure more expensive.

Tiburzi is comfortable with the crown caps. All the bottles in Domaine Chandon's library of old sparkling wines dating back more than thirty years have always been under crown cap. "If you have something worth protecting, you give it the best closure you have," he says.

CHAPTER EIGHTEEN

Trouble in the Cellar at Hanzell

*Hanzell's Jean Arnold found
herself over a barrel.*

At the California Wine Experience presented by *Wine Spectator* in October 2002, Jean Arnold, the president of California's Hanzell Vineyards, her husband, Bob Sessions, the retired winemaker and former president, as well as Frenchman Daniel Docher, the current winemaker, were staffing their company's table in a cavernous ballroom of the Venetian Hotel in Las Vegas. They were pouring their latest release: the 2000 Chardonnay. Hanzell is at the prestige end of the California wine market, with the Chardonnay selling for about $65 a bottle and the Pinot Noir going for some $80. The winery has an annual production of only about two thousand cases of Chardonnay and one thousand cases of Pinot Noir.

Early in the event, James Laube of the *Wine Spectator* passed by their table and was offered a sample of the Chardonnay. Jean Arnold poured him a glass and then she, Sessions, and Docher leaned back and waited for the anticipated effusive praise. Laube regularly gave the Hanzell marks in the high 80s or low 90s on the magazine's 100-point scale. Laube sniffed the wine, took a sip, and then said that he thought it was corked. To Arnold, it was like taking a cannonball in the stomach.

Unbeknownst to the Hanzell people, Laube already had the winery on his journalistic radar screen because he had been getting signs of TCA in its wines when he tasted them for reviews. Laube was the first American journalist to pick up the taint issue seriously. Only the month before, he had published a story on the *Wine Spectator*'s Web site about high levels of TCA at Beaulieu Vineyard. He had noted troubles with a variety of its red wines from the 1997, 1998, and 1999 vintages, including the Georges de Latour Private Reserve Cabernet Sauvignon, which sold for $100 a bottle. Laube had sent samples of fifteen Beaulieu wines to ETS Laboratories for independent verification. The results came back showing TCA levels ranging from 3.4 ppt to 4.6 ppt. Winery officials said the cause of the TCA was apparently a humidifier that had recently been installed in one cellar. Echoes of France two decades earlier.

After the shock of Laube's statement, Arnold quickly put that bottle aside and got another from an ice bucket where the Chardonnay was being chilled. The ritual of pouring, smelling, and tasting was repeated, and Laube said he thought the second bottle was also corked. This time Arnold tasted it as well. She admitted the wine didn't have the rich, fruity aroma that was a hallmark of Hanzell's Chardonnays but attributed that to its temperature, since cool wines often have an inhibited fragrance.

Arnold tried a third time with another new bottle, and Laube passed the same judgment: the wine was corked. Then without waiting for a fourth bottle to be opened, Laube walked away and continued his tour of the display tables.

The trio from Hanzell were surprised and dumbstruck. What was going on? Arnold and Sessions turned to Docher and began grilling him for an answer. Was Laube right? How could three bottles in a row be corked? Docher insisted the Hanzell wines were too cold and not corked, explaining that if they are too chilled the fruit flavors shut down and oak flavors dominate the taste. Laube was wrong; the wines were fine.

Just then, two master sommeliers passed by the Hanzell table, and Arnold poured samples of Chardonnay for them from the third bottle. Without any hints from the Hanzell group that something might be wrong, the sommeliers all said the wine seemed corked. The Hanzell team returned to California deeply worried about what had happened at the California Wine Experience.

Hanzell was one of the earliest pioneers in California wine, having been founded in 1953 by James Zellerbach, head of the Zellerbach Paper fortune and ambassador to Italy during the Eisenhower administration. He had a passion for Burgundy's two great wines—Chardonnay and Pinot Noir—and set out to make them in Sonoma. No expense was spared at Zellerbach's small, hobby winery that produced only those wines, and the results were the first outstanding California versions of those great French classics. The winery, which never made a profit even though its wines were great, has had three owners since Zellerbach. The current one is Alexander de Brye, who inherited it in 1991 at the age of sixteen when his mother died. At the time, his financial advisers suggested that he sell the money-losing property, but he kept it, although he lives most of the year in London.

Arnold had been in the wine business since 1979 after a short career as a dancer. She had a long history in sales and management at some of California's leading wineries, including Chateau St. Jean, Jordan Vineyards & Winery, and Chalk Hill Estate Vineyards & Winery. She was brought into Hanzell as president in 2002 to replace Sessions, who stayed on the board of directors and helped with winemaking. They married a year later. She reported to a board of seven—six men and herself.

By the spring of 2003, Hanzell was starting to get steady, although not massive, reports from the field about corked bottles of the 2000 Chardonnay. Arnold, though, was convinced that the white wine was fine, although she still couldn't figure out why the winery was getting the bad feedback.

Arnold was so confident that she didn't hesitate to send a bottle to Laube in May 2003 for his annual tasting panel of California Chardonnays. A few days later, she received a telephone call from Laube's assistant saying that her boss felt the winery had a problem. Arnold replied strongly, saying that she had discussed the matter with her winemaker, who said the trouble was that the wine was being served too cold. Arnold told the assistant that they should decant the wine and that she would send another bottle. By now, though, the scenario was becoming painfully familiar. Laube's assistant called a few days after getting the second bottle and said he had troubles with it as well.

While before this Hanzell had had few bottles of Chardonnay ever returned for corkiness, Arnold was starting to get reports from her broker, Lucy Malocsay, of a number of corked bottles of 1999 Pinot Noir. Arnold asked if there were also complaints about the 2000 Chardonnay. Malocsay replied that there were a few, but she thought those seemed to be due to *Brettanomyces.*

The reports of troubles with the Hanzell wines had now become so strong and so consistent that Arnold had to take them seriously. After the second call from the *Wine Spectator,* the Hanzell staff pulled thirty bottles of Chardonnay at random from the cellar and tasted them. If there was any question about the wine—"if it didn't sing" in Sessions's words—then the bottle was put aside. In the end, Arnold sent fifteen bottles to the ETS Laboratories in St. Helena for chemical analysis.

A few days later, Arnold received a call from Gordon Burns, the head of ETS, who was already familiar with TCA in wine facilities. Using the scientifically preferred nomenclature of nanograms per liter, he said the Chardonnay bottles had an average of 2.3 parts per trillion or 2.3 nanograms of TCA per liter of wine. Burns tried to give the vague numbers some meaning by saying, "It's like taking two steps on a walk to the sun or having two grains of salt in a swimming pool." That, however, was hardly reassuring for Arnold. Then she sent ETS a second sample, this time including some bottles of Pinot Noir. Those were also tested for *Brettanomyces.* The results for that came back negative, but the TCA level of the Pinot Noir was 3.2 nanograms per liter.

Shortly after the results for the second sample were known, Arnold got a call from owner Alexander de Brye in London.

"I understand we have a problem with the wine," he said.

"Yes, we do," Arnold replied.

"Is it a health issue?"

"No, it's a TCA issue. It's a chemical-flavor issue."

"I think we should stop sales."

After the call, Arnold got on the phone with other board members and told them de Brye had said sales should be stopped. In a series of meetings and phone calls the board debated the issue, with a majority of the group disagreeing on the need to halt sales. Finally, Arnold concluded that she and the other company officers simply didn't know enough about TCA to make an intelligent decision on an issue that could determine their winery's future.

So Arnold and the entire board went to St. Helena for a meeting with Gordon Burns at ETS and a crash course in TCA. With the patience that had been honed by years of explaining complex technical issues to winemakers more interested in tastes than test tubes, Burns walked the group through some of the basics of wine chemistry.

At one point Arnold said she couldn't understand how some of their wines were corked while some others "sang," as Sessions said. She said that the random nature of the problem indicated it might be a problem with corks.

Burns replied, "No, there is a low level of contamination—more than two nanograms per liter—in all the bottles." That wasn't much TCA and probably less than the average consumer would pick up, but it was there nonetheless.

At the recommendation of Burns, Arnold and the board then met with Leslie Norris, a flavor chemist and sensory scientist who had previously done work for the Ernst & Julio Gallo Winery and had just done a study on the consumer rejection threshold of TCA for several New Zealand winemakers. She put together a group of wine connoisseurs from COPIA, the food, wine, and arts center in Napa, and tested their sensitivity to TCA in a variety of wines. Most of the group started picking up the TCA at about 3 parts per trillion and clearly got it at about 7 ppt.

Since Laube had set off the original concern of TCA at Hanzell, Arnold decided to go back to him with an offer: would he like to join them in the search for the cause of the contamination? She had always enjoyed good relations with Laube, and only the year before he had done a flattering article on Bob Sessions's retirement, writing, "Sessions leaves a legacy of magnificent wines few of his contemporaries could hope to match." Laube says he replied that if Hanzell sent him any test results, he would take a look at them.

In late May, Arnold put a hold on selling any more wine until it determined what had caused the TCA problem. At the same time, she hired ETS to do a thorough search of the winery's entire facility to get to the bottom of the matter. Soon white-coated lab technicians were climbing into rafters, looking down drains, and inspecting barrels at Hanzell.

Finally later that month, Burns told Arnold that Hanzell had a winery problem. If there had been only trouble with the corks, the scientists would have found random bottles with high levels of TCA. But they were finding signs of it in the air, on barrels, and in hoses. In short, everywhere.

Arnold and Sessions decided to call Laube because they thought he was "a good friend and I forgot he was a journalist" and told him that ETS had determined that Hanzell had low-level TCA contamination in the winery. Laube put out the news on the *Wine Spectator* Web site and also reported it in the next issue of the magazine. Both stories quoted Arnold extensively.

The pressing question now facing Hanzell's management was how to handle the news with the wine-consuming public. By this time, Arnold was learning that other leading California wineries had suffered through similar problems in previous years. The Beaulieu case was well known, but a similar one at Chalone, a leading winery near Monterey, hadn't yet been made public. Beaulieu's strategy had been to minimize its problem in hopes that it would go away. Chalone's was to bet the news would never get out, and it didn't for a long time.

How was Hanzell going to react? Half the board of directors favored going public with the news, but the other half wanted to say nothing, hoping that the bad publicity would fade away given a tincture of time. Those members told Arnold just to ignore the problem, say nothing, and promote their wines even more aggressively.

Arnold replied to her all-male counterparts, "Gentlemen, how can I promote the wine when everyone will read soon in the *Wine Spectator* that we have TCA?" She explained that her sense was that this problem was going to be controversial and would not be going away.

Some board members suggested Arnold could just call Laube and say she had been mistaken, but Arnold replied that she would not lie to the press. Others said Hanzell was too small a winery to undertake the monumental task of going public with that kind of bad news. It would take a wine giant like Robert Mondavi to handle such a case of crisis management successfully.

A second time several board members urged Arnold to tough it out and tell Laube that she had been mistaken. This time she replied, "I won't do it. And if you say it a third time, I'll quit because I'm not going to lie to the press."

Around this time, the sorry saga of the energy company Enron's duplicity with the investing public was being played out on the front pages of newspapers. Arnold at one point told the board, "We're in the era of Enron. If we do nothing, it will smack of nondisclosure; and we will risk losing all our brand trust. This isn't just about two vintages of our wines. It's about our entire legacy of pioneering and quality winemaking. We have nothing to hide because we did nothing wrong."

As tempers rose, Arnold said bluntly, "With all due respect, gentlemen, you're acting like patriarchal dinosaurs. You can't do that anymore."

One board member finally broke the tension with a laugh and a quip: "Where's the respect for us in that?"

Board chairman Bill Britton swung the group to Arnold's position by announcing his support and saying, "As the old saying goes, you can't make a silk purse out of a sow's ear." Hanzell had been working on a multiyear plan to get to profitability in 2006 by slowly increasing production. But Alexander de Brye said his newborn son, Sebastian, might be the first member of the family to see the winery turn a profit.

On June 16, Arnold officially "pushed the pause button," as she called it, on future sales of the 2000 Chardonnay. In a memo labeled a "Customer Communication" that was also e-mailed to key clients, Arnold announced that Hanzell had "suspended all sales of the current release wines until the source and ramifications of this concern have been determined." In an attempt to explain it more clearly, the e-mail read, "This is NOT a complete recall of the 2000 Chardonnay. However, if anyone has a bottle/bottles they feel are not 'right' or are deeply concerned about the bottle variation issue, we will absolutely refund or give credit for the wine." Arnold and her staff also called around that day to wholesalers, retailers, and important customers to explain personally what had happened and what the winery was doing to get to the root of the problem.

Almost immediately, Arnold received support from some of her best customers, who said they were going to pour the wine by the glass so they could taste each bottle. Catherine Fallis, a master sommelier and the wine director of Aqua, a top San Francisco restaurant and Hanzell's largest account, e-mailed her back, "Are you kidding. I love this wine! I have been pouring 2000 Chardonnay by the glass for six months. I have gone through 30 cases without complaint. . . . Send me three more cases."

Bill Harris, the wine director and sommelier of the Ritz Carlton Hotel in Naples, Florida, sent an e-mail saying, "Don't push the pause button with me! I want to pour this wine by the glass now and I will taste every bottle!"

One distributor urged Arnold to stop talking so openly about her problem because that was only making a bad situation worse. She replied that people were going to learn about it eventually and she'd rather that they heard it first from Hanzell rather than through the press.

The strategy of total disclosure worked, and in the end only twelve cases of 2000 Chardonnay from five customers were ever returned out of the national distribution of two thousand cases.

During the early summer of 2003, ETS technicians were all over the Hanzell winery searching for the source of TCA contamination. They tested the air in the cellar and the fermentation room as well as all the equipment. Burns reported to Arnold that although his people had found several different sources of trouble, they weren't yet uncovering any single "smoking gun." But he was sure they would.

A California winemaker who had suffered through the same problem but without the glare of publicity became a high-priced consultant. His immediate advice to Arnold: "Test the hoses." Burns also suggested Arnold hire France's Pascal Chatonnet, the world's top expert on cellar cleanups following his work with French wineries in the 1980s, to get a second opinion and some recommendations on eventual remediation of the facilities and wines. Hanzell now had a small army of consultants on call, and the cost of the TCA recovery shot past $100,000.

ETS staffers eventually found the highest level of contamination in the drains and hoses. One red-stained pipe under an iron floor grate in the fermentation room was particularly suspect. But the ETS technicians also found TCA in the upper winery, the barrel-aging cellar, and the bottling room. Wooden pallets used for moving cases of bottles or other goods were loaded with TCA. It was even on plastic bungs, the stoppers in the top of barrels. Clearly, the contaminant was airborne. Areas of dampness or little ventilation had particularly high levels of contamination. The problem, though, had nothing to do with the corks Hanzell put in bottles, even though many people were saying the wines were "corked."

The ETS technicians finally concluded that the most likely cause was years and years of using chlorine as a disinfectant. Since Hanzell's earliest days in the 1950s, chlorine had been widely used to sanitize equipment. Disinfecting with chlorine was a mantra among California winemakers, although their counterparts in Europe rarely used it as a cleaning agent. According to stories widely repeated in the California wine industry, Hanzell crew members admitted that one worker just that year had poured undiluted chlorine onto a particularly tough stain on a floor in the winery. Most of the liquid had probably gone into the drain, and any remnants would have vaporized into the air and landed on anything and everything. It was the equivalent of letting off a chemical time bomb in the winery. The ETS conclusion was bad news, but now at least Hanzell knew the likely source of the TCA and could take remedial measures and get back to business.

On August 7, Arnold sent out another press release outlining in great detail what TCA was all about. She also announced that Hanzell was again putting its 2000 Chardonnay on sale since the level of TCA in the wine was below the threshold of consumer awareness that Leslie Norris had determined from her consumer testing at COPIA. Said the release,

"The low levels of TCA in the Chardonnay were not observed or recognized by nor changed the acceptability of the wine for the qualified, wine-knowledgeable consumers who were tested."

The winery was also going to sell the 1999 Pinot Noir, which had a slightly higher level of TCA, but only in response to "individual, expressed customer demand." Arnold concluded the main part of the release saying, "In any case, as has always been our policy, we will stand behind our wine and guarantee a refund to anyone who is not happy."

Arnold then took off on a two-month trip across the country as a kind of professor of TCA to the wine industry and wine consumers. To wholesalers, retailers, restaurant owners, and top customers she explained everything she had learned from Hanzell's research during the painful ordeal. All the information about TCA, how it developed through use of chlorine in cleaning, and its effects on wine, was also put on the Hanzell Web site for both consumers and other winemakers. Arnold ended her marathon tour with a luncheon on September 22 at the Fifth Floor restaurant in San Francisco, where she hosted a group of wine reporters and professionals. Master Sommelier Catherine Fallis presented a three-page "TCA Update" for them that also went out to people in the trade. At the lunch sixteen wine experts tried both the 1999 Pinot Noir and the 2000 Chardonnay. None of them detected any TCA in either wine.

While Arnold was traveling around the country, a new $4 million harvest of grapes for the 2003 vintage was waiting to be picked and brought into the winery for fermentation. No one wanted to bring the new crop into the facility and thereby risk ruining it, so winemaking equipment was moved out into the open air under rented party tents, where TCA formation would be much less likely than in the damp, closed environment of the old contaminated winery. In addition, many other changes were made. The staff was already using a peroxide-based cleanser to replace chlorine, but now old hoses, used pallets, and numerous other pieces of equipment were also thrown away and replaced with new. French oak barrels were sanded twice at a cost of $100 each to remove TCA from the wood, and the dust from the operation was collected in bags and discarded.

The 2001 and 2002 Hanzell Chardonnay were being stored in tanks before going into barrels for aging, while the Pinot Noir from those years was already in barrels. Winemakers Sessions and Docher were not sure whether the wines could be salvaged, but Pascal Chatonnet told them to leave small amounts of lees, the dead yeast remaining after fermentation, in the barrels because they would pull TCA molecules out of the wine. In addition, he advised them to fine the wine in tanks using a mixture of half milk and half cream. That would also attract TCA and fall to the bottom of the tanks, where it could be removed. Those steps, he said, would reduce the TCA level to less than 1 nanogram per liter. Even the best instruments or professional tasters could not reliably detect it below that level.

On March 15, 2004, Hanzell put the 2000 Pinot on sale, its first full release since the TCA contamination struck. Three months later, the winery began selling the 2001 Chardonnay. James Laube reviewed the Chardonnay in the *Wine Spectator* and gave it 78 points out 100. He wrote, "A troubling musty character robs the freshly squeezed lime and the pippin apple flavors within. Difficult to recommend. Tasted four times with consistent notes." That was the lowest score a Hanzell Chardonnay had ever gotten from the magazine. The following year, Arnold sent Laube a bottle of the 2001 Pinot Noir with a note that read, "New and Improved Formula—Less than 1 Part per Trillion TCA." He gave that an 82, still low by historical standards. Other publications rated both Hanzell wines much higher.

As part of the program to achieve profitability by expanding production, Hanzell had been planning for several years to construct an additional winery and cellar. That project was dramatically accelerated when the TCA crisis broke, since everyone concurred it was necessary to get winemaking out of the quaint, wooden facility that Zellerbach had built in the 1950s as a replica of the famed Clos de Vougeot in Burgundy. In July 2004, Arnold and the Hanzell staff unveiled their new winery and caves, which cost $4.1 million.

By going so public with the Hanzell story, Arnold did a major service to the American wine industry. Enology professors at places such as UC Davis knew the dangers of using chlorine for cleaning wineries. After all, Hans Tanner had zeroed in on the chlorine connection to TCA as far back as 1981. But starting with the chairman of the cork company who told Tanner he had made a mistake by publishing his TCA research and through the 1980s silence by the French wineries about their taint problem, the wine business had resorted to cover-up rather than full disclosure about any taint troubles. If there had been more open discussion, there might not have been the chlorine-caused crisis at Hanzell twenty-two years after Tanner. That was the price of silence.

After Jean Arnold told the Hanzell story in full and painful detail during 2003, no one in the industry could be unaware of the dangers in using chlorine. Several wine trade journals published stories about cellar problems that drew heavily on her experience. *Vineyard & Winery Management* headlined its article "Hanzell's Magnanimous Gift to the Wine Industry." The story included an eight-point program to avoid similar troubles starting in capital letters: "BLACK LETTER RULE: NO CHLORINE IN THE FACILITY EVER." Soon ETS was doing a booming business testing wineries for TCA contamination and recommending remedial action.

No one will ever know the number of California wineries that had chlorine-caused TCA problems, but there are doubtless many. On July 1, 2003, shortly after the story broke, James Laube wrote in an e-mail to Arnold, "Today we had eight bottles with TCA, so it's a serious problem at several wineries. . . . Your discussing it may help others look for similar problems."

Within the California wine industry, Arnold received countless kudos for her action. Lew Platt, the former CEO of Hewlett-Packard, the technology company, and then head of Kendall-Jackson, sent her an e-mail in August 2003 saying, "I think you handled this beautifully. . . . Careful handling of situations like this is what builds long-term loyalty and you've given people lots of reasons to trust you and the brand. I'm proud to say I know you."

One winemaker who had been driven by the Hanzell story to inspect his own facility and to change the way it was cleaned told Arnold simply, "Thank you. You saved my winery."

MESSAGE IN A BOTTLE:

GULF MILLS, PENNSYLVANIA

Sheldon B. Margolis was the longtime owner of Margolis Wine & Spirits, once Pennsylvania's largest wine distributor. Like many young people in the 1950s, when he started drinking wine, the only thing he could afford was Wild Irish Rose, a strong sweet wine. After graduating from the University of Pennsylvania's Wharton School of Business in 1956, he drifted into wine, first selling Roma wines from California. One of his mentors was John Dennis, who worked in New York City, and Margolis regularly took the train to see him and taste his wines.

One day in 1966, Dennis told him that if he really wanted to learn the subject, he should take $200 and buy some of the best French offerings to see what great wine was all about. Margolis didn't have $200 to spend that way, but he went to a liquor store on Fifty-ninth Street in Manhattan and bought two cases that cost him less than that. He bought three bottles each of Château Lafite Rothschild, Château Margaux, and other prized 1961 wines. None of them cost more than $10 a bottle. Margolis stored his treasure away in a homemade wine refrigerator that he kept in his kitchen in Gulf Mills, Pennsylvania, a suburb of Philadelphia.

One night in 1979, Margolis decided to open the first bottle of the 1961 Margaux for three wine buddies who regularly joined him to enjoy special tastings. So with his friends watching, he took the bottle out of his wine refrigerator and, sitting at the table in his kitchen, turned a corkscrew into the neck and began to pull. His hand suddenly shot up when the cork broke off with half of it still in the bottle.

For the next half hour, the four men tried everything they could think of to get the cork out of the bottle, including a two-pronged opener named an Ah-So, which was supposed to open any bottle with a cork. Nothing worked. One of the wine buddies then remembered he had a glass cutter at home and suggested they try that. There was nothing to lose at this point, so the friend brought back the new tool and started to saw off the neck. With gallows humor, the four agreed they were probably going to be killed by glass chips in the wine.

When the cutting was finished, the neck was tapped and fell smoothly off the bottle. Nonetheless, Margolis decided to pour the wine through cheesecloth to catch any bits of glass. Margolis knew that when corks crumble like that, the wine inside the bottle would often be dead. But they'd gotten this far, so why not give it a try?

"The wine was wonderful," recalls Margolis. "The best way to describe it, 'elegant.' The edges were not brown, as you often see in an old wine. It was magnificent, soft, and luscious. It was the best wine experience of my life."

When the four looked back at the remaining cork in the neck, they realized the cork had originally been at least an inch and a half long. The top of it crumbled, but the bottom half held the seal and protected the wine.

Margolis told his friends that Margaux is often described as having an iron fist in a velvet glove. They decided that in this case, the cork had been the iron fist that protected the 1961 Château Margaux.

CHAPTER NINETEEN

The Problem of Reduction

*Alan Limmer's dog Lou Lou gave
him some solace when the battle
grew fierce. Says he: "She knew very
little about closures, but was very
good at opening biscuit packets."*

Alan Limmer, the owner and winemaker of Stonecroft Wines in the
Hawke's Bay area of New Zealand, does not step away from challenging situations. Many young New Zealanders head off to Britain to enjoy
a European experience by working there for a year or so before returning
to spend the rest of their lives at home. In the late 1970s, Limmer and his
young wife, Glen, did just that. When they were finished, though, Alan
decided to take a long overland way home. After piling all their earthly pos-
sessions into a green-and-white Volkswagen Westphalia camper, Alan
and Glen set off first to North Africa. The only maps they had were in a

1950 high school atlas, but they convinced themselves that they could get good Michelin maps once they got to Morocco. They didn't, but they set off nonetheless on a yearlong trek that took them first through the battle lines of Morocco and Algeria, who at the time were at war, and then into numerous encounters where they could have been killed in Turkey, Iran, Nepal, and India. When they finally got to Calcutta, Limmer put the camper on a ship to Australia, while the couple backpacked across Burma, Southeast Asia, and Indonesia. At last, and virtually broke, they arrived back in New Zealand. That kind of fortitude has been handy during the past five years, as Limmer has waged a lonely fight against the use of screw-caps to seal wine bottles.

Most winemakers have studied a little chemistry; Limmer has a Ph.D. in the subject from the University of Waikato. In 2001, he received the New Zealand Order of Merit for his services to the wine industry and, the following year, was elected a fellow of the New Zealand Institute of Chemistry. With perennially tousled rust-colored hair and wearing Levi's instead of a lab coat, Limmer wasn't cut out for the academic life. So after a short stint as a wine chemist, he started Stonecroft, making his first vintage in 1987. His goal was Rhône-style wines like Hermitage, and he was quickly credited with making New Zealand's best Syrah.

Limmer used all the latest technology of the day, which included fermenting grapes in stainless steel tanks and keeping young wines as far away from air as possible. He filled his tanks to the brim with wine, then sealed them tight to make sure no air reached them. He noted that when he bottled the wine, it seemed perfect. But after only a few months, it often took on a foul smell. He later discovered that the offending odors came from a range of sulfides caused by a process technicians call reduction. ETS, in a technical bulletin, lists eight offending sulfur compounds that give tastes ranging from sewagelike and burnt rubber to rotten egg and garlic.

Reduction is not unique to screwcaps. French winemakers had been struggling with the problem for a long time if their corks provided too tight a seal. Many people, though, did not understand reduction well, and some even incorrectly thought corks caused it. Only recently have enologists been able to measure the amount of air getting into the bottle, and it is still unclear whether the air comes through or around corks.

Digging into standard wine textbooks, Limmer found the treatment of sulfur compounds was twenty years old and of little help to him. "I just couldn't figure out what was happening," he recalls. "I was beating myself up pretty bad, but nothing would fix the problem." He then began a long search through technical literature in scientific journals—a journey that has taken him several years and still continues.

Limmer finally concluded that the problem originated from the sulfide fingerprint yeast leaves behind after fermentation. Wine is a living product that continues to develop in its container for decades. Limmer concluded that oxygen has a role postbottling. If the winemaker eliminates it totally, sulfur smells will likely develop in some wines. While he didn't totally master all his problems, Limmer finally got them under control and his wines began winning prizes. He won the gold medal in the aromatic class for a Gewürztraminer at the 1997 International Wine Challenge in London.

In mid-2001, when Limmer began hearing about the New Zealand Screwcap Wine Seal Initiative, he immediately became concerned about the claims its leaders were making about how screwcaps were the perfect closure because they provided an airtight seal and got rid of cork taint. Because of his own experience, he knew that the anaerobic environment could lead to trouble. Limmer started an e-mail exchange with Michael Brajkovich, the winemaker at Kumeu River and the best researcher in the Initiative's leadership. "I warned Michael to be careful about what he was saying because it was more complicated than it appeared," says Limmer.

Brajkovich responded that the "closure doesn't cause the problem but exposes a problem that was already there." He also sent Limmer papers written by father and son Jean and Pascal Ribéreau-Gayon as well as Émile Peynaud from Bordeaux University, which had become the standard line of defense against corkscrew critics since the Clare Valley winemakers launched their screwcap movement. Brajkovich explained that as a student in Australia's Roseworthy wine program he had learned all about hydrogen sulfide and that he actually liked a touch of reduction in his Chardonnays. He also maintained that if winemakers were careful and their wines were clean going into the bottle that was going to get a screwcap, there would be no problem. Later Bob Campbell, a Master of Wine and spokesman for the New Zealand screwcap group, and Dr. Paul Kilmartin, who ran the new wine program at the University of Auckland, joined the e-mail discussion. The dialogue finally petered out, though, because neither Limmer nor Brajkovich was convincing the other of his case.

When Limmer read the section of the first report of the Australian Wine Research Institute closure study, which warned that wines under screwcaps were "exhibiting a reduced or sulfide/rubbery aroma," he felt vindicated. That was not only consistent with his own observations but also with the predictions he had been making to Brajkovich. The bad odors were not there at the beginning, but they formed after about a year in anaerobic conditions.

In his winery's February 2002 newsletter, Limmer wrote for the first time about his concerns with using screwcaps with high-tannin wines such as Syrah and Cabernet Sauvignon because of the airtight seal. "If they do not have sufficient access to oxygen, the wines develop reductive characters which have a significant deleterious effect on the sensory qualities." Shortly thereafter, the local Hawke's Bay newspaper ran a story about Limmer's charges against screwcaps. The photograph accompanying the story showed Limmer aiming a bottle with a cork at John Hancock, the winemaker at nearby Trinity Hill and a founding member of the New Zealand Initiative, who had a bottle with a screwcap pointing back at him. The battle was engaged.

Limmer had been stewing over the issues in reduction chemistry for about a year without reaching any clear conclusions when, in late 2002, he finally got around to reading the proceedings of the September Romeo Bragato Conference, New Zealand's annual technical wine meeting. A paper by Roger Boulton of UC Davis caught Limmer's attention because it raised some of the same issues that were bothering him. "I suddenly realized that I wasn't the only guy on the planet thinking about this chemistry," recalls Limmer. "Someone else was out there thinking the same way."

The New Zealander quickly found Boulton's e-mail address and opened a dialogue. "In my first message I told him his paper was bloody brilliant," recalls Limmer. For the next eighteen months, Boulton and Limmer exchanged e-mails at least weekly, sometimes even daily, bouncing ideas off each other. By late 2003, Limmer felt he had his arguments together and wanted to publish some articles in respected wine publications to explain the issues he thought the screwcap advocates were refusing to admit even existed. Limmer had never before published an article in such journals but felt it was now his duty to alert New Zealand winemakers to what he had learned. He was undaunted by the task. Talking his way through the battle lines of both the Moroccan and Algerian armies was certainly more difficult than this.

In his Stonecroft newsletter, Limmer set out what he called "Alan's Thoughts as at November 2003." He started with a full broadside against cork, writing, "There is no doubt the performance from cork producers has been less than it should have been. In fact it has been so poor, in terms of responding to customer requirement, they hardly deserve to stay in business." He went on, "I have read pretty well everything I can find on the subject, which is not much, and with a degree in chemistry, have more questions than answers at this point." One of his fundamental questions, he wrote, was whether corks breathe. If they do and screwcaps do not, then the wines under the two closures would be different wines. He concluded, "So far, there is a serious lack of science and trials to evaluate this important matter."

Limmer's first technical article appeared in *New Zealand Winegrower,* an industry magazine, in November 2004, and was followed by two more. The first one was entitled "Redox Reactions, Sulfides, and General Misconceptions." It laid out the basic issues in sulfide chemistry and how sulfide compounds behave in wine. The title of the second was "Do Corks Breathe? Or the Origin of SLO [Sulfur-Like Odors]." It was an update on cork research and took the subject beyond the Bordeaux work from the middle of the twentieth century. It also discussed the importance of small amounts of air in stopping reduction and helping wines age. The third, "Possible Ways of Dealing with Post-Bottling Sulfides," gave winemakers practical options for dealing with redox issues. Limmer repeated the basic arguments from the three articles in somewhat different versions in the *Australian & New Zealand Grapegrower & Winemaker* and the American magazine *Practical Winery & Vineyard.*

The essence of Limmer's message is that sealing wines in an airtight atmosphere under screwcaps leads to the formation of off odors, but minute amounts of air, which get to the wine through corks, will remove those offensive smells. Limmer's case is not easy going for a nonscientist. These are technical papers written by a Ph.D. chemist about complicated issues. I asked dozens of winemakers in New Zealand and Australia if they had read and understood Limmer's theses. One of them said bluntly, "Ninety-five percent of people don't understand what he's saying. It's my bedtime reading, but I'm asleep after the first paragraph." Limmer was disappointed in that kind of reaction, since he had painstakingly worked to translate scientific material into something winemakers could understand. He nonetheless received numerous compliments from winemakers in New Zealand and Australia, and the articles published in Australia were the most frequently reprinted the magazine had ever had.

The final sentence of the third paper stated Limmer's conclusion succinctly and is easy for winemakers or wine consumers to understand: "In a nutshell, the screwcap impermeability is encouraging a specific, unfortunate, post-bottling sulfide reaction (thiol accumulation), while cork's permeability discourages it."

Wine flaws are not always easy to recognize, and even some so-called experts do not recognize small amounts of cork taint or the spoilage yeast *Brettanomyces,* although anyone will certainly identify high doses of them. Reduction has been known to winemakers for a long time. Limmer was concerned about sulfur compounds that can be formed by reduction or other reactions. He suspects that all wines under screwcaps eventually have those problems. Many other wine professionals say such estimates are far too high, but no one has an accurate number.

Limmer was surprised in early 2006 when a Gewürztraminer he had tasted three weeks before and thought had sulfide problems won a Hawke's Bay wine competition. He asked Kate Radburnd, the winemaker at the nearby C J Pask Winery and a judge, if she was picking up much reduction in the wines. She responded that she wasn't, so Limmer invited her to stop by his winery to taste again the wines he thought were reduced. When Radburnd and her assistant winemaker arrived a few days later, Limmer opened a bottle of the suspect wine and poured two glasses. He then put a small amount of copper sulfate in one of them, which was similar to what would be accomplished by copper fining the wine. The three then tasted the wines side by side. They all agreed that the one with the copper sulfate had a more attractive aroma and tasted better. The original wine was suffering from sulfides. Limmer said this was proof the problem was much bigger than anyone realized.

After I had spent nearly half a day talking with Limmer for this book in September 2006, I asked him if we could do the same experiment. He agreed and said he knew that the 2005 vintage of a neighbor's Gewürztraminer was reduced, so that would be a good example. We hopped into a car, drove down the road, bought a bottle of the 2005 Gewürz, and returned to the Stonecroft tasting room. Limmer placed the wine and four glasses—two for him and two for me—on a plain pine table that also had on it the book *Wine Dogs: The Dogs of Australian Wineries.* Limmer started by pouring two glasses of the Gewürztraminer for each of us. Then he pulled out a small bottle of copper sulfate and with an eyedropper put a few drops into one of each of our glasses. Finally he swirled those two glasses around for a few seconds and suggested we try both wines. After taking a sip of each, I had my own impression, but I waited for Limmer to react first. "I taste the reduction first in the palate," he said. "This wine, the one without the copper, is both hard and kind of flat. The one treated with copper is fresher." My impression was that the wine with copper was livelier and more agreeable, while the other by comparison was dull. The difference between the two wines was not as great as if one had been badly corked. If I had tasted each wine separately, I might not have noticed the difference. But side by side, they were distinct.

Although the vast majority of New Zealand's wine media was in lock-step support of screwcaps after the initial press conference in 2001, one journalist began raising questions about the same issues Limmer has been zeroing in on. He was American Paul White, who wrote a weekly wine column for the *Dominion Post,* one of New Zealand's two national papers. He also writes feature stories for leading wine publications in Australia, Britain, and the United States.

After doing his undergraduate work at Portland State University, White went to Oxford in 1986 to get a Ph.D. in music. His specialty was the Baroque-era bassoon as both a player and instrument maker, and his thesis was on its development between 1635 and 1810. While at Oxford, White developed a love of wine and became a member of the university's tasting team, which competed against Cambridge in fierce contests of identifying wines by varietal and vintage. Jasper Morris, a British Master of Wine, taught White about what he called the "shitty flavor" that developed in some wines—the same phenomenon winemakers and scientists like Limmer call reduction. One day Jasper presented White with a glass of a dreadful-smelling wine and said that was an example of reduction. In a demonstration similar to the one John Forrest did for the Marlborough winery owners, Jasper put a copper penny into the glass and the offensive odor disappeared.

In 1993, when White's Kiwi wife wanted to return home, he moved from Britain to New Zealand. After a brief stint as a wine buyer, he moved over to writing about the country's booming wine scene. White's suspicion about wines under screwcap was first raised in 2002, when he was doing a blind tasting with two wine judges of thirty recently released Kiwi Gewürztraminers. The three tasters quickly eliminated eight wines under screwcap. Four of them had been sealed with screwcaps, and White described them as "malodorous" with "rubbery, rotten-egg-like characters." In an article that appeared July 5, 2003, White wrote a column in the *Dominion Post* pointing out the redox problem with wines under screwcap, which is believed to be the first time the issue was raised in the popular press. In it he concluded that as a result of switching from corks to screwcaps, "One problem may simply have been traded for another."

Shortly thereafter, White went on an industry-sponsored trip to Hawke's Bay and met Limmer for the first time. The winemaker told him he had read his story on the smelly wines and offered to help him understand reduction chemistry. Then in October of that year, White wrote an article for *Gourmet Traveler,* an Australian magazine that circulates widely in New Zealand, which laid out the case against screwcaps and Limmer's views in much more detail. White says that shortly after the story appeared, a member of the Screwcap Initiative came up to him at a meeting in Auckland and told him that what he was writing was "bollocks" and he had better stop it or he'd be ostracized by the New Zealand wine establishment. Soon the wine samples wineries routinely sent writers for reviews stopped coming to White, and at the end of the year the *Dominion Post* informed him that his column was being dropped.

Although he could no longer get published in New Zealand, White was still able to sell stories to wine publications abroad, particularly in Britain, where there were some skeptical observers. In June 2004, White published a short story in *Decanter* magazine, and the following month he did a much more detailed one for the *World of Fine Wine,* which quoted Limmer extensively. The subhead written by the editors summed up White's case well: "It should be increasingly clear by now that screwcaps aren't all they've been cracked up to be. A growing body of evidence suggests that they're as potentially faulty, albeit in different ways, as either corks or synthetic stoppers, and as much a downward spiral as a glorious revolution."

While the New Zealand wine establishment did not take on Limmer because of his prestige in both winemaking and science, White was fair game. Not only was he frozen out, as threatened, stories began to circulate widely that he was a shill for cork companies. Charges were loosely thrown around in both New Zealand and Australia that White must be in the pay of the cork industry. He defended himself from those kinds of allegations in the very first sentence of the article in the *World of Fine Wine*: "Before I dig myself any deeper into this hornet's nest, let me declare that I have absolutely no preference for cork over screwcap." White in his writings has never specifically endorsed cork, but rather simply raised questions about screwcaps.

Doubts about the closure were also being expressed in other respected quarters, although not as loudly as by Limmer and White. The most esteemed critic is Australia's Brian Croser, the *Decanter* Man of the Year in 2004 and a universally respected winemaker with more than thirty vintages in his cellar. After losing control of Petaluma—the winery he founded— in a hostile takeover battle in 2001, Croser started Tapanappa, which many are already predicting will become one of the world's great wine estates. He purchased the thirty-two-year-old Cabernet Sauvignon and Shiraz vines of the Whalebone Vineyard in Wrattonbully near the northern boundary of Coonawarra and gets Chardonnay grapes from the Croser family's thirty-year-old Tiers Vineyard in the Piccadilly Valley. In 2006, he also planted a new Pinot Noir vineyard in the Fleurieu Peninsula on the edge of the Great Southern Ocean. The winery is a joint venture by Croser and two French partners, Bollinger Champagne and Jean-Michel Cazes, owner of Bordeaux's Château Lynch-Bages. Tapanappa bottles all its wines with corks.

After studying agriculture in Australia and working for the wine company Thomas Hardy & Sons, Croser went to UC Davis in 1972 to undertake the master's program in viticulture and enology. In those early days of California wine, he learned as much outside the classroom from people such as André Tchelistcheff at Beaulieu Vineyard, who tried to hire him away from his Australian employer, as he did in the Davis lecture halls. Shortly after returning home, Croser started Petaluma, a wine consulting and research business that he named after a town in Sonoma County. He wrote his thesis at Davis on the measurement of sulfides in wine and, when he returned home, introduced copper fining to Australia as a way to remove them. Few winemakers know their sulfide chemistry any better.

Croser, who is currently deputy chancellor at the University of Adelaide, has always leaned toward academia, and in 1976 he set up a wine program at Australia's Riverina College. As part of his money-raising efforts there, he approached ACI, the company that then had the license for Stelvin screwcaps and had done the earlier studies of the closure. ACI agreed to help fund him if he would do tests with wines under screwcaps. Croser thought it was a reasonable request and was also interested to see how the closure performed. So in 1977 and 1978, Croser bottled four white wines, Chardonnay, Riesling, Sauvignon Blanc, and Gewürztraminer, and two red Shirazes, under both cork and screwcaps. The first year he made a particularly large amount of Gewürztraminer because his daughter Lucy was born in 1977, and he wanted to have lots of it around for her in future years. Looking back on wines from those two vintages, Croser says today, "When they were young, the Stelvin wines were more closed and marginally stinky compared to those under cork." He says he had a high degree of failure among wines under cork, but blames that on the low-quality ones he used. "When they held, the bottles with cork were wonderful. There is a complexity you get from cork—when the cork is behaving itself—that you don't get with Stelvin."

Over the years, Croser has tasted the Gewürztraminer made for his daughter many times. When I asked him to compare those under cork with those under screwcap, he replied, "The ones under Stelvin have a vibrant yellow color with no sign of browning, smell like canned pineapple, but are slightly metallic. They are simple. The ones under cork have a much more complex aroma, more spice, and a deeper color."

Croser left Riverina in 1978 and turned his consulting company Petaluma into a winery, which soon became one of Australia's most highly regarded. Based on the testing he had just completed, Croser decided to use only cork at his own winery. Says he, "I left convinced that cork matures wine properly. With Stelvin, there is a different kind of maturation."

Croser does his best to stay out of the line of fire between the various factions in the closure wars. "If you say anything in favor of cork, you are immediately ostracized, isolated, and accused of being in the pay of cork interests." But he extensively reads wine research papers and is familiar with Limmer's writings, which he says are founded on the basics of wine chemistry. Unfortunately, those articles are not well understood by winemakers, much less by winery owners. "You need to understand chemistry to understand Limmer," he says. "Chemists have got to take back this discussion from the fanatics. This whole discussion should be about the interaction of oxygen and wine in the aging process."

The Australian winemaker is clear on one point: "Oxygen is important in the development of red wine both in barrel and in bottle. I can't tell you exactly what happens with the cork during bottle aging, and that is one of the huge gaps in our knowledge. But that's being ignored by the passionate Stelvin advocates."

Croser is particularly interested in recent research showing that oxygen comes out of the cellular structure of the cork quite slowly and at a diminishing rate over a fairly long time. "If you let a little bit of air into the bottle over a long time, oxygen can play a cementing role in the development of the wine," he says. "I very strongly believe that some oxygen is a necessary part of wine aging and wine holding."

Even though he introduced copper fining to Australian winemaking more than thirty years ago, Croser is now concerned about the excessive and almost routine use of it by winemakers using screwcaps, who see it as a simple way to avoid reduction. For starters, heavy application of copper before bottling does not guarantee that smelly odors won't develop later. In addition, copper fining can have the unintended consequence of stripping wines of attractive aromas. Croser says he has been using copper fining less and less in his own winemaking.

Other leading winemakers share that point of view. Paul Draper at Ridge Vineyards in California told me that he was opposed to copper fining because it was a step away from the natural winemaking he practices. At a time when consumers, as well as wine critics, are demanding natural wines with little, if any, intervention by winemakers, extensive and routine copper fining seems to be going in the wrong direction.

Australia's Terry Lee, who now splits his time in retirement between Gallo and the boards of two organizations that fund and undertake grape and wine research in Australia, shares many of Croser's views. Lee says Limmer has put forth a "rational hypothesis" for what may be happening in wines under screwcap. At the same time, he believes much more research needs to be done and adds that only recently have some analytical tools become available that will help do those studies. Lee says the whole topic of what happens between the bottling of the wine and the consumer opening it has been a "neglected area of wine science."

Like Croser, Lee says the research should start with studies on the impact of oxygen on the development of wine in the bottle. Some research done at AWRI in the 1970s showed that red wines sealed in totally airtight ampoules for long periods underwent flavor changes. A 2005 AWRI study of wines aged in ampoules also reported serious redox problems with sulfurlike odors. So preliminary evidence seems to indicate that a totally hermetic situation is not ideal for wine development. And even AWRI's Peter Godden, a screwcap advocate, in May 2006 told a London meeting, "I don't think zero permeation is ideal for many, if any, wines. I wouldn't use such a closure to seal my wines."

Lee, like Croser, is critical of the deteriorating tone of the closure debate, saying that conferences of screwcap advocates sometimes remind him of religious revival meetings. Lee adds, "Too many people are taking sides and then grabbing hold of any bit of information that seems to justify their position."

From his perch in the Napa Valley, Eric Herve of ETS Labs told me after reviewing Limmer's thesis, "Anybody with some understanding of sulfur-compounds chemistry and reduction reactions would agree he totally makes sense. Anybody who has some knowledge of wine sulfur compounds knows it not only makes sense but also is predicable. In the wine industry, it is amazing to see how innovations can sometimes be quickly adopted on a wide scale, without being adequately tested first."

Britain's Jamie Goode, a wine writer with a Ph.D. in plant biology, says, "Most people would now agree that a degree of oxygen transmission is needed for the successful development of wine in bottle." Limmer is perhaps finally being heard.

The drumbeats about possible problems with screwcaps are certainly not as great today as those condemning cork. But some of the strongest supporters of screwcaps are beginning to raise the kinds of questions that Limmer and White were alone in asking earlier.

One surprising critic is John Hancock, the winemaker at Trinity Hill who was the Hawke's Bay representative to the Marlborough screwcap group and a strong early supporter of that closure. He had a cork disaster with his 2000 Chardonnay, when he had a 20 percent cork failure and lost two thousand cases. Yet at a press luncheon in December 2004, he said, "Our experience with screwcap is, frankly, that they reduce the quality of our better quality wines." As a result, Hancock continues using cork for his best wines. In 2006, he bottled 70 percent of his production with screwcaps and the other 30 percent with Diam, the agglomerated cork. When I talked with him in September 2006, Hancock told me of his doubts about screwcaps, saying, "I don't think screwcaps are the be-all and end-all for every wine."

Another unexpected critic was Brent Marris, one of the early supporters of the New Zealand Screwcap Initiative. At the end of 2004, he was chairman of the judges at the annual Air New Zealand Wine Awards. In his comments after the event he wrote, "Some obvious concerns were that too many wines were showing sulphides that were under screwcap. Something to watch."

In the *Wine Front Monthly*, Australian Campbell Mattinson wrote, "This is the article I never wanted to write—about screwcaps. It's a negative article. . . . In my mind, screwcaps are a glorious trend. Or they were—until I noticed, and heard of, significant variation between newly released bottles—variation that is not related to storage conditions." He complained in particular about a bottle of Hunter Shiraz under screwcap that "reeked of smelly reductive, rubbery scents." He admitted he had been hearing for years about how the reduction problem was not in the closure but with the winemaker who wasn't doing his job right, but felt that argument was starting to wear thin.

Paul Mooney is the winemaker at Mission Estate Winery, New Zealand's oldest winery, dating back to 1851 when French missionaries founded it. Mooney produces seventy thousand cases a year and has probably tested more closures than any other winemaker in the country—or maybe in any country. Mooney used natural corks for many years; then he tried Supreme Corq synthetics. He tested Altec, then used the technical cork Two plus Two, which had two disks at each end, rather than one. He tried Amorim's Twin Tops and most recently was the first winemaker in New Zealand to use Diam. Mooney has kept careful notes of all his tests, which he read to me as we sat at wooden table outside his Hawke's Bay winery. It was a tale of disappointment after disappointment.

Mooney in 2006 reluctantly moved most of his production to screwcap. The reality of the New Zealand marketplace today is that it's hard to sell wines without a screwcap. You can't fight the market, and the wine-consuming public is demanding them. "The screwcap guys have done a fantastic job and got all the wine writers behind them. Everyone bought into it," says Mooney. "Now a lot of winemakers are wondering about these reductive qualities, even though they're not talking about it in public. While winemakers know there are some problems with the wines, the public loves them because the convenience is wonderful."

The International Wine Challenge in London is the world's largest wine competition with some nine thousand wines. For years organizers such as Robert Joseph protested loudly about the high incidence of corked wines, which was usually at least 5 percent and sometimes even higher. At the 2006 show, however, the judges had a new complaint. While 4.4 percent of bottles showed signs of cork taint, 2.2 percent were suffering from rotten-egg or onion odors caused by reduction. Wrote Jonathan Ray, the *Daily Telegraph*'s wine correspondent, "In my mind screwcaps are brilliant. They have eliminated almost all cork taint, but this shows they are not infallible."

CHAPTER TWENTY

France Remains Hesitant

*Michel Laroche turned against cork
after a test in which only three bottles
out of forty met his standards.*

Screwcap advocates around the world long said they will know they have won the battle over how to close a wine bottle when the first of Bordeaux's famed Classified Growths of 1855 announces it's moving to screwcap. Despite recent problems of overproduction and declining domestic consumption, France remains the North Star that winemakers around the globe look to for direction in many things, including bottle closures.

On April 1, 2007, Bibendum, a British wine merchant, began distributing one thousand cases with screwcaps of 2004 Les Tourelles de Longueville, the second wine of Château Pichon-Longueville Baron, a classified growth. Second wines are made with estate grapes that are not considered good enough to go into the winery's top product. The winery annually produces about twelve thousand cases of Les Tourelles. Bibendum had been pressuring the château to let it try screwcaps. The wine will be used exclusively in restaurants and bars. Bottles of Les Tourelles sold in wineshops will still have a cork in them. It's not a First Growth, and it's not the entire production. But it may be a beginning.

In France, less than 4 percent of wines carry screwcaps. Nonetheless, three high-end wineries became the Three Musketeers for the new closure. One is Domaine Paul Blanck & Fils, a family-run winery in Kientzheim, Alsace, specializing in Grand Cru white wines. Among those top-quality products are four Riesling, two Pinot Gris, two Gewürztraminer, and one Pinot Noir. Although the family has been making wines in Alsace since 1610, it only got its name on a winery in 1975 when Marcel and Bernard, the winemaking sons of Paul Blanck, who was also a *vigneron,* took over a winery with only four hectares (9.9 acres) of vines. By the time they handed over management of the property in 1985 to their respective sons Frédéric and Bernard, the property had now grown to twenty hectares (49.4 acres). Frédéric is now in charge of winemaking, while Bernard runs the business side. The vineyards have expanded to thirty-six hectares (89 acres), with one-third of its eighteen-thousand-case annual production being Grand Cru wines. Andrew Jefford in his guide *The New France* gave Paul Blanck & Fils a star rating, writing, "The overall style is one of elegance and purity; after a sometimes steely, inarticulate youth, the wines age well."

Although Frédéric has never had a disaster with cork, he began being unhappy with its performance in the late 1990s. The occasional bottle of corked wine was a nuisance, but he was more concerned with the inconsistency of his wines under cork. "After a year or two in the bottle, if you had twenty bottles of the same wine in front of you, they were actually twenty different wines. Some were excellent, while others were only okay," he says. "I wanted to have greater consistency with my wines."

The winemaker received his wine training in Alsace, but in the early 1990s he became a big fan of Australian wine and started going there at least once a year to learn what was happening. He usually went during Australia's harvest and crush in the spring before things got really busy at home. Blanck naturally tended to visit Riesling makers in areas such as the Clare Valley, but he also liked the Yarra Valley, just outside Melbourne. A favorite stop was at Jeffrey Grosset in the Clare Valley because of the international reputation of his Riesling.

At home Frédéric was already experimenting with alternative closures by 2000, when he sealed a few test bottles with plastic corks. But he quickly decided he didn't like them because he didn't think his wine would age well under them and they seemed like only a poor imitation of cork. As a result, he never sold any wine with synthetic closures and soon dropped the tests.

During his 2001 visit to Australia, however, Blanck heard about the Clare Valley Screwcap Initiative and that New Zealanders were going to follow up with an even more ambitious screwcap program. He says Grosset was more than happy to share the results of his testing and the favorable reaction he was getting in the marketplace. Grosset even found some old bottles with screwcaps from the Australian experience in the 1970s, including Pewsey Vale Riesling, which he shared with his French visitor. Blanck had heard that an Alsatian winery had been part of the Stelvin experiments in the 1960s, but it was now out of business and the old bottles were all gone.

Blanck returned to Alsace anxious to start bottling at least part of his production under screwcaps. Since he had studied the recent Australian tests so closely, he felt he didn't need to do his own. Following the Clare Valley model, Blanck picked out one of his better wines, a Cru level, although not a Grand Cru, to be his first sold under screwcap. In the fall of 2001, Paul Blanck & Fils bottled one thousand cases of Rosenbourg Riesling with screwcaps. The wines went on sale in September 2002. Simultaneously, Blanck began putting his Grand Crus partially under screwcap.

Paul Blanck & Fils in 2006 did 60 percent of its production in screwcaps. The market acceptance, says Frédéric, was good in the United States and Britain, and after a slow start also in Germany and Scandinavia. The winery now exports 95 percent of its screwcap wines.

The French market, though, has been slow to embrace the alternative closures. When I asked Frédéric when he would be 100 percent under screwcap, he replied, "As fast as I can. If I could do it next year, I would. But I have to take into account the French market, which is still twenty-five percent of our sales. France and Belgium are our two toughest markets for screwcaps."

For the past four years, Frédéric has regularly been doing comparative tastings of his wines under both screwcaps and cork. His conclusion to date: "The screwcap bottles are better; they have much more aroma."

André Lurton, a pillar of the Bordeaux establishment, shocked the French wine trade in 2004 when he became the first producer to put a white Bordeaux Cru Classé, Château Couhins-Lurton, under screwcap. At the same time he also bottled two other lesser whites, Château La Louvière and Château Bonnet, with that closure.

The Lurton push to screwcap started with the younger generation.

While André Lurton is running the family's heritage properties in Bordeaux, sons Jacques and François have set up a company that bears their names, which is making wines around the world and challenging old traditions. They are now producing wine in the Languedoc region of France as well as in Argentina, Chile, Spain, and Uruguay. Half of their production is bottled with screwcaps, 30 percent with natural corks, and 20 percent with plastic corks.

In the early 1980s, while he was still studying accounting, François Lurton worked for a short time for a small winery in Switzerland near Geneva that was making Fendant wine sealed with a screwcap. When he returned home, François brought some of those wines, put them in his cellar, and promptly forgot all about them. After a meeting with some Stelvin representatives in 1988, though, he remembered them. When he opened a few, he was pleasantly surprised. "I thought they would be oxidized by then, but they weren't. In fact, they were very good," he recalls.

François asked the Stelvin people if he could do a small experiment with some of his wines, but they said they didn't have the equipment to do it. So he again forgot about screwcaps as he went about setting up a new business with his brother. At first they were flying winemakers, consulting in far-flung places from Moldavia to Mendoza, but they soon began buying up property and starting their own wineries.

Shortly after the turn of the new century and after noticing that New Zealand and Australian winemakers were making significant advances into screwcaps, François again remembered those old Swiss bottles, which had by now been under screwcaps for nearly two decades. He wanted to convince his father to give screwcaps a try, so he pulled out some of the wines and also some 1992 bottles of the family's Château Bonnet that had been bottled in early 1993 under both natural cork and screwcap. In September 2001, the two Lurton brothers, their father, the head winemaker plus his assistant, and two board members gathered in the cellars of Château Bonnet to see how the wines had aged. First they tried the two-decades-old Swiss wines. "Some of them were a little tired, and the quality of the old Swiss screwcaps had not been good," says François. But for wines that old, the group was still impressed. The bottles of nine-year-old Château Bonnet were very different. Those in cork were "dead, totally oxidized," says François, while those under screwcap had "lost some of their freshness, but were not oxidized." After the test, the company's top management unanimously wanted to switch at least some of its dry white wines to screwcap. The following vintage, the winery offered their wines in both screwcap and natural cork. Today more than half of the sales of Lurton dry whites are in screwcap.

François Lurton now feels confident that he understands how white wines will age under screwcap, and he is comfortable continuing to push for more and more of his wines to be under that closure. The red wines, however, are another story. "With the reds, we don't have the experience," François states candidly. For the past few years wherever in the world the Lurton brothers are making red wines, they are bottling some in screwcap and some in cork to see how they will age. They have already started testing these at six-month intervals, but have not to date seen any significant trends. "Sometimes the cork is better; sometimes the screwcap is better," he says.

Looking out at the global consumer market for wine, Lurton says that his experience varies greatly from country to country. The inexpensive end of the market in Britain and Scandinavia has already accepted noncork closures, and it's only a question of whether plastic or screwcap is better. In Argentina, Chile, and Spain he says, "It is very difficult to sell wine with screwcaps." In Argentina, for example, he exports half his total production and all of that is in screwcap. But in the domestic Argentine market, all but one wine are still in natural cork. The situation for his Chilean wines is similar—exports in screwcaps, but domestic in either natural cork or plastic. The Lurton brothers now send their wines from Languedoc to Britain, Scandinavia, and the United States in screwcap, but domestic sales are still in bottles with natural corks.

Although his brother is primarily responsible for winemaking, François stays familiar with what's happening there. He warns that vintners cannot just put a different cap on a bottle without adjusting their winemaking regimes. "From the beginning of vinification to the end, wines have to be treated differently," he says. He adds that wineries also have to be much more careful in both the bottling and the transportation of screwcaps because of the danger of damaging the seal. "It's a bigger problem than screwcap advocates admit," he says.

In the Chablis section of northern Burgundy, winemaker Michel Laroche, a demanding perfectionist, is pushing screwcaps the most aggressively. His family winery dates back to 1850, but when he took over management in 1967, it had just six hectares (14.8 acres) of vines. Today it owns 130 hectares (321.2 acres). He has also expanded its holdings to southern France, Chile, and South Africa and even did some experiments in California. Located in a former monastery appropriately named

"Place of Obedience," Domaine Laroche's most prized properties are its two Chablis Grand Cru: Réserve de L'Obédience Les Blanchots and Les Clos. Always trying to push the quality not only of his own wines but also those of Chablis in general, Laroche was the driving force behind the formation in September 2000 of the Union des Grands Crus de Chablis, which set new quality standards for its thirteen members that own the top 2 percent of Chablis vineyards.

At the turn of the new century, Laroche was also unhappy with corks. At his own wineshop in Chablis and in internal tastings, he found 4–5 percent of his bottles adversely affected by TCA and another 6–10 percent prematurely oxidized. "We were tired of being disappointed when we open gems from our cellars only to find that they have been destroyed by what is effectively a packaging fault," he says. "More than ten percent of our production was reaching the client in an inferior state." He put some of his wines under Nomacorc plastic stoppers, which he felt sealed as well as natural cork, but at the same time was looking for something better.

Then a tasting in April 2004 of the 2001 vintage of Réserve de L'Obédience Les Blanchots, one of his two best wines, sent the winemaker over the top. Laroche and three staff members opened forty identical bottles that were all under cork. The four judged fifteen bottles to be totally unacceptable, while twenty-two were considered acceptable for sale but showed wide bottle variation. "The most striking result was that only three bottles reflected optimum quality—three out of forty," he laments. In view of that level of failure, Laroche decided not to release the wine to the market. It was a major financial hit, but the damage to his reputation would have been even greater.

Laroche, though, was already taking action. For the 2002 vintage, he bottled 10 percent of his two Grands Crus as well as 5 percent of his Premier Cru Chablis wines in screwcap. He decided to go out with his best wines to make sure consumers realized he was making the move to protect his top wines, rather than trying to save money on closures. He also believed that winemakers such as he, who know their wines best, should make the decision on closures, not marketing experts or even consumers. "Would an architect accept that buyers decree which type of clay should be used for their houses?" he asks.

The winemaker, though, is careful in handling his screwcap wines, saying that they require a different style of winemaking. Laroche maintains that if you bottle the same wine on the same day under both cork and screwcap, "you risk reduction." He adds, "Bottling with screwcap requires the wine to be more mature because the bottle is completely sealed." It's like cooking, he says. "When you believe the wine is ready by tasting it, you bottle."

After being the Old World's representative at the International Screwcap Symposium in November 2004, Laroche became an even stronger screwcap advocate. He returned to Chablis determined to keep pushing the envelope on closures, while recognizing the French market would be slow to leave cork.

Laroche in 2005 moved his entire American exports to screwcap at the urging of his importer. He now sells only screwcaps in Scandinavia, Britain, Ireland, Canada, and the United States. In fiscal 2006, Domaine Laroche bottled 60 percent of its production of 750,000 cases in screwcaps, an increase from 3 percent in fiscal 2004, and 32 percent in fiscal 2005. At his wineshop in Chablis, he sells 80 percent in screwcap.

Laroche wishes he could sell more wines in France in screwcaps, but as the master of his Domaine says, "People are inherently suspicious of change." In 2006, only 5 percent of Laroche wines sold in France were in screwcaps. Up to now he has offered the French a choice of screwcap or cork, but he is contemplating taking a leap into the unknown and offering one quality wine only in screwcap. He strongly believes the breakthrough in his native country will start with three-star restaurants offering screwcaps. "Then consumers will be brave enough to put the bottle on the table when they have friends at home for dinner."

The most sacred wine properties of France are along the two-lane D2 road north of the city of Bordeaux. There can be found the elegant châteaux that generally open their doors for visitors only by appointment. Undoubtedly, some testing of new closures is going on behind tightly guarded gates, but little news of that is getting out. It is known that Château Margaux in 2004 put two cases of the 2002 vintage of its second wine, Pavillon Rouge, under screwcaps as a test to see how it aged. No results have, though, been announced. At the time winemaker Paul Pontallier told Britain's *Decanter*, "I can certainly see the benefits of screwcaps for whites and would be very interested in using them for young reds that will be drunk within five years. But we are far from knowing how red wines will age under screwcaps after twenty-five, thirty, even fifty years, which is essential for us at Margaux."

A few miles up the road at Château Lafite Rothschild, Charles Chevallier, who has been directing winemaking for nearly a quarter century, is confident he has a system that guarantees his consumers quality cork to match his quality wine.

Lafite has records showing that King Louis XIV drank its wine from a bottle at his palace in Versailles in the early eighteenth century. Those bottles were almost certainly sealed with a cork stopper. The winery, though, did not sell the majority of its wine that way until the late 1920s after Baron Philippe de Rothschild at nearby Château Mouton Rothschild introduced the system of estate bottling with the statement *mis en bouteille au château* (bottled at the chateau) on bottles as a way to fight counterfeit wine.

The oldest wines in the Lafite cellar date back to 1797, but the corks on them haven't been changed since Chevallier took over management of the winery. "There's too big a danger of exposing the wines to air during the process of changing the corks," he says. "You'd do more harm than good in doing it." The stoppers were changed several times in the past, but he doubts that will ever be done again in the future. Other old Lafite bottles are examined regularly, and the corks are sometimes changed after thirty or forty years. If the level of wine in the bottle is high, however, the cellar master assumes the cork is holding well and leaves the wine alone.

Chevallier makes a distinction between wines to be cellared and those for current consumption. He cites Beaujolais Nouveau as the perfect example of a wine that's meant to be drunk young and could easily be sealed with a plastic cork or a screwcap. "It goes on sale in November and is considered dead two months later," says Chevallier. "Why bother with cork for that kind of wine?" And while some winemakers recommend putting all whites under screwcap, he cautions against it, noting that "high-quality Chardonnays" and certainly all Sauternes should be considered cellared wines. For those, Chevallier says, he "wouldn't change the system we have."

Lafite buys some 1.2 million corks annually from Italy, France, Spain, and Portugal. A decade ago, it significantly tightened up its cork-purchasing system, demanding much more information from its roughly ten suppliers. "They now have to provide very detailed reports to show us there is no TCA in their corks," he says. Chevallier looks for corks that are particularly dense as a result of growing slowly in a hot climate. His favorites come from Sardinia and Catalonia, but he can't get enough from those locations, so he brings in some from other areas.

Lafite made a significant change in its corks two decades ago, shortening them from 54 mm (2.1 in.) to 49 mm (1.9 in.). Chevallier had grown concerned that the corks were too long and could be a risk for contamination. The neck of the bottle is about 50 mm long before it starts to widen out at the point known as the shoulders. So the bottom of the cork was actually sticking in the air, rather than forming a tight seal against the side of the bottle. "We shortened the cork to get a better seal," Chevallier says. "Everyone thinks we did it to save money on corks, so it was not a good move from the point of view of marketing. But that's the truth."

Chevallier says he has no idea how much corked Lafite reaches consumers, while insisting it is "undoubtedly very small." Nonetheless, "We want to know if there is a problem." He says consumers with a bad bottle should return it to the winery with the cork and the wine still in the bottle, if possible. Each bottle is coded, so it's possible to trace the source of the cork. "If we get the bottle back fast, we can do the analyses and see whether the problem is TCA or something else."

For now, at least, Chevallier is confident in his system of cork selection and just as happy to let others do the testing on how wines will age under other closures. "One doesn't know what the evolution of a bottle of Lafite would be under another closure in fifty or sixty or seventy years. That's a risk I can't take."

Tim Johnston, who runs Juveniles, a popular wine bar and bistro at 47 rue Richelieu in Paris, thinks that other French winemakers should join the pioneers and embrace screwcaps. After starting in the wine business in Britain four decades ago, he moved to France in the 1980s and has witnessed at firsthand the troubles of the French wine business caused by declining domestic consumption and growing foreign competition. He says winemakers who used to say haughtily that they couldn't provide him any wine because all their production was under allocation are now coming around and begging him to take some cases.

Johnston, a big fan of screwcaps, in November 2006 bottled his house brand of Beaujolais Nouveau in screwcaps and quickly sold out. He dismisses synthetics out of hand, saying consumers are tired of breaking their corkscrews trying to get them out of bottles.

With the insight of an insider who is also an outsider, Johnston says that if the French do not move to screwcap, it will be "catastrophic" for the country's already badly weakened wine sector. "Some people say the market is not ready for this," he adds. "But if they don't get a move on, France will once again be left behind."

Slowly, ever so slowly however, some wineries are starting to follow the three French pioneers. On Bordeaux's right bank, the small St.-Émilion winery Magnaudeix now releases part of the production of two Grand Cru reds, Château Vieux Larmande and Vieux Château Pelletan, under

Stelvin. In February 2007, Burgundy's Maison Jean-Claude Boisset became the first winery in Burgundy to use screwcaps on a Grand Cru red. It had been bottling some of its lesser wines with that closure since 2003. The winery sealed half of its fifty-case production of 2005 Chambertin, a Pinot Noir, with screwcaps and half with corks. The wine retails for about $200 a bottle.

MESSAGE IN A BOTTLE: NEW ZEALAND

On September 12, 2006, I flew into Hawke's Bay, New Zealand, to do research for this book. My first night there Alan Limmer, the owner and wine-maker at Stonecroft Wines and the country's leading wine chemist, invited me to join him for dinner. We were scheduled to have a formal interview two days later, and this was going to be just a comfortable evening to get to know each other. He picked me up at the motel where I was staying, and we drove to the Thai Silk, a restaurant he liked.

The restaurant was nearly empty when we arrived. At the door Limmer showed the hostess two bottles of his own wine and asked her if it was okay if he brought them. She said that was fine and took the wine from him. Limmer and I went to a table at the far side of the restaurant, where we could have some privacy.

We had just started looking at the menu when the waitress came to the table with the two bottles already opened. One was a 2004 Stonecroft Old Vine Gewürztraminer, and the other was a 2003 Stonecroft Syrah. Since Limmer is a well-known critic of screwcaps, I joshingly told him that I noticed the wines didn't have screwcaps. He pointed with pride to the Gewürztraminer, saying that it went well with spicy Thai food. He added that the 2004 was a partic-ularly good vintage and was the last year he had used natural cork as a closure. He is now sealing his bottles with Diam, an agglomerated cork.

Limmer poured a small amount of Gewürztraminer into a glass and smelled it. He then said sadly but firmly, "It's corked." He tasted the wine and repeated, "It's corked." Then he poured a small amount for me. There was no doubt; the wine was badly corked.

The winemaker finally asked the waitress to bring the wine list and ordered a bottle of Montana Gewürztraminer to go with dinner along with his Syrah. After that minor change of plans, Limmer and I had an animated din-ner conversation about current wine research around the world and the future of closures.

Four nights later, I had dinner with Wayne Edwards, a New Zealand sales representative for Oeneo, the maker of Diam. We dined at the Elevation Café in the Waitakere Ranges outside Auckland, as the city lights shone bright in the distance in front of Hauraki Gulf. It was strictly a business affair, and we were quickly discussing the future of closures.

When the waiter came by with the wine list, I left the choice to Edwards, figuring he would undoubtedly know more about his country's wine than I. We each said what we were going to order, and then Edwards asked if I minded a 2002 Trinity Hill Chardonnay. I had visited the winery just the day before and met winemaker John Hancock, so I agreed that was a fine choice.

When the waiter brought the wine, I was a little surprised to see a cork because Hancock had been one of the early advocates of screwcaps, but I also knew he had developed some misgivings about them. The waiter poured a small amount for Edwards, who said the wine was fine. Then the waiter poured a full glass for me. As soon as I tasted the Chardonnay, I had a flashback to the wine from a few nights before. The varietal was different, but there was some of that same musty taste, although not nearly as strong.

I immediately told Edwards that I thought something was wrong with the wine. He then took another sip from his glass and agreed. It wasn't terrible, but just not right either.

Edwards called the waiter back and said we thought the wine was corked. The waiter quickly brought another bottle of the same wine, and this one was wonderful. Since the two bottles were opened, both Edwards and I tasted from each, and there was no doubt about the difference between the two wines. One was tired and flat, while the other was fresh and lively.

During the rest of the research trip through New Zealand and Australia, I lugged the two corked bottles around in my suitcase, planning to have them analyzed when I got back to the United States. After I got home, I sent a sample of each wine to ETS Labs in the Napa Valley, asking for a TCA analysis. Cost: $120 per test. A day after the samples arrived, I received an e-mail report of the analysis. The Stonecroft Gewürztraminer had a 2,4,6-TCA level of 16.2 ng/L or nanograms per liter; the Trinity Hill Chardonnay level was 5.3. The Gewürtz was badly tainted; the Chardonnay much less so but still a corked bottle.

CHAPTER TWENTY-ONE

American Experiments with Closures

*Ridge Vineyards' Paul Draper
has a soft spot for both cork
and his dog Bodhi.*

In thousands of wineries around the world, owners are conducting countless experiments with closures. Even the most conservative vintners are trying out different ways to seal wine bottles in the hope of finding the perfect solution that will at the same time be accepted by consumers and also improve the quality of their wines. Here are four such experiments at leading American wineries.

RIDGE VINEYARDS,
SANTA CRUZ MOUNTAINS, CALIFORNIA

Paul Draper of California's Ridge Vineyards is perhaps the most respected American vintner. He is one of only three Americans to be named Winemaker of the Year by the British magazine *Decanter,* the other two being André Tchelistcheff and Robert Mondavi. Draper's Monte Bello Cabernet is an icon wine, and the 1971 vintage was the winner of the thirtieth anniversary reenactment of the Paris Tasting against top French and California wines. As would be expected from a philosophy major from Stanford University, Draper is as comfortable around ideas as he is around grapes. With tongue firmly planted in cheek, Bonny Doon's Randall Grahm calls him "Saint Paul."

Ridge uses only natural corks from Spain and Portugal. Eric Baugher, the winemaker at Monte Bello, has set up a rigorous inspection program. Both coated and uncoated samples of cork lots from three or four suppliers are soaked in a top-quality white wine for eight hours and then the wine is blind-tasted. Baugher looks not only for TCA but also for unwanted flavors from the original washing or from the coating material. Samples also undergo outside analysis, and if there is less than 1 part per trillion TCA and no negative taste from the soaking, the corks are accepted and Ridge orders them. After arriving in California, the corks are again subjected to random sampling, soaking, and tasting and can still be rejected. Ridge once shipped back a batch of some fifty thousand corks branded with the Ridge logo after it failed that final test. Based on bottles opened in its tasting room and at off-site events, Draper has concluded that Ridge has a TCA incidence of less than 3 percent.

Beginning with the 2001 vintage, the winery has bottled two to four cases of each vintage of wines under several closures, and since 1992 the Ridge staff has quietly been running experiments with a variety of closures. The first experiments involved Ridge's three top red wines: Monte Bello Cabernet and two Zinfandels, Lytton Springs and Geyserville. Several cases of each wine were sealed with both natural cork and a molded-plastic cork. The synthetic performed poorly, and after several years the wine was so badly oxidized that the Ridge staff stopped testing that closure. Since then it has added different types of screwcaps, and most recently a glass stopper joined the testing. The closure experiments are tasted several times a year.

Draper and Baugher have a strong affinity for natural cork, which in the experiments to date seems to help a wine develop greater complexity, particularly age-worthy ones such as the Monte Bello. Draper is not closing his mind to new developments and is interested in how his wines will age under new closures as they are developed. At the same time, he is not rushing to change without extensive study, believing that "if you care about whether your wine improves in the bottle, then you should be doing experiments to see what happens under different closures. You shouldn't just jump to a new closure without testing it for at least five years."

Draper invited me to participate in one of the closure tastings with him, Baugher, and Karen Schmidt, the Ridge lab director. All are members of the regular Ridge tasting team. Their standard practice is that with an even number of wines, the judges give half the wines a positive and half a negative rating. If an uneven number are tasted, one is given a neutral. In this tasting there was an uneven number of wines. All the wines had been taken out of their original bottles and placed in either clear bottles or decanters. On each container was a piece of masking tape with the name of the closure and another piece of tape over that to hide that identity. The tasting took place in the old redwood-paneled production tasting room around a rectangular table. While they were judging, the three tasters sipped from bottles of Crystal Geyser mineral water and nibbled on pieces of baguette. Draper particularly likes to dip the bread in olive oil, and the brand that day was San Giuliano Alghero extra virgin.

The first wine was a 2004 Santa Cruz Chardonnay that had been bottled only three months before. The judges were told only that one was sealed with cork, one with a screwcap with a tin liner, and one with a glass stopper. Baugher noted that the wine had been aged in oak for ten months. Chardonnay, he said, would likely show up the differences in closures more quickly than red wines because it is more delicate.

After simply smelling the three wines, Draper was shocked by the differences in the three glasses in front of him, saying, "These are already three different wines in only three months. I'm astonished."

Following the tasting of the wines, the tasters then began to read their notes one after another, which included many favorable phrases such as "long finish," "great acid," and "creamy." There were also some negative comments, with both Schmidt and Baugher saying that one wine was "no longer fresh."

When the results were announced, two of the three had picked as their favorite the wine with the cork, while one selected the glass closure. Overall the order of preference was cork, screwcap, and then glass.

Baugher, though, had strong views on the glass closure, saying, "There's too much air penetration. I don't think it makes a good enough seal." Since this was the first trial with the glass stopper, he said he was anxious to see what the wine would be like after one year in the bottle.

Draper concluded that the cork had actually improved the wine in the bottle, while the screwcap had kept it the same as it had been at bottling. He concluded, "This is the first time I've tried whites under various closures, and I was not expecting to see such differences so quickly. I find that fascinating."

As the first red wines were being poured, I asked Draper about the old saw of the wine business that there are no great wines but only great bottles of wine because of the bottle variation caused by the different quality of cork. He didn't agree with that, saying he thought the differences in old bottles were primarily due to the conditions under which they had been shipped, stored, or cellared. He said that Ridge, for example, has had "very few disappointing bottles" of the award-winning 1971 Monte Bello. "Great vintages are quite consistently great," he said.

The next wine tasted was a 1992 Lytton Springs Zinfandel, which had been bottled in 1994. This was part of the first group bottled under several closures. Baugher announced that one wine was sealed with a natural cork and the other with a plastic cork. Although they were no longer testing synthetics because of their poor experimental results, a few bottles from the experiment were still in the cellar. Again comments from the tasters were both positive and negative, but with a lot of uncomplimentary views on wine identified as bottle A. Schmidt said of A, "lots of heat on the nose and a cooked taste," but said of B, "rich, chewy." Draper said A was oxidized and was not "just an old wine that's over-the-hill." He described B, on the other hand, as "fruity, complex, spicy, and complete."

When the pieces of tape were removed, no one was surprised. All three judges agreed. The A wine had been sealed with an extruded-plastic cork. The B wine had been sealed with a Portuguese cork.

The final tasting was of a 2001 Monte Bello that had been bottled in 2003 and sealed with cork, a screwcap with a tin liner, and a screwcap with a plastic liner. This was a ripe year and had the highest alcohol level, 14.2 percent, of any of the forty-four vintages of Monte Bello. Baugher explained that the plastic liner was more permeable and let in too much air. As a result, it had already been dropped from more recent tests, but it was still being included in this tasting for comparison.

As befitting Ridge's top wine, the judges were deadly serious, speaking little as they tasted. When the comments were revealed, Draper gave poor ratings to both the permeable and tight screwcaps, saying that they lacked the "complexity and depth of Monte Bello." The clear winner was the natural cork. Said Draper, "The tannins are firm, but not hard. It still needs more time, but this is the fullest and most complex wine on the table." Said Baugher as he pulled off the label of the top-rated wine: "Spanish cork. The best cork comes from Spain."

As the three judges compared the results, it had clearly been a good day for cork, which won all three flights. They were a little disappointed with the glass stopper on its first time in competition. The tin-lined screwcap received generally good marks, but there were clear doubts about whether it allowed the wine to develop its full complexity.

Draper concluded by noting the price difference between the high-quality cork, which they buy for fifty-five cents each, while screwcaps would be only thirteen and a half to fifteen cents. That is a significant cost savings for any winery and cannot lightly be dismissed. Ridge briefly entertained the idea of bottling its least expensive wine with screwcaps, while reserving corks for all the rest. In the end, though, they decided against it on the grounds that it would be an explicit message to the market that that wine was not as good.

For now, Ridge will stay with cork—but the testing goes on.

CHALONE VINEYARD, GAVILAN MOUNTAIN RANGE, CALIFORNIA

Chalone Vineyard, high in the Gavilan Mountain Range near the end of a one-lane road 140 miles south of San Francisco, was the first U.S. cult wine in the 1970s, when its Pinot Noirs and Chardonnays won a loyal band of followers. Chalone champions such as Julia Child trekked up to the mountaintop to taste its wines with Dick Graff, the Harvard music-major-turned-winemaker. Diageo, a British spirits-and-wine empire, now owns it.

Former Chalone winemaker Dan Karlsen is a blunt-talking, no-nonsense guy who started out studying science at Sonoma State University in the early 1970s and had dreams of becoming a biologist or epidemiologist. But he soon discovered that he didn't like labs or working indoors, so he switched to marine biology. He then kicked around at several jobs in the late 1970s, including starting a brewery and working as a carpenter. Karlsen got his first job at a winery at Dry Creek Vineyard in Sonoma County as a carpenter and mechanic before moving over to cellar work and becoming an assistant winemaker. In 1984, he moved to Dehlinger Winery, a boutique shop in Sonoma's Russian River area that sells its wines mainly to twenty-five hundred people on its mailing list. Pinot Noir is one of its most prized products.

In 1987, Karlsen left Dehlinger to help Taittinger, a French Champagne company, set up a California outpost in the southern Napa Valley to make first sparkling wine and then Pinot Noir. He stayed there for nine years until Augustin Huneeus, who ran Napa Valley's Franciscan winery, hired him because of his record of producing knockout Pinot Noirs. He was the winemaker at Estancia, a new producer near Soledad in the Central Coast region, which was soon making a half million cases a year. In 1998, Karlsen moved again, this time to Chalone.

During the past few years, Chalone has experimented with several closures in real time on real vintages that were sold in wine stores across the country. When Karlsen arrived at Chalone, the winery was using prestigious two-inch natural corks. These were expensive; and Karlsen soon learned, just as the winemaker at Château Lafite Rothschild had, that long corks did not actually provide a good seal. Chalone then switched to the highest-quality 1.75-inch natural corks and had great success with the 1998, 1999, and 2000 vintages.

For the 2001 vintage, the Chalone Group, which included several other wineries, switched to inexpensive grade-C corks. The whole restaurant trade suffered from the post-9/11 drop in entertainment, and management wanted to cut costs. It correctly said that the quality of cork is not determined in the market by its ability to seal a bottle but whether it looks good, and so it seemed logical that the less costly cork could do the job just as well as the more expensive ones. But within eight months of bottling, Chalone wines were beginning to show serious oxidation. First it was one bottle out of ten, then it was two in ten, and soon half the bottles were oxidized. "We began getting calls from retailers and restaurants saying that the wines were dying," recalls Karlsen.

That experience led Karlsen to look carefully at the Australian closure studies. He also read reports on the comparative advantages of natural vs. synthetic corks. He concluded that the problem with natural corks was not TCA, which is rare, but random oxidation, which is much more prevalent, and decided that a screwcap or a dense natural cork was the best closure. His personal choice was the screwcap. "The evidence all points in that direction, but who makes the decision?" Karlsen asks. "It's probably not the winemaker unless he owns the place."

For the 2002 and 2003 vintages, the Chalone Group switched to synthetic corks, trying both the Supreme Corq molded style and the Neocork extruded version. Karlsen vociferously disagreed with the decision for two reasons. The first was the Australian studies showing high oxidation with synthetics. The second was his experience with bottles at Taittinger. Champagne or sparkling-wine bottles have to be much more robust because of the intense internal pressure caused by the carbon dioxide, and at Taittinger he was in constant discussion with bottle makers and knew the shortcomings of wine bottles. Glassmaking technology is at best flawed because there are relatively large variations in the diameter of the necks. Natural cork is forgiving and can accommodate those differences because of its unique cellular structure. Synthetic cork, Karlsen argued, could not adjust that way. "I don't like cork, but if I had to choose between natural cork and synthetic, I would always choose natural," he said.

Karlsen had predicted that Chalone would go from random oxidation with natural cork to uniform oxidation with synthetic, and that is what happened in 2002 and 2003. Chalone soon started getting more complaints from the marketplace.

During the 2004 vintage Chalone was in the middle of its protracted sale to Diageo, and Karlsen had more freedom of action, so he bought dense, high-quality cork. The incidence of both TCA and oxidation fell dramatically and to an acceptable level. Karlsen's preference, though, is still not natural cork. "I would go to screwcaps in a heartbeat," he says.

CALERA WINE COMPANY, HOLLISTER, CALIFORNIA

Josh Jensen makes wine in one of the most inhospitable areas of California: a parched region outside Hollister in San Bonito County, which gets only about one-third as much rain each year as Napa and Sonoma counties. Jensen, however, found there the ingredient that winemakers in Burgundy had told him was the secret to making good Pinot Noir and Chardonnay: limestone.

Jensen grew up in Northern California, the son of a dentist, before going East to Yale University to major in history and minor in rowing. After graduating in 1966, he went to Oxford University for graduate work, majoring this time in anthropology and minoring again in rowing, participating in the fabled Oxford-Cambridge Boat Race. While living in Britain, Jensen made a long list of things that he didn't want to do in life such as teach or be a lawyer. But he eventually stopped that negative list and started to concentrate on which things had really turned him on and that he might enjoy doing for the rest of his life. One of those was wine, and he thought that since he had grown up in California, maybe he should go back there and open a winery. Says he, "I liked the culture of wine, the people, the physical work as well as the artistic element."

So after earning his master's degree at Oxford in 1968, Jensen went to Burgundy and got a job picking grapes during the harvest. He jumped in literally with both feet, and one of his jobs was stomping down the cap of fermenting wine with his feet to increase the extraction of flavor and tannins. He recalls the job was like climbing a skyscraper three stairs at a time, as he sank to midthigh into the mixture of juice, seeds, and pulp. Jensen was particularly taken with Burgundy, working the 1970 harvest for Domaine de la Romanée-Conti, the region's most famous vineyard, as well as the 1971 harvest at nearby Domaine Dujac. He also worked in the northern Rhône Valley for Château Grillet near Condrieu, which makes a wine that writer Andrew Jefford has called "the most show-stopping Viognier of all." Winemakers at various places were taken by the eager American and explained their craft to him in detail. Burgundians such as Andre Noble, the *maître de chai* at Romanée-Conti, told Jensen that their wines got their greatness from the limestone soil in which the vines grew.

Shortly before Thanksgiving 1971, Jensen returned to California with plans of making Burgundy-style wines in California in limestone vineyards. Unfortunately California soil is predominantly made up of granite and other geologic materials. But with the help of geologic maps from the California Bureau of Mines, he spent the next two years driving a yellow Volkswagen camper up and down California looking for limestone. He found none in the primary wine regions of Napa and Sonoma counties. When he did locate a deposit in other counties, it was usually at the bottom of a canyon or on a cliff, where vines could never grow. Jensen carefully looked for names of streets and hills that contained the word *lime* in either English or Spanish. Finally in 1974, about three miles from Lime Kiln Road on Mount Harlan near the farming town of Hollister, Jensen found his prized limestone formation. It was on the opposite side of the Gavilan Mountain Range from Chalone, and he paid $18,000 for 324 acres at twenty-two-hundred-foot elevation. On the property next door, which he bought eight years later, there was an abandoned thirty-foot-high limekiln dating back a century to the time when limestone was mined and kilned there to make lime. Jensen named the winery Calera, the Spanish word for limekiln.

Jensen's plan was to make Pinot Noir and Chardonnay, Burgundy's two great wines, and Viognier, which he had discovered while picking grapes in the Rhône Valley. He had been taken by Viognier's flamboyance and considered it the most aromatic and fragrant wine made anywhere. "Viognier has so much personality and exuberance," he says with his own exuberance. Viognier, though, was not being grown in California, so even before he closed on his limestone property in March 1974, Jensen paid the Foundation Plant Materials Service, a joint venture of the UC Davis wine school and the federal Department of Agriculture, $75 to import cuttings of Viognier from France. It took the bureaucrats fifteen years to get the plant material imported through quarantine and then certified to be free of disease, but by that time Jensen had already obtained some from the New York State Experimental Fruit Station in Geneva, New York.

Like many winemakers, Jensen is unhappy with the failure rate of his corks, calculating that about 5 percent of his bottles are corked. "You may get an entire case with no problems, and then the next case will have two messed-up bottles," he laments. "That's a failure rate that would never be tolerated in cosmetics or ketchup." Jensen says he buys only top-quality corks, "so it's not a question of getting better results by getting better corks."

After attending an Australian conference on Viognier in August 2002, where he heard repeatedly from his hosts about how the wine was much livelier when bottled with screwcaps, Jensen returned to California determined to bottle some of his production of some seven hundred cases of Viognier in screwcaps. His staff thought he was crazy, but Jensen was the boss and had the final say. Calera Viognier, which many critics consider the best among the growing number of California producers, sells at a premium price of about $36 a bottle. Viognier accounts for only 5 percent of the company's production, so Jensen wasn't betting the business on the new closure. Calera bottled 50 percent of the 2002, 2003, and 2004 vintages with cork and 50 percent with screwcaps. In May 2007, Jensen switched to 50 percent of the 2006 Viognier in screwcaps, and the other 50 percent with the Alcoa glass closure. He sees the glass closure as the "perfect final solution," which doesn't come with the historical cheap-wine image of screwcaps.

The market reaction to the Calera experiment with screwcaps has generally been good, although its Japanese importers, who buy 20 percent of Calera's total production, have refused to take screwcaps. Calera offers both its distributors and customers at the winery a choice of Viognier with a cork or a screwcap, each priced the same. With the 2002 vintage, the company sold out of the bottles with corks first, but in 2003 it was just the opposite. In the 2004 vintage, cork went first largely because of the wine's strong sales in Japan.

Sitting under a vine-covered pergola and looking out over what geologists call the Central Creeping Portion of the San Andreas Fault, the source of so many California earthquakes, Jensen in August 2006 opened for me two bottles of the 2002 Viognier, his oldest wines with both cork stoppers and screwcaps. The bottles had just been pulled out of the winery's underground cellar and were slightly chilled. The wines, which went through exactly the same wine production, had been bottled on April 29–30, 2003, the cork being bottled the first day and the screwcaps the second. The wines had thus been under the two closures for three and a half years.

With no fanfare Jensen first pulled the cork from one bottle and turned the screwcap of the other. Then he smelled the two wines and rendered an instant opinion: "The screwcap has a much fresher and fruitier nose. You can smell it right away." After tasting the two Viogniers, he gave his final judgment: "The screwcap wine tastes fresher. The bottle with cork is fine, but the other one is a little livelier."

As Jensen and I continued to sample the two bottles, he said that with either glass stoppers or screwcaps, "you don't need a special tool to open the container." He believes that the need for a corkscrew is an inherent "impediment to wider wine consumption." With cool ocean breezes rolling across the valley toward the Diablo Range that separates the Central Coast from the hot San Joaquin Valley, Jensen asked, "How many cans would Coca-Cola sell if you needed a special tool to open them?"

HOGUE CELLARS, COLUMBIA VALLEY, WASHINGTON

Every winery has a unique personality, which usually comes from its founder. The personality of Washington State's Hogue Cellars is academic. Brothers Mike and Gary Hogue founded the company in 1982. Their family had long been farming the eastern part of the state in the Columbia Valley, where soils are rich and the rainfall is much less than in the western side of Washington. The chilly nights and warm, but not hot, days are considered ideal for grape growing.

Over the past quarter century, Hogue has been chockablock with UC Davis graduates, usually with advanced degrees. Longtime director of winemaking David Forsyth has a master's from Davis, and Wade Wolfe, another longtime employee, has a Ph.D. from there. Co Dinn, now the director of winemaking, also has a master's from Davis, as does Jordon Ferrier, the winemaker. So it's not surprising that Hogue has done some of the most thorough research on wine-bottle closures of any American winery. Perhaps only Gallo, which never releases the results of its studies, has done more.

Hogue largely makes inexpensive, fruit-forward wines that sell for less than $10 a bottle in retail shops. Those make up some 70 percent of its annual production, with Riesling being its most popular white wine, and Merlot its best-selling red. In addition, it has a line of premium wines, Genesis and Reserve, which sell for slightly more. Hogue is now part of Constellation, the world's largest wine company.

Like many other wineries, Hogue initially used natural cork closures but began having problems with taint and inconsistency among bottles in the late 1980s and early 1990s. The winery in 1996 first experimented with plastic SupremeCorqs, which came from a fellow Washington company with which it worked closely. From 1998 to 2003, Hogue used the synthetics on most of its wines. The results were, however, disappointing. The wines oxidized quickly and aged too rapidly.

Hogue launched its closure study in May 2001 with two of its most popular products, a 2000 Chardonnay that sold for $8 and a 1999 Genesis Merlot that retailed for $15. At that time, the Chardonnay was being bottled with a SupremeCorq, and the Merlot had a natural cork.

Jordon Ferrier, who had also done work in statistics and computers as well as enology, headed the research project. The wines were sealed with five different closures: natural cork, extruded synthetic Neocork, molded synthetic SupremeCorq, Stelvin screwcap with the less permeable tin liner, and Stelvin with the more permeable plastic liner. The plan was to test the wines every six months, with the first taking place in November 2001. Every six months, the same seven members of the Hogue production management group with one exception tasted the wines in three or four flights. And every six months eight bottles of each closure treatment were opened in random order for analysis. Levels of SO_2 and CO_2 as well as phenolics, the building blocks of wine found most commonly in red wines, were also measured. All the tastings were blind, meaning the tasters did not see the type of closure used. Nontasters poured the wines in advance in random order into coded glasses. Testing was done over a few consecutive days. The first day was a training session, so the tasters could become familiar with the wines and the descriptive terms being used; the next days the tasting was for the record. Each day the white wines were presented first, followed by the red. The wines were tasted every six months between November 2001 and December 2003.

Some differences were noted early. For example, wines with the synthetic closures quickly showed the effects of oxidation, from loss of fruit early on to tired, mildly oxidized wines in the later tastings. TCA was also detected early in the cork-sealed wines.

After the December 2003 testing, the Hogue staff drew up their conclusions, which were presented in June 2004 at the annual meeting of the American Society of Enology and Viticulture:

- Wines using natural cork generally had some incidence of cork taint from low to high depending on the individual cork, while those with synthetic cork or screwcaps had none. The cork wines also had correspondingly less fruit flavors.
- Wines with synthetic cork showed oxidation as well as browning in both the Chardonnay and Merlot wines. Those also became excessively aged and had the lowest fruit tastes. Wines using the SupremeCorqs generally showed more oxidation than the Neocorks, although the differences were not statistically relevant.
- Wines under screwcap kept more of their fruit flavors and were fresher than those under either natural or synthetic cork.
- Already at twenty-four months and thirty months and for both the Chardonnay and Merlot wines, the judges' closure choice was screwcaps. Synthetic corks came in second, and natural corks were the least favorite.
- Between the tight tin screwcap and the looser plastic one, the tasters clearly preferred the plastic, which lets in a little more air. Some reductive, flinty tastes were also noted in the Merlot bottles with the plastic liner.
- Natural cork was best at preserving the SO_2 in the wine, but screwcaps were a close second and were not statistically different. Synthetics did poorly in that criterion.
- Wine-taste problems caused by closures were more noticeable in the Chardonnay than in the Merlot.

At the same time as the study results were released, Hogue announced that its entire line of 2004 fruit-forward wines, 70 percent of its total five-hundred-thousand-case production, would be sealed with screwcaps using plastic liners. The remainder would be closed with high-quality cork.

Despite that ringing endorsement, the case at Hogue was not entirely closed. No one could predict how Hogue's customers were going to react to screwcaps. So the company's top management asked the winemakers to come up with a backup plan just in case at the end of the first year sales were down significantly. Co Dinn got the job of formulating the emergency plan. After closely studying the test results, he proposed that if sales went over the cliff, Hogue should seal its wines in the best synthetic corks it could find.

In the end, though, the backup strategy was not needed. Business in 2005 held firm, and at the beginning of 2006, with sales statistics for the entire year in hand, Hogue decided it was sticking with screwcaps. In fact, the winery began slowly moving its more expensive brands from natural cork over to that closure. The premium Genesis Riesling was the first to go that way, and others are expected to follow. "It's nice to be on the other side of the chasm," said Dinn.

Now with substantial experience making wines destined to go into screwcap bottles, Hogue winemakers say they have had to adjust their winemaking practices. Wines react differently in the bottle under screwcap than they do under either synthetic cork or natural cork. Says Dinn, "Winemakers have been using cork as a crutch for a long time because it is so forgiving."

The wine that goes into a screwtop bottle has to be perfect, according to Dinn, because it's going to change much more slowly due to the lower amount of oxygen it will receive in the bottle. "If it's not ready and you're hoping for it to develop further in the bottle, you're going to be disappointed." That may mean moving the wine from barrel to barrel to expose it to more oxygen prior to bottling. White wines are less forgiving than red ones, and faults will be magnified by the airtight screwcap. This may require more work, but for Hogue the research clearly showed screwcaps are the preferred closure.

CHAPTER TWENTY-TWO

On the American Front Lines

A merican consumers are deciding the future of wine-bottle closures with the millions of decisions they make every day in wineshops and restaurants around the country. It is expected that the United States will soon pass France to become the largest wine market in the world. Many countries have a higher per capita annual wine consumption than the United States, but the total yearly value of American wine purchases will soon be greater. That is why winemakers from around the globe pay special attention to what happens in the American market, and insiders say this will be the decisive battlefield in the conflict over closures. The following three people are professionals working on the front lines of the American wine business and are daily witnesses to the attitude of consumers to various closures.

THE SOMMELIER

Paul Roberts is a master sommelier, as well as corporate wine and beverage director for the Thomas Keller Restaurant Group, which includes some of the brightest stars in the constellation of American restaurants such as the French Laundry in Napa Valley and Per Se in New York City. Annual beverage sales for the group come to $15 million, with $11.5 million just for wines. The price spread of wine offerings at Keller restaurants goes from the teens to $15,000 for a bottle of 1947 Château Pétrus or a 1947 Château Lafleur. The Keller Group employs thirteen sommeliers and has several more in training.

More than 90 percent of Keller wines still have corks, although the restaurants also have some screwcaps, synthetics, and even a few glass closures, primarily on German Rieslings. Virtually every New Zealnd wine on the list, from inexpensive Sauvignon Blancs to expensive Pinot Noirs, has a screwcap. Likewise every bottle from France has a cork in it.

Roberts says that in about 2000, first sommeliers and then consumers became increasingly aware of corked wines. Sommeliers today all recognize it, although sometimes the level may be so low it is difficult to spot. Consumers are now asking a lot more questions about closures and are also much better informed. Regularly, though, some people may think a wine is corked when they just simply don't like it.

The Keller Group keeps close tabs on the incidence of corked wines. The day before I talked with Roberts, there had been a case in the French Laundry and another at Per Se of corked bottles of wines that cost the restaurants $2,000 wholesale and would sell for two to three times that retail. One was a 1990 Montrachet, and the other a 1989 French First Growth. Roberts estimates that restaurants have 3–5 percent problem bottles caused by "cork or something else."

If the corked bottle is of recent vintage and comes from a California winery, the restaurant can get compensation, but in the case of an old vintage it has no recourse. The annual wholesale cost of corked wines for the entire Thomas Keller group is between $75,000 and $85,000.

While everyone is talking about corked bottles, Roberts says the term has become a catchall for any problem with a wine. "Cork gets blamed for a lot of things it shouldn't be blamed for," he maintains. Roberts says the bad odors or taste may come from faulty barrels, incorrect winemaking, or a touch of *Brettanomyces.* Consumers may have become better at distinguishing good wines from bad ones, but few are adept enough to spot exactly the cause of the problem. When in doubt, they blame the cork.

At the French Laundry and Per Se, sommeliers taste every bottle they open, so they can stop obviously corked ones from ever reaching the table. If the sommelier passes on the wine, but the customer thinks there's a problem with the bottle, the customer is always right. "We train all our sommeliers not to get in a fight with the customer," says Roberts. "Even if you're right, you can't dig in your heels and destroy the sense of hospitality. We never want to make a person suffer through a meal with a wine he didn't like." Roberts adds that it's not the sommelier's role to tell the customer he's wrong.

The sommelier might suggest that the wine needs time to develop after opening and to wait for a while to see if that happens. If the guest still disagrees after that, the answer is probably that the person simply doesn't like that wine. In that case there is no use opening another bottle of the same wine. The sommelier would usually then take back the first wine and recommend a different one in the same style and price range.

Since the rejected wine is perfectly good, Roberts says the sommelier might use a football term and "call an audible." They tell their colleagues that the wine is available by the glass. If it's a bottle that was selling for $2,000, it might be $100 for a glass. The guests get an unexpected opportunity to enjoy a rare wine that they might never have had—and might never be able to afford as a bottle. The goal, if possible, is just to get back the bottle's wholesale cost, so the restaurant is not out any money. Given the flow of diners at Keller restaurants, it's usually not difficult to find people interested in having that kind of special wine experience.

While many people now can spot corkiness, few recognize reduction—the burnt-rubber/rotten-egg smells associated with some screwcap wines. Roberts says he only learned about that wine fault during a 1996 visit to Burgundy, when the winemaker at Jean-Jacques Confuron explained it to him using his Romanée-St. Vivant as an example. The winemaker wanted to achieve some reduction because it helped his wines age for a long time. "Most people don't know what reduction tastes like, and they may even think the wine is corked," says Roberts.

Roberts has no personal closure preference. He says a Sauvignon Blanc from New Zealand or a Kabinett Riesling from Germany is generally so light that any flaw is going to be magnified because there is neither a high alcohol level nor long aging in oak barrels to mask it. As a result, he thinks a screwcap or plastic cork might be the best. For a classic red wine such as a Domaine de la Romanée-Conti La Tâche or a great aged Chardonnay or Riesling, he considers cork the best closure because it helps the wine "achieve its greatness." The one closure Roberts doesn't like is the agglomerated cork and has most often had problems with them. He thinks the glue that binds the cork particles together often ruins the wine.

THE IMPORTER

Leonardo LoCascio is the founder of Winebow, a New Jersey–based wine distributor and importer. Robert Parker in 1998 called him "one of the most influential wine personalities of the last twenty years." Born in Italy and educated in the United States, he's at home anyplace in the world where wine is made. LoCascio, a dapper dresser, looks as if he just stepped out of a Milan fashion show, but crunches numbers like an MBA. He started out in business working in finance for such giants as Rockwell International, McKinsey, and Citibank. He got the money to launch his own business by playing the credit-card game, borrowing the maximum amount on a small mountain of plastic. It worked, and now his company has annual sales of $175 million. LoCascio in 2002 bought 165 acres of prime land in Bolgheri south of Pisa, where his neighbors include such wineries as Sassicaia. He is doing the project with the Allegrini family, the producers of Amarone, a rare wine made from dried grapes. LoCascio named his property Poggio al Tesoro and will by 2010 be producing forty thousand cases a year. He bottles his own wines with corks.

Looking out at the international wine market, LoCascio sees continued good growth despite the weak dollar, which makes it hard for European producers, in particular, to raise prices. Pinot Grigio has consolidated its position as the world alternative to Chardonnay in white wines, he says, and new producers in Argentina, Spain, and Greece are "here to stay." He notes that Spanish wine is now "where Italy was fifteen years ago."

As LoCascio goes about finding new wines to import, he spends a lot of time answering questions from winemakers about the closures they should be using. Producers both large and small constantly ask him whether the U.S. market will accept screwcaps. LoCascio's answer is that the American market has now split into two segments. "Up to twenty dollars a bottle, it is increasingly accepted to have screwcaps," he says. "In fact, now it's even hip to have a screwcap." He says he tells uncertain winemakers that if they are making wines meant to be drunk young and where there's lots of volume, then "don't be afraid." While screwcaps started in New Zealand and Australia, he's seeing more and more from Germany, Chile, and Argentina. "It used to be just whites, but now there are reds as well," he adds.

Above $20 retail and for the restaurant trade, though, LoCascio says American consumers still want a cork in the bottle. "People are afraid that not enough research has been done, and they're uncertain about whether the aging potential is there."

Italy poses a special problem because of its law that high-end appellation or DOC (Denominazione di Origine Controllata) wines must be sealed with a cork. "That's a huge segment of the market that can't play in screwcaps; you simply can't now get a Barolo or Chianti Classico with a screwcap." LoCascio doubts there will be any movement soon to change that law. As a result, he thinks there will be export opportunities for Italy's IGT (Indicazione Geografica Tipica) wines that come from larger regions and can use screwcaps.

As a distributor, LoCascio gets only a fraction of 1 percent returned bottles. Winebow's policy on returned bottles is to replace them with no questions asked. Most people, he says, unfortunately don't have a high sensitivity to corked wines. As a result, they often think a mildly corked bottle is just an inferior product from a bad winery. "That's the real problem because people blame the winery instead of the cork."

THE RETAILER

Given its location in a 1950s strip mall in Canoga Park, California, a working-class suburb of Los Angeles, it's a little hard to believe that the Duke of Bourbon has been ranked by several publications as one of the top wine stores in the United States. Celebrities from the movie and music industries as well as serious wine collectors, though, regularly make their pilgrimage to Canoga Park because of the store's extensive selection of the world's great wines, especially those in large-format bottles such as a twenty-seven-liter, 1995 Justin Isosceles, the equivalent of three cases. Despite its hard-liquor name, 95 percent of sales are wine.

Dave Breitstein, along with his wife, Judy, founded the store in 1967, after Dave worked at his father's nearby liquor business for several years. Along with many of their contemporaries, the Breitsteins' first experiences with wine were the popular Blue Nun and Cold Duck. But at the same time Dave was interested in then little-known quality wineries in the Napa Valley such as Inglenook and Louis M. Martini. The first time Dave's father left him in charge of the store while he went on vacation, the young Breitstein ordered several cases of those two wines.

When he opened his own store, Dave Breitstein quickly zeroed in on California wines, although he also carried such French stars as Château Margaux and Château Lafite. Between 1969 and 1971, Dave and Judy made their first trips to California's wine country, where they met winemakers such as Joe Heitz at Heitz Cellars, Dave Bennion at Ridge Vineyards, and Bob Travers at Mayacamas Vineyards. He bought ten cases of Schramsberg sparkling wine after a phone call with owners Jack and Jamie Davies, as well as the first vintages of Stag's Leap Wine Cellars and Chateau Montelena, the two wineries that won the Paris Tasting of 1976. When all those wines became hot items, for example, after President Richard Nixon took Schramsberg to China on his historic 1972 visit to open diplomatic relations, the wineries remained loyal and kept the Duke of Bourbon stocked.

From his vantage point, Breitstein says American consumers "don't have a strong opinion one way or another about closures." A day before we talked, a customer had come into the store and bought a bottle of Layer Cake, an Australian Shiraz that sells for $16 with a screwcap. As the person was checking out, he said, "I don't know what to think about this screwcap, but I guess it's here to stay, so I'll live with it." Breitstein says that is a common attitude. People are neither opposed to the cork alternatives nor demanding them. "We're going through a transition right now."

Breitstein was surprised when one of his managers told him that while twenty years ago only 1 percent of wines under cork might be tainted, that number is now about 10 percent. Dave's own experience is that the problem is not nearly that big. But if it were, he said, people paying $150 for a bottle of a superpremium wine might want to consider a screwcap to protect their investment.

Screwcaps still make up a small segment of the Duke of Bourbon's inventory. Breitstein has several high-end white wines from Australia, New Zealand, Germany, and California that carry screwcaps, but the only premium red wine with that closure is PlumpJack Reserve Cabernet Sauvignon. "We need another twenty or thirty Napa Valley wineries to go to screwcaps to get the dialogue going," he says. "Not enough American consumers have tried them to have a good discussion."

In the classic story *Peter Pan*, the hero wants to remain a child forever and defiantly says he "won't grow up." Some wine people worry about Peter Pan wines, particularly reds, that "won't grow up" under screwcaps because they don't get a little bit of air during bottle aging. Judy Breitstein says that while she can imagine wines made to be enjoyed in two or three years under screwcaps, she wonders whether the great red wines will age.

Dave Breitstein remembers a visit he once had from Baron Philippe de Rothschild of Château Mouton Rothschild, who said he never drank one of his prized wines until it was at least a decade old. "Wine improves with age, and millions of cases are in people's cellars aging so they will get better," says Dave. "The experience of drinking something aged is very special."

While winemakers and wholesalers frequently complain that their wine gets blamed when the cork is the problem, Breitstein says people often simply don't like a wine and condemn the cork. "A bum wine went into the bottle, and when they taste it, they blame the cork."

The Duke of Bourbon rarely gets a returned bottle. When it does, the store will almost always replace the bottle, no matter what caused the trouble. While it's rare to get a $100 bottle returned, it can happen. The day after I interviewed the Breitsteins, a customer called to say that a bottle of 1997 Diamond Creek Volcanic Hill Cabernet Sauvignon he had taken to a Los Angeles restaurant had been corked. The person was not angry and understood such things happen, but just wanted the store to know and asked about its policy on corked wines. Breitstein immediately said he would replace the bottle.

MESSAGE IN A BOTTLE: SAN FRANCISCO

Robert Devlin, a San Francisco investment counselor and money manager, some years ago learned that John Daniels, proprietor of Inglenook Winery in the Napa Valley, had set away a generous supply of wines for his two daughters from the years of their birth to be later served at age twenty-one, graduation from college, or some other special occasion. Devlin was so impressed that in 1963 and 1966 with the births of his daughter and son, he followed suit and cellared liberal quantities to celebrate the major events of their lives. In 1999, his son married, and so father broke out four cases each of 1966 Château Lynch-Bages and 1966 Robert Mondavi unfined Cabernet Sauvignon. Both wines had been stored in the same location for the previous twenty-four years at temperatures varying between fifty and fifty-five degrees.

Devlin had sampled the wines every five or so years and knew their condition and that of their all-important corks. At a dinner following the wedding rehearsal, he watched the wine steward attempt to open the wines with his single-leverage steward opener only to break off the cork in the initial French wine. "I had come prepared with numerous openers and salvaged the broken cork with an Ah-So opener," says Devlin. He then demonstrated the proper method of cutting the seal below the lip of the bottle and using the double-leveraged opener to smoothly remove the corks from the remaining bottles. Both wines required decanting because of moderate sediment deposits evident at the bottom of bottles. The corks were sound after more than thirty years, and ullage was at a minimum of less than an inch. The wines proved to be a high point of the evening's festivities.

As he thought about that wonderful event of old wine, Devlin recalled two equations that had haunted him since his study of architecture forty-five years before that dealt with design and materials: Change = Progress and Newness = Goodness.

"We have the evolving trends of closures on wine away from the traditional cork-finished product, but what's up with this change from a centuries-old tradition?" he asks.

Increasingly, he thought, the wine trade has been producing its products for early consumption, which in part nullifies the long-standing presumption that a cork assists in the aging of wines to be laid down for future maturity and consumption.

"Most of us have been hybrid wine consumers, with many of our cellars oriented toward a cross between what we expect to consume over the coming year or more and those select wines for future special occasions," he says. "In the former category, it doesn't seem of importance which method or how the closure of the bottle is accomplished. The wines have been selected for current consumption, and aging does not come into play." In the second category, however, with wines that have been acquired for later consumption, the cork has played "an important function to the keeper of these wines laid down for a more mature and often with age softer tasting."

CHAPTER TWENTY-THREE

The Penfolds Recorking Clinic

*Peter Gago rescues old Penfolds wines
with failing corks.*

For the past fifteen years, Penfolds, the Australian winery, has held free
recorking clinics around the world. Anyone owning a Penfolds red wine
that is fifteen years or older can bring the bottle in and have it examined to
see how the cork is holding up. Usually, but not always, the old cork is
exchanged for a new one, and the Penfolds fan goes home happy. More
than eighty thousand bottles of Penfolds wines have already been recorked.
This is most frequently done to a Grange, a Shiraz that is the winery's flag-
ship wine and has been called the southern hemisphere's only First Growth.

I attended the second day of a two-day clinic in Adelaide on September 21, 2006. The event was held in the old Spirit Bond Room of the original 1844 Penfolds Magill Estate Winery. The room was already abuzz as
I walked in shortly after 10:00 a.m. A dozen plain tables had been set up
around the large room with stone walls painted white. At each table
were several Penfolds employees wearing white aprons with the bright red
Penfolds logo.

Peter Gago, Penfolds' Chief Winemaker, was at one table, also wearing an apron and consulting with the owner of a 1982 Bin 820, a blend of Shiraz and Cabernet Sauvignon from Coonawarra. Speaking rapidly with intensity and enthusiasm, Gago resembled a teacher talking to a student, which is not surprising since he used to teach secondary-school science and math. Gago told me he uses this opportunity to give a lesson in the proper cellaring of wines. He explained that when old wines fail, the cork is usually not the problem. More often than not the wine has been improperly stored. The two keys to successful aging are constant temperature and no light. It pains him when people come in and brag about how they've kept the wonderful bottle they want recorked in their den where the sun hit it every afternoon. Gago said with a properly stored bottle, the cork should last fifty years. He added he had recently opened a bottle of 1953 Grange, and the wine was "perfect."

The first thing Gago did was take the capsule off the bottle so he could get a good look at the cork. He said that fortunately it looked fine and still seemed to be doing its job. Then he looked closely at the level of wine in the bottle. Ideally it should be only about a half inch below the cork. "If it's down as low as the shoulders of the bottle, there's trouble and signs of leakage," said Gago. "Every millimeter down into the shoulder area is a day of borrowed time." The level on this one was nice and high.

Gago then asked an assistant to remove the cork. If the cork is in good shape, the level in the bottle is high, and the wine has reached its peak of aging, he occasionally recommends that it not be recorked lest the owner risk ruining a good thing. But he thought this one might need a new cork. The assistant had a panoply of corkscrews in front of him, but he used Gago's favorite technique to minimize cork crumbling: two separate screwpulls went into the neck of the bottle on opposite sides. The ex–science teacher noted that the screwpulls intertwined to form the shape of a double helix. The corkscrews went in just to the point where they stuck out the bottom of the cork, then were smoothly pulled out. A small piece of cork had, though, broken off, and the assistant went after it with a fine stainless steel device and pulled it out.

After a mixture of carbon dioxide and nitrogen was shot into the bottle, Gago poured a small amount of wine (fifteen milliliters or a half an ounce, he said) into a simple wineglass. A T-top cork stopper was placed into the bottle as a temporary stopper while the wine was examined.

Gago said that at this point the great temptation is to smell or taste the wine immediately. Instead he swirled it around in the glass and held it up to the light. The winemaker noted it has "a touch of brown, but it should have that at twenty-four years." He also remarked about the wine's brightness.

After carefully examining the wine, Gago tasted it and said, "Bin 820 can be an idiosyncratic wine, but I think this one is admirable. It has beautiful fruit, magnificent fruit. It smells of cassis and black olives." Then he quickly added, "But let's see what the experts say." He pulled out the fifth edition of the Penfolds book, *The Rewards of Patience*. Every few years, the winery has a group of international wine judges independently taste Penfolds' so-called museum wines, which go back uninterrupted to the 1950s, to determine when they should ideally be drunk. Some are honestly declared over-the-hill; fortunately many are not, and drinking windows and tasting comments are recorded. Gago looked up the 1982 Bin 820 and seemed happy to learn that it should be drunk now.

Gago finally handed the remaining wine in the glass to the bottle's owner and suggested he try it. After sipping it, the owner said, "It delivers everything it should."

It was then time to top the bottle up with some new wine and recork it. Bottles are normally topped with the current vintage of that same wine. New Grange tops old Grange; Bin 707 tops Bin 707; and St. Henri tops St. Henri. Bin 820 is so unusual that there is not a topping bottle of it, so Bin 707 was used. The T-top was removed, the new wine was poured in almost to the top, another shot of carbon dioxide and nitrogen was added, and the T-top was placed back in the bottle.

Gago then signed the certificate testifying that the bottle had been recorked at the clinic and put a similar coded label on the back of the bottle. He also explained that a bottle can only be recorked once. The addition of fifteen milliliters or less (less than 2 percent of the content) of new wine to the bottle once is acceptable, but it would alter the wine's integrity to do it again.

The last stop was the corking machine. Bottles of Grange wine get a cork inscribed with the Grange stamp and date, but all others get one with the Penfolds name. The recorker first took a little more wine out of the bottle to the correct fill height, lowered the handle that pushed the cork in under vacuum, then applied the red Penfolds capsule on top of the bottle and crimped it into place. "The bottle is now good for another twenty years," Gago told the owner. "But you might want to drink it earlier. Many people hold wines too long."

After the demonstration, I wandered around the room for two hours watching people as their prized bottles were judged and in most cases recorked. There were young people and old. Men and women. Some brought their own bottle; others were carrying ones for a husband or friend. Many people had only one bottle, but a week before a collector had brought in ninety-six bottles of Grange.

Steve Lienert, Penfolds Senior Winemaker, who has worked with Grange for more than two decades, helped Helen Renfrey with eight bottles of Grange from 1982 to 1989. Every year she gives the current release to her husband for Father's Day. Lienert and Renfrey decided not to open the 1987 bottle because the cork was holding well and *Rewards of Patience* said it should be drunk now anyway. They did open and tried the 1983, which Lienert said was "just sensational." After all the bottles had been checked and Renfrey had tried most of them, she said with a sigh, "It's too bad my husband missed out on the tasting. He should have taken the day off from work and come himself."

David Proud brought thirty bottles in a makeshift collection of cartons. One bottle, a 1968 Grange, was a disappointment because it was oxidized. He said he buys Grange every year but now mainly for his children, so they can open the bottle from their birth vintage on their twenty-first birthday. He was delighted with the taste of the 1970 Grange, which is ready to drink now—and he clearly was ready to follow that advice.

At one table a young Penfolds employee accidentally pushed a whole cork into a bottle of 1983 Grange while trying to get it out. But then in a feat that seemed to defy the laws of physics, he quickly pulled the cork back out of the bottle using several devices.

At another table, an owner proudly passed around a bottle of 1970 Grange for everyone to see and admire. The bottle still had the original sales sticker on it: A$11.75 (US$9.27). That bottle would today sell at auction for about A$300 (US$237).

Greg Stevens, a collector who buys wine at auctions, owns eighty or ninety—he wasn't quite sure how many—bottles of Grange as part of a collection of three thousand bottles. He brought to the clinic a potpourri of twenty-two old wines. He told me he was really there to get advice on when to drink the wines. By the time I got to that table, the Penfolds crew and Stevens had handled all but the three oldest. The assistant asked him if he really wanted to open the last ones, saying it was his call. There was no way of knowing what was inside. The wine level on one was clearly down into the shoulders. Said Stevens, "When you buy at auction, you really don't know how it's been stored."

After a short hesitation, Stevens said to go ahead. The first was a 1964 Grange. When the tin capsule was pulled off the top, you could see mold growing on the cork. The cork came out smoothly, but it was nearly soaked through. After he tried it, Andrew Baldwin, another Penfolds winemaker, smiled and said with some surprise, "This has derived fruit characters of plums and berries, as well as tobacco and leather. It's wonderful." Then he handed the glass to Stevens, who tasted it with the reverence reserved for history.

Bottle two was a 1965 Bin 2 Shiraz Mourvèdre that was simply gone. When the glass with a sample was passed around, I tried it and was immediately reminded of a 1950 Château Haut-Brion that a friend had given me three years before that had also been well past its prime and a huge disappointment. Like that wine, the taste of this 1965 had faded, and it tasted like dried grapes that had been left too long on the vine. There was even some tannin bitterness. "Nothing's left on the palate—it's completely dried out," said Baldwin.

Finally, the last bottle. Baldwin again asked Stevens if he wanted to open it, but after a few seconds of hesitation he replied, "The only way to find out if it's any good is to open it. No guts, no glory."

The last bottle was a 1962 Bin 389 Cabernet Shiraz. The label on it was handwritten and said it had been bottled on July 11, 1964. It was in a heavy Burgundy-style bottle that might first have been used for a Pinot Noir. The Penfolds staff called over John Bird, a retired Penfolds Senior Winemaker who had probably helped make the wine, to look at the bottle. He examined it closely and pointing to the bottom said, "It's a real strong one; look at that punt." Bird then explained that he recognized the handwriting as that of Max Schubert, legendary Penfolds winemaker and the father of Grange. Bird said the bottle was never meant to be sold commercially and had probably been made for a special company function.

In swift order, off came the capsule and out came the cork. Baldwin poured a small amount into a glass and examined the wine's brownish color. Then he tasted it and said, "It's an interesting wine. It survived, and it's a sterling effort." Then Stevens suggested that Bird taste it since he probably had a hand in it. After he took a sip, Bird said simply, "The wine stood up; it stood up well." The bottle was recorked, and Stevens said he was probably going to drink it in the next week or so.

Before Peter Gago left for lunch, I talked with him about what Penfolds was doing with closures these days. He said the company has been examining various wines under a variety of closures since the 1990s, first with only white wines. Then at mid-decade they began setting aside Grange and Bin 389.

With infectious enthusiasm that seemed to make his dark, curly hair curlier, Gago said that starting in 2005 Penfolds was doing all its whites for the Australian market and "other willing markets" in screwcaps. He added that the United States was one of the markets slow to accept them. He said Penfolds is also gradually introducing various red wines under screwcap "as we gain more confidence and have more experience with them."

Gago became really excited, though, when he started talking about something still very much in the development stage: a glass closure. When I asked him if it was the Alcoa Vino-Lok, he replied, "No, although we looked at Vino-Lok, we're also looking at another glass option. If it can be perfected, then it will be a no-brainer." He said developers were having some troubles getting the seal to hold, but he thought they could solve that. Then in a musing way he added, "Screwcaps may end up being a transitional closure, not the final solution. They're not one hundred percent perfect."

There are no plans at present for putting Grange under screwcap. But it's hard to imagine that consumers a generation from now, coming to a Penfolds clinic to put a new screwcap on a bottle of old Grange, would be as excited as those at the 2006 recorking clinic in Adelaide.

CHAPTER TWENTY-FOUR

Battle for the Wine Bottle

The market for wine-bottle closures is a $4 billion battlefield where an epic confrontation is now taking place. Arrayed to slug it out, in a struggle where only a few closures will survive, are both giant corporations such as Alcoa, Amorim, and Alcan and small companies hoping to capture their tiny piece of a lucrative market.

The conflict has already become both emotional and vicious. Fans of screwcaps disparagingly call corks "tree bark," while advocates of corks call plastic stoppers "polluting petroleum by-products." Some winemakers, wine writers, and wine scientists have turned into shills for one camp or the other, often making unsubstantiated and outrageous claims about their favorite products, while self-righteously condemning someone else's. Charges of payoffs are tossed around like confetti with no supporting evidence, and motives of anyone who doesn't agree with the attacker's point of view are impugned.

Friendships wither away when people can no longer carry on a civilized dialogue about something that in the large scope of things is pretty inconsequential. Opponents are not just wrong; they are evil. Australian Brian Croser only half-jokingly compares the current atmosphere to the Salem witch trials. When will they be burning people to death on pyres of old corks?

Australian wine critic James Halliday says that wineries still using corks are members of the flat-earth society, while Britain's Andrew Jefford in *Decanter* writes, "The ayatollahs of screwcap have made it seem morally defective to speak up for cork." John Buck, the CEO of Te Mata Estate in New Zealand, says he was personally offended when a wine columnist wrote that any winery that still used cork "doesn't care about his customers." Te Mata uses screwcaps, natural corks, and agglomerated corks; and Buck cares a lot about his customers.

In this Internet age, many of the battles are waged in breathless blogs. Tyson Stelzer, an Australian who has written several effusive paeans to screwcaps including *Screwed for Good?* and *Taming the Screw,* in 2005 led a blog on RobertParker.com that was white-hot with emotion and opinion, but weak on facts and research. Stelzer, a science teacher at an elementary and secondary school, elevated himself to "senior oenophile" and claimed his "research has been recognized both locally and internationally." With the passion of a true believer, Stelzer wrote in his kickoff posting, "The great thing now is that we have solid, scientific, quantitative evidence, and it is no longer conjecture."

In the blog Stelzer trotted out an old and widely discredited study on the variation in oxygen transmission in corks compared with screwcaps that showed corks had a 1,227-fold variation. If true, that would make them totally unreliable as a closure. Stelzer repeated that supposed fact like a mantra.

Alan Limmer points out that the 1,227-fold statistic comes from a study done using dry corks. But corks are supposed to be kept wet to maintain their seal. Limmer maintains the variation is about threefold, or about the same as screwcaps. Jim Peck of California's G3 Enterprises has performed preliminary tests using a wet cork and found there to be a difference of less than one order of magnitude. More research is obviously needed. Throwing around "solid, scientific, quantitative evidence" of a 1,227-fold variation, when the real number is perhaps one, shows the degradation of this debate. Michael Pronay, an admitted "cork bark hater" from Vienna, brought a voice of reason to the blog when he pleaded, "Calm down, please."

Some in the wine business believe staff members of the normally above-the-fray Australian Wine Research Institute have damaged the organization's reputation by abandoning rigorous scientific objectivity and becoming crusading zealots for screwcaps. Managing Director Sakkie Pretorius took nearly twenty-seven hundred words in a letter to the editor to attack Paul White's article in the British wine magazine *Harpers* that raised questions about screwcaps. It would be enough for Shakespeare to think he "doth protest too much." Later, threats of lawsuits and cries of press freedom were tossed around in a confrontation that made no one look good. The editor eventually lost his job.

The tone of the discussion was seen in a September 6, 2006, e-mail from Stelzer to the contributing editors of his *Taming* book, where he wrote, "Godden said that they have unearthed some dirt on White and Limmer which reveals some less than scrupulous motives which are relevant to this issue, and they won't be afraid to put them on the table if White comes back fighting."

Fortunately, some of the extraneous characters in this melodrama provide brief comic relief. In 2002, Britain's Prince Charles, who may never personally have pulled a cork in his life, came out strongly against what he called "nasty plastic plugs" and in favor of natural corks for environmental reasons. In May 2006, the World Wildlife Fund, the conservation group, published a thirty-four-page study on the ills that would befall the earth and the animals on it if cork stoppers were replaced by alternatives. It ended with the ringing cry, "WWF calls on the wine and the cork industries to reverse the current and potential threats that affect the survival of cork landscapes."

Given growing public interest in ecology and global warming, cork industry executives think this might be their trump card. They stress at every opportunity that their product is more environmentally friendly and that the carbon footprint of a cork is less than that of a screwcap. The Rainforest Alliance, an international ecology group, created a certification for wineries that use cork from what they determine to be properly controlled forests. Says Jamie Lawrence, the alliance's European forest division manager, "Cork stoppers that come from responsibly managed forestlands are the only choice for wineries that want to have a positive environmental and social impact." The first winery to be so certified was Willamette Vineyards in Oregon.

Some 20 billion wine-bottle closures are used annually around the world. Despite the major inroads alternatives have made in the past few years in some important markets, about 13 billion of those are still natural corks, and another 3 billion are technical corks. So 80 percent of the closure market is still in the hands of cork. That's down from a virtual monopoly two decades ago, but it remains a commanding position. Plastic corks total some 2.5 billion. And screwcaps, despite all the hoopla and recent success, are only about 1.5 billion.

The Portuguese cork industry obviously has the most at stake and the most to lose. As the biggest dog in this fight, Amorim has been taking the lead, although it is not alone. After paying scant attention to cork problems for more than three centuries, the Portuguese, and in particular Amorim, have recently been investing heavily in research and new equipment to improve the quality of their product.

The most important part of that effort is being done in the Amorim labs run by Miguel Cabral. With a staff of seven and an annual budget of €6 million (US$7.9 million), he has been working hard to get that promised statue built in his honor at the company headquarters. Cabral has established a two-path strategy for solving cork's problems through what he calls "preventive and curative solutions."

The preventive approach, which has now been implemented, involved a total overhaul of cork production operations. Starting in the forests, research showed that contamination was most likely in the tree bark growing near the earth, so cutters were ordered to stop harvesting low on the tree. When the bark is brought into the factory, workers now cut several inches more off the base and send it to be used in industrial cork products. In the past, bark was left on bare earth for months while it dried out. Research determined this could be another source of trouble, so the bark is now often stored on concrete.

Cork boiling has been completely overhauled and new stainless steel equipment installed. Instead of water being used over and over, it is now continuously replenished to reduce the danger of infecting fresh batches of cork. The drying period after cork is boiled, an ideal time for dangerous mold to form, has been cut from three weeks to three days. At the same time, the moisture level is much lower, thus minimizing another cause of mold growth.

The quality-control system developed by ETS Labs has become the industry standard and is widely used by Portuguese companies. The Amorim Lab now gets sample corks from twelve factories around the country on a random basis and does nearly six hundred TCA tests per day. In June 2006, Eric Herve and Peter Weber made a presentation at the Culinary Institute of America to report on the Cork Quality Council's program of testing corks. Since the start of testing, nearly 5 million corks had been soaked. The percentage of corks brought into the United States with more than 2 parts per trillion of releasable TCA dropped from 42 percent in the fourth quarter of 2002 to 6 percent in the first quarter of 2006. In addition, the average releasable TCA level in corks tested went from just over 4 ppt to 1 ppt, a 76 percent decline, from the fourth quarter of 2001 to the third quarter of 2005. Now 80 percent of incoming cork shipments have scores of less than the minimum reporting limit of 1 ppt.

The curative solution has taken longer to develop and is still not complete. Cabral's goal was to find a way of cleaning cork material to remove, or at least dramatically reduce, the level of TCA. It took him and his staff three years before they came up with a process that uses pressurized water and steam to eliminate most TCA. They started cleaning granular cork material and have been slowly working up to larger and larger pieces of material.

In October 2001, Cabral was getting ready to go to an AWRI conference in Australia where he was going to unveil the preliminary results of his research. In searching for a moniker without revealing sensitive secrets, he named it Rosa after the wife of Stephan Dahl, a Swedish scientist who worked for him. Since that's a common Portuguese name, he was also able to tell lab colleagues that he had named it after their wives or even after them. Marketing Director Carlos de Jesus then reverse-engineered the name and said it was an acronym for Rate of Optimal Steam Application.

The following October, Cabral unveiled the ROSA process at the annual Amorim general manager's meeting at the Serralves Museum of Contemporary Art in Oporto, claiming it reduced TCA by up to 80 percent. The next month Cabral and Marketing Director Carlos de Jesus traveled to Australia and New Zealand to unveil ROSA to their most hostile markets. Ever the careful scientist, Cabral never said he could eliminate the compound entirely, saying he was striving to reduce it to an insignificant level. Confident of his new process and anxious to get the endorsement of wine scientists around the world, Cabral commissioned several independent research institutions, including AWRI, Research Institute Geisenheim in Germany, and Campden & Chorleywood Food Research Association in Britain, to do their own tests to see how effectively ROSA removed TCA. They all came back with results similar to the 80 percent first announced.

Amorim introduced ROSA into its manufacturing process in October 2003 on its Neutrocork, an agglomerated cork made of cleaned-up granular material that the company was touting as its inexpensive answer to plastic stoppers, and Twin Tops, where it was used for both the granular center and the natural-cork disks on the top and bottom.

In the middle of 2005, Cabral began testing what he calls ROSA Evolution, a method to clean up entire corks. The initial steam-cleaning process deformed both the length and diameter of whole corks. The improved procedure, however, eliminates that problem, while removing as much as 85 percent of TCA. In late 2006, the first industrial production of whole corks cleaned with ROSA started, and trials of those corks began in wineries around the world.

With his basic work done on ROSA, Cabral has turned his attention to other cork-related issues, sponsoring studies at wine research institutes from Bordeaux to Australia. Researchers in Spain studied TCA-causing molds in forests, and some in Bordeaux looked at air ingress in wine bottles. "We still know little about how corks work," Cabral laments with obvious frustration.

The impact of all the capital investment is most evident at Amorim facilities, but it can also be seen at other major cork producers in Portugal who are taking similar steps. The Alvaro Coelho & Irmãos cork-handling plant in Ponte-de-Sôr, which belongs to the family that left Amorim in 1996, started production at the beginning of 2005 with modern high-tech equipment as advanced as one would see in the United States, Germany, or Japan. Every lot of cork is bar-coded, so it can be traced through production, shipping, and sales. Engineers and technicians watch computer display screens that monitor development from the time the raw cork arrives from the forests to its departure for the finishing plant near Oporto. Raw cork is boiled at a constant 100°C (212°F) for exactly one hour. The only human involvement is to open and close the door on the boiler. Everything from the boiling equipment to the pallets carrying cork around the factory is stainless steel to avoid possible TCA contamination through wood. Computers also control the production of technical cork material.

The Santa Maria de Lamas offices of the Cork Supply Group, another large exporter, looks like a high-tech company, and Ana Cristina Mesquita, the head of Quality R&D, uses an elaborate PowerPoint presentation to show how the company has systematically increased the level of control over cork production. The back of her business card promises "Quality from Forest to Bottle."

The quality-cork producers have established industry standards as a way of getting less advanced companies to live by the ones they follow. In 1987, they formed the Confédération Européenne du Liège (European Cork Confederation) and in 1996, began setting the International Code of Cork Stopper Manufacturing Practice, a set of rules that govern cork production. They have also steadily been raising those standards. Currently about 280 of Portugal's some 400 cork companies profess to follow the code, and they represent more than 90 percent of the country's cork output.

The weak link in the Portuguese cork chain is not Amorim or Coelho or the Cork Supply Group. They all use basically the same modern procedures, with their own versions of ROSA cleaning and stainless steel machinery. The problem is in the hundreds of small cork companies that operate in the backstreets of cork towns south of Oporto and still produce some 10 percent of output, which has a good chance of being shoddy. They are still operating as a peasant industry from ages past. They don't have the modern equipment to control quality—and they don't have the money to buy it. They also don't follow Cabral's preventive and curative steps to improve quality.

Wine consumers in California, Australia, or France getting a corked bottle of wine don't, however, know whether the tainted cork came from a modern company or a peasant one. All corks look virtually alike. To the consumer the problem is just a bad cork. The backstreet operations are rapidly going out of business because they can't keep up with needed investments. The question is whether they will be gone before they destroy cork's reputation.

Both Italy and Spain have attempted to protect their own cork producers by passing legislation that requires natural corks only be used on certain high-level wines. Such measures, however, are likely to have little effect in changing the attitudes of winemakers and consumers.

Natural cork's best chance for future success may come from a new generation of corks made with industrial methods and controls that provide more product reliability. As man-made products, they have a consistency that natural corks can never achieve, which should help eliminate the problem of random oxidation. A casual consumer might not even notice the difference between a natural cork and an agglomerated one and could still enjoy the romance-of-the-cork experience. Since they are made with no wasted cork material, the cost of agglomerates is also attractive.

Diam, which rose from the ashes of Altec, is getting lots of attention, especially in Australia and New Zealand. Oeneo now makes and sells Diam, and any links to Sabaté are long gone. Even some vehement anticork wine critics are now giving it good marks. The supercritical CO_2 treatment appears to remove TCA effectively from cork material, and the new adhesives to reconstitute the stopper do not impart off-tastes. Diam also retains the many favorable characteristics of cork. Diam's worldwide sales were 100 million in 2006 and are expected to double in 2007. In France, Louis Jadot is a strong advocate. Use in the U.S. has so far been limited, but Kendall-Jackson has them on five of its brands.

Amorim uses its ROSA process in the production of Neutrocork, which has become a big seller. In addition, Amorim and other Portuguese cork manufacturers are extending steam-process treatments that remove virtually all TCA in natural corks. Until recently, they could not be used on whole corks.

As cork companies struggle for their very survival, perhaps their greatest asset is the hard-to-describe, but impossible-to-deny, factor that can only be described as the romance of the cork. For whatever reason, many, many people are enthralled by the ritual of pulling a cork. Screwcaps may appeal to the left side of the brain because they are so logical, but corks appeal to the right side for millions because of the mystique that engulfs them. For the latter group, the pop of a cork is like mainlining adrenaline. It may not be rational, but then lots of life is not rational. How many people around the world keep collecting old corks in fishbowls or wastebaskets as fond remembrances of things past? Captured forever on gossamer wings in every one of those corks is the recollection of a special experience. Is anyone out there now collecting screwcaps? Probably not. In any battle between the heart and the head, either side can win, but the romance of the cork cannot, and should not, be dismissed lightly.

Corks are also part of a change that may be taking place in the world's attitude toward wine. Since the days when Plato with his friends and pupils reclined on couches at symposia, drinking wine from a krater and discussing the meaning of life, wine has enjoyed a special role in society as a beverage of mystique and magic. It wasn't just something to quench your thirst or get you drunk. It was an elixir, the nectar of the gods. In more recent times, corks became a participant in that, as wine lovers opened old bottles with great anticipation, but also terror that perhaps the cork hadn't held. It was like playing Russian roulette with a bottle. If you won, the price was even more meaningful. But some New World wine lovers today want to take the magic away. If they succeed in making wine just another commodity drink, cork will lose its prestige position as well.

The pressure on cork, though, remains relentless. In the spring of 2002, Gallo officials contacted the top cork companies and told them they wanted to meet with all of them together to discuss what they were doing about TCA. The owners of Portuguese companies called around to each other saying that it was outrageous that the arrogant Americans were demanding a command performance. After the panic phone calls, though, the cork barons realized they didn't have much choice. Gallo was then the world's largest wine producer, turning out some 70 million cases under a variety of labels. António Amorim told his colleagues, "I'm going to give it my best shot and my best PowerPoint to change their attitude about cork." So all the producers agreed to meet in July at the Praia Golfe Hotel in Espinho for the joint meeting. In this intimate conclave, Amorim had to go back to being a translator for some of his Portuguese counterparts whose English wasn't up to the job. The meeting went well, and Amorim later traveled to California to meet with Joe Gallo, the company CEO, where the two also talked about the special problems involved in running large family companies. For a while Gallo used Amorim's Twin Top, but eventually switched most of its wines to Nomacorc plastic stoppers. Saving just one penny on each closure of 1 million cases of wine adds $120,000 to Gallo profits. For a company making 70 million cases a year, closures are big money.

Many wineries self-righteously proclaim they are making the switch in closures because it's all about the wine. Don't believe them. H. L. Mencken, America's curmudgeon laureate, once said, "When you hear somebody say, 'This is not about the money,' it's about money." John Buck of Te Mata told me he could add NZ$100,000 (US$70,450) to his winery's annual profits by shifting entirely to screwcaps. A winery easily saves about twenty-five cents a bottle, or $3 a case, in switching from a good grade of cork to screwcap. Even for small wineries, that's a significant savings.

That kind of cost cutting is attractive to wineries struggling to make a profit—or a bigger profit. When the Mondavi family ran into financial problems before they sold out to Constellation, one of the cost-cutting measures was to switch to plastic corks for a large part of production. The official explanation was that it was all about the wine, but it seems clear that it was really all about the money.

A synthetic stopper usually costs only a few cents, and competition is driving the price down all the time. Agglomerated corks can get close to that, but plastic always wins in a price shoot-out. Plastic corks have the additional advantage that consumers don't realize they are even getting one until they return home and open the bottle. On a store shelf the normal bottle with a capsule over the stopper looks the same whether it has a natural or synthetic cork.

Plastic corks are certainly an adequate closure for short-term wines that consumers, especially in the New World, drink most of the time. Michael Martini, the longtime winemaker at Napa Valley's Louis M. Martini Winery, quips that an American's idea of the length of time needed to age a wine is the time it takes to drive home from the liquor store. According to a study done by Supreme Corq, 90 percent of all wine is consumed within forty-eight hours of purchase, and 95 percent is consumed within two years of bottling. If a wine is going to be drunk within a few months of bottling, it doesn't make a lot of sense to pay the extra money to use a quality natural cork that will last for forty years.

Significant technical progress has been made in synthetic closures since the early days of Cellucork and Supreme Corq. Supreme Corq in late 2006 released results of a test showing that its new X2 model kept air out of the bottle better than the best natural cork over two years.

Nonetheless, synthetics still face the same problems they had two decades ago. No man-made plastic has yet been developed that has the magical qualities of natural cork. Plastic lacks the elasticity to bounce back quickly when the cork goes in the bottle. There is also a trade-off with plastic between a good seal and ease of extraction. The better the seal, the tougher it will often be to get the plastic cork out of—or back into—the bottle. Britain's Jancis Robinson in June 2006 wrote in her *Financial Times* wine column, "Wine producers of the world, please, please, *please* stop using plastic corks. They are utterly infuriating." While still a fan of screwcaps, Robinson has also written, "I feel sure we are far from throwing away our corkscrews."

Synthetics will continue to have a good share of the closure market, being used for low-priced wines designed to be drunk young. But you are unlikely to see many wines selling for more than $20 and intended for cellar aging with plastic closures. If a wine with a plastic cork stays around for more than a couple of years, it's likely to be oxidized.

The biggest synthetic producer is Belgium's Nomacorc, which claims to have 30 percent of the market for plastic corks. Both Gallo and Robert Mondavi are big Nomacorc users. The company currently sells about 1.2 billion annually in more than thirty-five countries. Supreme Corq remains a major player in the synthetic market, but under new ownership it has lost the entrepreneurial enthusiasm of the early 1990s and has been losing market position. Perhaps a hundred companies are now making either molded or extruded plastic corks, and they have been driving down prices. Italian companies that used to make plastic shoes lost that market to the Chinese, and some of them turned in desperation to making plastic corks. The lowest-cost producers, of course, are in Asia and Eastern Europe, and they are likely to gain market share. If the customers are big enough, a synthetic producer can prosper with only a few of them. Australia's NuKorc makes plastic stoppers for the hugely successful Yellow Tail brand, which annually sells some 12 million cases worldwide, but the company has been diversifying the sources of its closures.

Having a plastic cork or screwcap is no guarantee that the wine will be free of TCA-type odors. In the early 1980s, Switzerland's Volg Weinkellereien, an early user of screwcaps, had taint problems after liners in the closures became contaminated after TCA got into the winery via wooden pallets. Heineken beer once had a similar taint problem with its bottles, and in 1999 and 2000 Canada's Labatt's brewery had troubles that were traced to a variety of causes, including the water used in brewing. Nomacorc in 2004 received customer complaints that bottles with its closures smelled like horse stables. Studies revealed that the cause was talc used in producing the polyethylene products. That same year, a shipment of Nomacorc plastic stoppers was hit with TBA during shipment to Switzerland. Wooden planks in the walls of a shipping container were found to contain the offensive compound, which spread to the plastic.

The most rapidly growing part of the closure market is screwcaps. Since 2000, when the Clare Valley Riesling producers switched to that closure, its market share has soared and no one knows at this point where it will top out. A growing market has brought in lots of new producers from Asia and Eastern Europe. At the beginning of 2005, only one plant produced screwcaps in Australia and New Zealand; at the beginning of 2007 there are six. Not all of them are going to survive.

Stelvin was slow to take advantage of getting to market first and is now battling against Guala Closures, an Italian company, for screwcap leadership. Guala was founded in 1954 and originally made a wide variety of plastic products but soon began concentrating first on plastic and then also aluminum bottle closures. It became the largest supplier of those closures to the spirits industry. It entered the screwcap business for wine bottles in 2003 by buying its fellow Italian company GlobalCap. Guala then continued expanding aggressively by acquisition. In December 2006, it bought Australia's Auscap and in March 2007 picked up the screwcap operation of Stephan Jelicich's company, Esvin Wine Resources in New Zealand.

Franco Cocchiara, Guala's Global Wine Coordinator, says that in five years screwcaps will have 20 percent of the market thanks to growth primarily in Australia and the United States. He admits that the European sales are growing only "slowly, very slowly." Italian firms have a forte in design, and in 2006 Guala introduced the attractive WAK closure.

In 2005, Gallo, which has more experience than anyone else with screwcaps, began selling such closures to other wineries through its G3 subsidiary. It now offers both short screwcaps, which it traditionally made for jug wine, and the longer Stelvin-style ones. Other screwcap producers think Gallo is testing the waters before making the plunge. It already sells wines with screwcaps under other brands in the United States and under its own name in Britain.

While many companies are making screwcaps, the all-important liners for them are produced by just a few firms, with the biggest being Meyer Seals in Germany and MGJ in France. That may change, though, as the market gets bigger. The companies currently make only a few types of liners, mainly one that contains just plastic material and one made of plastic, paper, and tin or aluminum. The metal liners generally provide the tighter, less-air-permeable seal. It varies from winery to winery which liner is used. New Zealanders use only the tin, while Americans use both plastic and metal liners. Liner makers and screwcap manufacturers have been experimenting with different kinds of products, particularly ones for red wines that let a little more air in the bottle. The delay in delivering them seems to indicate technicians are running into some problems.

Outside of the big three in the closure market, new companies keep popping up promising that they have discovered the perfect closure. A UC Davis professor came up with MetaCork, a twist-to-uncork closure that was used briefly in California by Fetzer and Kendall-Jackson. The company's supposed deal with Robert Mondavi fell apart in the Constellation merger and ended up in court. Zork, a plastic stopper with a pull tab developed in Australia whose claim to fame is that it pops just like a cork, got a lot of attention when it was introduced in 2003. A few wineries down under such as d'Arenberg, and Don Sebastiani & Sons in the United States, used it, but the product never made a market breakthrough and has been losing momentum. Another new stopper out of Australia is ProCork, which has been called a condom for corks. It is a natural cork with a fine, five-layer membrane on both ends that protects the wine from any TCA in the cork. After four years of research, it went on sale in 2003. W. L. Gore and Associates, the inventor of Gore-Tex fabric, has developed a product called Gore Siglio to block TCA from getting out of the cork. The company says it uses an "ultrathin selectively permeable barrier" around the cork. Siglio is already being tested in wineries, and Gore hopes to have it out in 2008.

The challenge for all the new closure companies is that the business has become a game of giants. It takes huge research and marketing budgets to compete, and only large, international companies have that kind of money. A company such as Zork, which operates out of a small office in Adelaide, can't compete with Amorim or Guala. It's not good enough just to develop a better product. It has to be promoted and sold globally to companies that are buying mainly on price.

One new product that has big backing is Alcoa's glass stopper. Many winemakers or winery managers told me they liked it because it was an "elegant solution" to the TCA problem. It has a clean, modern look. The price, which is as much as for a top-quality cork, scares off some wineries looking for an inexpensive taint-free closure, but the less expensive acrylic version might work for them. The stopper is still not widely used outside Germany and Austria.

Some wineries have moved back and forth among closures, partly in reaction to the owner's mood or emphasis on profits. Most of the switches have been back to natural cork after a move to plastic. Such leading California brands as Acacia, Behrens & Hitchcock, and Chalone all returned to cork after a short time with plastic. Moving to screwcaps and then back to either natural cork or synthetics is much less common. The Australian market, though, got a jolt when Peter Lehmann, a high-end producer in the Barossa Valley, moved its 2006 Riesling back to cork after troubles with screwcaps.

Looking out at the world closure market from country to country, it is surprising how much national markets vary. New Zealand is far and away the most monolithic. In 2006, some 90–95 percent of all its closures were screwcaps. While natural cork is trying to make a comeback, it's now used by only a handful of the very best producers such as Dry River and Te Mata. Diam has also earned a reputation in New Zealand for offering a safe cork alternative.

Australia actually uses more screwcaps than New Zealand, but does not have as high a proportion under that closure. About half of the Aussie market is now in screwcap. The share of exports under screwcap is much smaller because producers feel some important markets, the United States in particular, are not yet ready for screwcaps. Wineries send bottles to the United States with plastic corks that they sell at home with screwcaps.

The British market is bifurcated. At the large, less-expensive end where wine is sold mainly by supermarkets, screwcaps predominate. Cork, though, still reigns almost supreme at the upper end, which is made up of perhaps the most knowledgeable, although traditional, wine consumers in the world. These people usually buy at specialty wine shops.

British supermarkets still play the same role as they did in the early days of Supreme Corq. They are the gatekeepers that determine which closures get used, and they still don't like natural cork. After first being enthusiastic about synthetic corks in the mid-1990s, their ardor waned. Simon Thorpe, the wine buyer of the Waitrose chain, said in late 2003 that synthetics would make up "less and less" of his product line.

Tesco, Britain's leading wine retailer, first jumped on the Screwcap Initiative after it was started in Australia and New Zealand. In September 2001, Tesco worked with big Australian producers such as Hardy, Southcorp, and Rosemount to bottle a line of six wines that would sell under the Unwind label and go on sale the following year. Learning from the New Zealand experience, stores priced the wines just above £5 (US$9.79), so that they would not have a cheap image. Phil Reedman, a Master of Wine and formerly product development manager for Tesco, says it helped that

New Zealand wines such as Jackson Estate and Lawson's Dry Hills were then selling for between £7.99 (US$15.64) and £9.99 (US$19.56). Tesco eventually launched about forty wines under screwcap.

Tesco executives say their customers quickly adopted the new closure because of the convenience of not needing a special instrument to open a bottle and the ease of resealing it. Looking out to the future, Andy Gale, the Tesco technical manager for beers, wines, and spirits, sees the day when his wines will have mostly screwcaps, a few synthetic, and lot of agglomerated corks such as Diam. He predicts that in a few years he'll be selling few bottles sealed with natural corks.

In researching this book in Chile in January 2006, I visited Veramonte in the Casablanca Valley, which was the first premium Chilean winery to go with screwcaps when it switched its Sauvignon Blanc away from cork. When I asked winemaker Cristian Aliaga Coronel why he made the move, he replied simply, "Tesco."

While those other three Anglo-Saxon markets are moving strongly toward screwcaps, the United States has been much slower to follow suit. A 2006 study by ACNielsen, the market research company, showed that just 3 percent of American wines were sold with screwcaps. Only a few wineries such as Bonny Doon have switched almost all their production to that closure. Another is Quixote Winery, which was started by Napa Valley pioneer Carl Doumani. Since 2001, it has bottled its Quixote and Panza wines in screwcaps. A lot more are doing one or two wines that way, while waiting to see how the market develops. The first wine to go screwcap is almost always Sauvignon Blanc. Winemakers say privately that the New Zealanders have done such a good job of selling that wine to the world in that closure, it's easy to get consumers to make the shift with American Sauvignon Blancs. PlumpJack is still almost alone among high-end producers with a screwcap offering.

Back in the Old World wine countries of France, Italy, Spain, and Portugal, the move away from cork is the slowest. It's still rare to find a screwcap bottle for sale at a shop. In Italy, synthetic corks are a little more popular. The glass stopper is enjoying a lot of success in Germany with high-end wines and some Riesling producers.

The New Zealand experience, however, where the screwcap share of the market went from zero in 2000 to 95 percent in 2006, showed how quickly things can change. Even though New Zealand is a small market, that experience keeps Portuguese cork makers worrying late into the night.

CONCLUSION

Monopolies are bad not only for those who suffer under them but also for those who run them. Winemakers and consumers were unhappy prisoners of cork producers for more than three centuries because there was no credible alternative way to seal a wine bottle. No one was ready to go back to storing it in amphoras that had globs of wet clay for a closure. Less obvious, however, is that cork's long monopoly was also bad for cork producers. Fat and sassy, they became complacent. Innovation was virtually unknown, and prices only went up. Today cork companies are fighting for their lives, and the outcome of that struggle is anything but certain. It is not unthinkable that the use of corks in wine bottles will go the same way as their use in medicine and beer containers did early in the twentieth century.

Cork will likely still have a role; the question is how big a one. When I asked Robert Hill Smith, the proprietor of Australia's Yalumba Wines, if cork producers were belatedly doing a better job, he answered unequivocally, "The cork companies have finally improved their quality, and their investments are paying off." But they are still paying a high price for past hubris, and concrete results of the industry's research investments must be seen, for example, in lower numbers of TCA-rejected bottles at wine competitions.

During the past fifteen years, the pioneers of plastic corks and screwcaps turned the wine world upside down simply by providing alternatives and opening a much needed discussion about closures. It is too early to know where the business will end up, but a hard-fought battle in the marketplace of ideas and products can only benefit all members of the international wine community. People now have a choice, and the consumer is king.

The one certain thing is that no product will ever again enjoy a monopoly. Natural cork, synthetics, screwcaps, and still other closures will be fighting for their share of the market. The early skirmishes show there is no perfect closure. Each has its strengths and weaknesses, its fans and its foes. All are likely to find the market segment where they are strongest and those where they have a fighting chance. Winemakers will be experimenting with a panoply of choices to determine which best fits their variety of grape and their style of winemaking. Individual wineries may well end up using a variety of closures for a variety of wines. The concept that one closure fits all is dead.

Future generations of wine drinkers will consider it quaint that for several centuries the only way most people bought wine was in a bottle with a cork. A packaging revolution is on the horizon and rapidly rushing forward. Château Lafite may always be in a bottle with a cork, but that doesn't mean every other wine has to slavishly follow its lead. Wine should be judged by the quality of the product, not by its container. In December 2006, Australia's Hardy Wine Company introduced a plastic bottle-and-glass package designed for individual servings at outdoor events where glass is not permitted. In Australia, box wines—or, as the French say, *le bag in box*—have had more than 50 percent of the market for at least twenty-five years, and those containers are now also popular in Sweden. One of the hottest segments of the American wine business, albeit from a small base, has been premium wine in boxes or casks, as wineries like to call them. Movie-maker-cum-winemaker Francis Ford Coppola sells individual servings of his Sofia Blanc de Blancs sparkling wine in aluminum cans. Wines in Tetra Paks, Swedish-made paper containers with plastic linings, are big sellers in South America. The British supermarket chain Sainsbury in the summer of 2007 introduced wine in light PET plastic bottles that weigh only 2 ounces, compared to 14 ounces for a glass one. They had already been used in Australia. Coca-Cola and Budweiser over the years developed myriad ways to distribute their products to consumers, realizing the public has two priorities: content and convenience. Wineries should learn from their experiences. A group of California winemakers have formed the Alliance for Innovative Wine Packaging, which is promoting various new ways to sell their product. Clearly the last word has yet to be spoken on how to get wine into consumers' hands.

As winemakers experiment with different closures for various wines and new packaging, the role of research should become more and more important. Despite the work done by wine scientists going back to Pasteur, it is still surprising to realize how little is known about some of the most fundamental aspects of the field. How much air, if any, is needed for wines to develop properly in a container? How does air even get into a bottle with a cork in it? Does the formation of TCA start in the cork forests? The answers to those questions, and more, remain unknown. At a June 2005 seminar on closures at the American Society of Enology and Viticulture's annual meeting, UC Davis professor Roger Boulton irritated much of the audience by repeatedly barking, "Show me the data!" The uncomfortable truth is that there is still a lot more opinion than facts on important issues facing wine chemistry.

Not enough good wine science is being done. The AWRI study of Semillon under fourteen closures was excellent, but it should be only a beginning. It dealt with just one white wine. How would other whites and also red wines react in similar trials? The world of wine needs to know.

The questions New Zealand's Alan Limmer and others have raised about screwcaps are legitimate and should be addressed. It is not good enough for screwcap true believers simply to quote by rote Ribéreau-Gayon *père et fils* from the 1960s. Technology and research equipment didn't stop a half century ago. Everyone needs a much better understanding of sulfide chemistry and how wines develop under screwcaps. It seems only logical that winemakers, who have been preparing wine to go into a bottle with a cork that lets in a small amount of air, will need to change their enological procedures if it's going into one sealed with an anaerobic closure. Screwcap evangelicals are a little too glib when they say they won't have to change anything or just do a little copper fining of the wine before bottling.

The new emphasis on closures will be putting a lot more pressure on winemakers. It used to be easy to blame any and every fault in a bottle on the cork. Winemaking for screwcaps is much more demanding, and excuses are harder to make. In the past, too many vintners thought their job was finished as soon as the wine was delivered to the bottling line. They now realize their responsibility only ends when the consumer opens a bottle and tries the wine.

Fortunately, all of these developments are good for everyone from producers to consumers, just as the cork monopoly was ultimately bad for everyone. Unfettered competition remains a powerful driving force for good.

SELECTED BIBLIOGRAPHY

BOOKS

Amerine, M. A., and M. A. Joslyn. *Commercial Production of Table Wines.* Berkeley: University of California Press, 1940.

Beardsall, Judy. *Sniffing the Cork.* New York: Atria Books, 2002.

Blair, R. J., et al., eds. *Advances in Wine Science.* Glen Osmond, SA, Australia: The Australian Wine Research Institute, 2005.

Caillard, Andrew. *The Rewards of Patience.* 5th ed. Adelaide, Australia: Penfolds, 2004.

Campbell, Christy. *The Botanist and the Vintner.* Chapel Hill, NC: Algonquin Books of Chapel Hill, 2005.

Davis, Derek C. *English Bottles and Decanters, 1650–1900.* New York: World Publishing, 1972.

Debré, Patrice. *Louis Pasteur.* Baltimore: The Johns Hopkins University Press, 1998.

DeVilliers, Marq. *The Heartbreak Grape.* Port Medley, NS, Canada: Jacobus Communications, 1993.

Fetter, Richard L. *Dom Pérignon.* Boulder, CO: Fetter Publications, 1989.

Fleming, Stuart J. *The Story of Roman Wine.* Glen Mills, PA: Art Flair, 2001.

Gil, Luís. *História da Cortiça.* Santa Maria de Lamas, Portugal: APCOR, 2000.

Godfrey, Eleanor S. *The Development of English Glassmaking, 1560–1640.* Chapel Hill: University of North Carolina Press, 1975.

Goode, Jamie. *The Science of Wine.* Berkeley: University of California Press, 2005.

———. *Wine Bottle Closures.* London: Flavour Press, 2006.

Hooke, Robert. *Micrographia.* 1665.

Huysmans, J. K. *Against the Grain.* New York: Dover Publications, 1969.

Jardine, Lisa. *The Curious Life of Robert Hooke.* New York: Perennial, 2003.

Jefford, Andrew. *The New France.* London: Mitchell Beazley, 2002.

Johnson, Hugh. *A Life Uncorked.* Berkeley: University of California Press, 2006.

———. *Story of Wine.* London: Mitchell Beazley, 2002.

———. *Wine.* London: Thomas Nelson and Sons, 1966.

Kladstrup, Don, and Petie Kladstrup. *Champagne.* New York: William Morrow, 2005.

Leaf, Munro. *The Story of Ferdinand.* London: Hamish Hamilton, 1937.

Lukacs, Paul. *The Great Wines of America.* New York: W. W. Norton, 2005.

McGovern, Patrick E. *Ancient Wine.* Princeton, NJ: Princeton University Press, 2003.

McGovern, Patrick E., et al., eds. *The Origins and Ancient History of Wine.* London: Routledge, 1996.

Mendelsohn, Oscar A. *Drinking with Pepys.* London: Macmillan, 1963.

Oliveira Santos, Carlos. *Amorim: A Family History.* 2 vols. Mozelos, Portugal: Grupo Amorim, 1997.

Parker, Robert M., Jr. *Bordeaux.* New York: Simon & Schuster, 1998.

Pasteur, Louis. *Oeuvres de Pasteur, Tome 3: Études sur le Vinaigre et sur le Vin.* Paris: Libraires de L'Académie de Médecine, 1924.

Peynaud, Émile. *Knowing and Making Wine.* New York: Wiley, 1984.

———. *The Taste of Wine*. San Francisco: Wine Appreciation Guild, 1987.

Philips, Rod. *A Short History of Wine*. New York: Ecco, 2000.

Pliny. *Natural History*. Cambridge: Harvard University Press, 1968.

Pouillaude, Ch. *Le Liège et les Industries du Liège*. Paris: Les Impressions Techniques, 1957.

Purdue, Lewis. *The Wrath of Grapes*. New York: Avon, 1999.

Ribéreau-Gayon, Jean. *Traité d'Oenologie—Sciences et Techniques du Vin*. Vol. 3. Paris: Béranger, 1976.

Robinson, Jancis, ed. *The Oxford Companion to Wine*. Oxford: Oxford University Press, 1999.

Stelzer, Tyson. *Screwed for Good?* Brisbane: Wine Press, 2003.

———. *Taming the Screw*. Brisbane: Wine Press, 2005.

CONFERENCE PROCEEDINGS

Butze, Christian, and Adam Suprenant. "Implications of Odor Threshold Variations on Sensory Quality Control of Cork Stoppers." Proceedings of the 4th International Symposium on Cool Climate Viticulture and Enology, Rochester, NY, July 16–20, 1996.

International Screwcap Symposium, Marlborough, New Zealand, November 10–12, 2004.

Science of Closures Seminar. 56th Annual Meeting, American Society for Enology and Viticulture, Washington State Convention and Trade Center, Seattle, WA, June 20–21, 2005.

JOURNAL ARTICLES

Buser, Tanner, and Zanier Tanner. "Identification of 2,4,6-Tricholoranisole as a Potent Compound Causing Cork Taint." *Journal of Agricultural Food Chemistry*, 1982, 359–62.

Cabral, Mills, and Lopes. "Oxygen Brings New Life to Closure Debate." *The Australian & New Zealand Grapegrower & Winemaker*, Technical Issue 2006.

Chatonnet, Pascal, et al. "Identification and Responsibility of 2,4,6-Tribromoanisole in Musty, Corked Odors in Wine." *Journal of Agricultural and Food Chemistry*, Web release, February 14, 2004.

Conan and Géré. "L'Inavouable Maladie du Vin." *L'Express*, December 24, 1998.

Eric, Leyland, and Rankine. "Stelvin—Evaluation of a New Closure for Table Wines." *The Australian Grapegrower and Winemaker*, April 1976.

Godden et al. "Update on Wine Bottle Closures (30 months)." *Technical Review* 137 (April 2002).

———. "Update on Wine Bottle Closures (36 months)." *Technical Review* 139 (August 2002).

———. "Wine Bottle Closures (20 months)." *Australian Journal of Grape and Wine Research* 7, no. 2.

Leyland, Rankine, and Strain. "Further Studies on Stelvin and Related Wine Bottle Closures." *The Australian Grapegrower and Winemaker*, April 1980.

Limmer, Alan. "Do Corks Breathe?" *The Australian & New Zealand Grapegrower & Winemaker*, Technical Issue 2005.

———. "The Permeability of Closures." *The Australian & New Zealand Grapegrower & Winemaker*, Technical Issue 2006.

———. "Possible Ways of Dealing with Post-Bottling Sulfides." *The Australian & New Zealand Grapegrower & Winemaker*, December 2005.

———. "Redox Reactions, Sulfides, and General Misconceptions." *New Zealand Winegrower*, November 2004.

Lopes et al. "Impact of Storage Position on Oxygen Ingress through Different Closures into Wine Bottles." *Journal of Agricultural and Food Chemistry*, Web release, August 8, 2006.

Rauhut, Doris. "Volatile Sulfur Compounds: Impact on reduced sulfur flavor defects and atypical aging in wine." *New York State Agricultural Experiment Station*, February 25, 2005.

Tanner, Zanier. "Zur Analytischen Differenzierung von Mufton und Korkgeschmack in Weinen, Schweiz." *Zeitschrift Obst- und Weinbau*, 1981, 752–57.

ACKNOWLEDGMENTS

This book could never have been written without the help of many people around the world. More than 125 experts from the wine industry took hours out of their lives and away from their work to discuss with me their views about wine closures. Brian Croser spent most of a day outside Adelaide carefully explaining his views, while Pascal Chatonnet and his wife, Dominique Labadie, talked with me long into the night in Bordeaux. All those wine professionals represented every possible position in the debate and usually held strong opinions. This is not a topic for the weak of will. There's not enough space to thank each of them individually, but they all have my deepest appreciation.

For someone who got a gentleman's C in the only science course he took in college, the science involved in the cork debate was particularly challenging. Some of the world's leading wine scientists helped me find my way through issues such as redox chemistry and the oxygen permeability of cork. One of the highlights of my research was talking with Hans Tanner, the Swiss wine researcher who first identified cork taint as 2,4,6-TCA, about his historic 1981 research. Terry Lee, the former director of the Australian Wine Research Institute and later head of wine research at the E. & J. Gallo Winery, played a crucial role in my science education and was a prince of patience. He also read an early version of the manuscript and made many important contributions. Christian Butzke, formerly of the University of California, Davis, and now an enology professor at Purdue; Eric Herve at ETS in the Napa Valley; and Peter Godden at the Australian Wine Research Institute were all helpful.

My fellow wine writers in places far and near also provided generous support and counsel. Maggie Rosen did interviewing for me in London with wine buyers for large supermarket chains, who play a pivotal role in how bottles in that country are sealed. In the Napa Valley, John Intardonato was a great help in researching the California scene. In Auckland, I was lucky enough to dine, and share a bottle of Kumeu River Maté's Vineyard Chardonnay with Paul Tudor the night he learned he had been inducted into the Institute of Masters of Wine. An old friend, Elisabeth Kaiser, also helped me line up interviews in Germany and Switzerland. Pascal Deniau in France provided many insights. Paige Poulos and Joel Quigley of the Alliance for Innovative Wine Packaging in California were also very helpful

Behind every book there are invaluable supporters, who may be out of the limelight but whose work is essential to the final product. The first was my wife, Jean Taber, who read the first . . . as well as the fifth . . . version of every chapter and made countless valuable contributions. Brant Rumble, my editor at Scribner, provided encouragement and guidance along the way and a deft editing hand at the end. Harvey Klinger, my agent, was always there at the end of the phone line ready to help with problems large and small. Fortunately Robyn Liverant and my daughter Lara Taber, who both helped promote my first book, *Judgment of Paris,* signed up again for this one.

While all of these people gave invaluable help, any faults or errors in the book are mine alone. I tried to wend my way through the thicket of controversial and conflicting views about wine bottle closures without becoming a prisoner of any camp. Only the reader can determine whether I succeeded.

INDEX